Language and the Law

Language policy is a topic of growing importance around the world, as issues such as the recognition of linguistic diversity, the establishment of official languages, the status of languages in educational systems, the status of heritage and minority languages, and speakers' legal rights have come increasingly to the forefront. One-fifth of the American population does not speak English as their first language. While race, gender, and religious discrimination are recognized as illegal, the United States does not currently accord the same protections regarding language; discrimination on the basis of language is accepted, and even promoted, in the name of unity and efficiency. Setting language within the context of America's history, this book explores the diverse range of linguistic inequalities, covering voting, criminal and civil justice, education, government and public services, and the workplace, and considers how linguistic differences challenge our fundamental ideals of democracy, justice, and fairness.

DOUGLAS A. KIBBEE is Professor Emeritus in the Department of French at the University of Illinois at Urbana-Champaign. He is the author of *For to Speke Frenche Trewely* (1991), co-author of *French: A Linguistic Introduction* (Cambridge, 2006), and editor of *Language Legislation and Linguistic Rights* (1998).

Language and the Law

Linguistic Inequality in America

Douglas A. Kibbee

CAMBRIDGE
UNIVERSITY PRESS

CAMBRIDGE
UNIVERSITY PRESS

University Printing House, Cambridge CB2 8BS, United Kingdom

Cambridge University Press is part of the University of Cambridge.

It furthers the University's mission by disseminating knowledge in the pursuit of education, learning and research at the highest international levels of excellence.

www.cambridge.org
Information on this title: www.cambridge.org/9781107623118

First published 2016

Printed in the United States of America by Sheridan Books, Inc.

A catalogue record for this publication is available from the British Library

Library of Congress Cataloging-in-Publication Data
Kibbee, Douglas A., author.
Language and the law : linguistic inequality in America / Douglas A. Kibbee.
Cambridge, United Kingdom : Cambridge University Press, 2016. | Includes bibliographical references and index.
LCCN 2016015471 | ISBN 9781107025318 (hardback)
LCSH: Linguistic minorities – Legal status, laws, etc. – United States. | United States – Languages – Law and legislation. | BISAC: LANGUAGE ARTS & DISCIPLINES / Linguistics / General.
LCC KF3466 .K53 2016 | DDC 342.7308/7–dc23
LC record available at https://lccn.loc.gov/2016015471

ISBN 978-1-107-02531-8 Hardback
ISBN 978-1-107-62311-8 Paperback

Cambridge University Press has no responsibility for the persistence or accuracy of URLs for external or third-party internet websites referred to in this publication, and does not guarantee that any content on such websites is, or will remain, accurate or appropriate.

Contents

Preface

The cover of this book represents the Pledge of Allegiance, recited by school-children across the country, in its Arabic form. In January of 2013 the Cultural Arms Club of Rocky Mountain High School (Fort Collins, CO) read the pledge of allegiance in Arabic, one of many languages it used in an effort to break down cultural barriers. In March of 2015 a student at the Pine Bush High School in New York State recited this version. Both readings unleashed a firestorm of protest, with many websites and media outlets claiming that saying the pledge in Arabic forced students to embrace Islam. Christian Arabs as well as Muslims would use the same word, "Allah," in the translation of the phrase "one nation under God."

By design of the founding fathers of the United States, America does not have a national religion or a national language. Religious difference is explicitly protected in constitutional law, but linguistic difference is not. Linguistic inequalities affect an increasing number of Americans, from hundreds of linguistic backgrounds. Language and power are inextricably interconnected, with great potential for conflict and abuse, as the pages below will document.

The relation of language and power has been a focus of my work throughout my career. This research has explored how the preparation of grammars and dictionaries is related to political and social power, the relationship between French and English in England, and the elaboration and imposition of a standard language in France.

Most of my career has been devoted to studying this relationship between power and language relating to the use of French. In the early 1990s, I spent two summers in Quebec, at a time of great tension based largely on language. In 1994, I was teaching in France when the "Loi Toubon," designed to protect the French language against English encroachment, was debated, passed, and in part declared in part unconstitutional. These experiences led me to wonder how linguistic difference was treated in my native United States, which in turn led to the organization of a conference, "Language Legislation and Linguistic Rights," held at the University of Illinois in 1996 (selected papers published by John Benjamins, 1998). Subsequently, a series of reading groups with faculty and graduate students at the University of Illinois revealed the ubiquity of linguistic conflict and the variety of responses to it.

While ubiquitous, language conflict differs greatly from country to country, each with its own history and mixture of immigrants and indigenous peoples. The responses also vary according to the legal system and the political structures of each country. To cite only the other country I know best, France is a country of relatively recent immigration, which has never threatened the dominance and the legal position of the French language. The imposition of French on local languages (Basque, Breton, etc.) took centuries to complete; the survival and revival of local languages does not change their secondary and unofficial role in contemporary France. The creation of a standard language was part of a strong centralization of power that continues to this day. The local control that marks much of American-language conflict has far less impact in France. The protection of the national language from a foreign influence based on world economy and geopolitics is not a concern in the United States. The French legal code is based on very different principles that accord less influence to judicial precedent. Where some American cases we will consider took decades to be resolved in the courts, the political system in France includes a Constitutional Council that can overturn laws before they are enacted, a procedure invoked to reverse parts of the original Loi Toubon.

Eager to explore such differences and similarities, beginning in 2000, I offered a course on language and the law in the United States, and a few years later on language policies in the countries of the European Union. These opportunities deepened my understanding and my concern for the effects of linguistic inequality in a democratic society.

The philosophical issues are related through case law to individual experiences. These individual stories need to be remembered as the law seeks general solutions to particular problems:

- In 1919, August Bartels, in Bremer County, Iowa, and in 1920 Robert Meyer, in Hampton, Nebraska, gave their students religious instruction in the German language, in direct violation of their states' statutes forbidding instruction in any language except English.
- In 1965, Maria Lopez, a 21-year-old hotel worker in Rochester, NY, sought to register to vote; when she was denied registration based on an English-language literacy test, she filed a suit under the newly passed Voting Rights Act.
- In 1970, Kam Wai Lau complained to the Chinatown Neighborhood Legal Services in San Francisco that her son Kinney Kinmon Lau was not receiving meaningful education because it was all in English, a language he did not understand.

- In 1970, Jose Negrón, a Puerto-Rican farmworker in Suffolk County, NY, challenged his murder conviction because inadequate interpretation made him "not present at his own trial."
- In 1981, Manuel Fragante, a Pilipino-American, had the highest score on a civil service test for a position at the Honolulu Department of Motor Vehicles; he was denied the job because of the interviewers' perception of his accent.
- In 1991, Dionisio Hernandez challenged his felony conviction on the grounds that the prosecution had unlawfully used its peremptory challenges to exclude all Spanish-speaking potential jurors.

These are just a few of the stories that we will explore in the pages that follow. The picture that emerges is one of linguistic privilege and linguistic disadvantage. Long ignored in the American tradition, the power of language is one of the most intractable of inequalities in our society. The dominance of English, and of a particular variety of English, is taken for granted. Because language can be learned, there has been little sympathy for those disadvantaged by their limited knowledge of the dominant language.

Empathy is, however, a crucial factor in social cohesion. Political correctness is derided for its excesses, but the alternative lack of empathy is an invocation of privilege that destroys the social fabric. Accommodating those who do not speak English is a first step toward the realization of a true meritocracy and toward the needs of our society in its interactions with the broader world. The first act respecting the diversity of cultures is reaching across linguistic barriers, a "burden sharing" (to borrow from Rodriguez 2006) that must be equal if it is to be effective.

In my desire to present the full spectrum of language-related issues, I have been obliged to move quickly through complex matters that deserve fuller development. Many issues dealt with here in a paragraph merit a full book, and where possible I have referred the reader to more detailed sources. The bibliography is an invitation to explore these topics in all their complexity. There remain many areas deserving of fuller treatment. I hope future scholars will take up those challenges as we strive toward a more perfect union.

Acknowledgments

In a work covering so many areas, my first debt is to all the scholars who have delved deeply into specific parts of the study that follows. Access to their work has been greatly enhanced by the availability of materials online, through legal and other digital subscriptions of the University of Illinois Library. The interlibrary loan service of the University of Illinois and the Washington Island branch of the Door County Library has filled gaps in the digital record. I am eternally grateful to Kathy Danner and her fantastic staff at the University of Illinois and to Marcia Carr at the Washington Island Library.

Early explorations of this topic were developed in the context of a course designed for the Campus Honors Program at the University of Illinois. I am thankful to Director Bruce Michelson for this opportunity and to the students who suffered through the elaboration of the ideas presented in this volume. Thank you for your patience and your insights.

Language policy reading groups at the University of Illinois provided another forum to examine language policy issues. Zsuzsanna Fagyal, Braj Kachru, Rakesh Bhatt, Dennis Baron, Anna Maria Escobar, Marina Terkourafi, Eda Derhemi, and many graduate students participated in these meetings, enlightening me on the great diversity of problems and solutions in the politics of language. Similarly, participants in the conference "Language Legislation and Linguistic Rights," held at the University of Illinois in 1996, and in subsequent meetings on linguistic prescriptivism have shed much light on conflict between languages and between varieties of individual languages. John Joseph has been a constant inspiration for questioning issues of language, politics, and power.

More recently, a number of people have read parts of this volume, suggesting improvements and providing insights. Luis and Patricia Rivas read an early version of the chapter on bilingual education and shared their experiences in this domain. James Barrett and Robert Kibbee read other chapters, saving me from many errors of fact and logic. Throughout the elaboration of this book, Helen Barton, Editor at Cambridge University Press, and her staff have been extremely helpful; the comments of external reviewers contacted by the Press have helped me to clarify issues in my own mind, and in their expression in the pages that follow.

All errors that remain are strictly my responsibility. I hope that readers will help correct remaining mistakes and misconceptions as we all pursue a greater understanding of the linguistic issues that hinder the pursuit of our national ideals.

The first reader, to whom I owe everything, is Jo Kibbee. Her family's story is incorporated in this work: the strength and courage of immigrants to overcome the challenges of a new world. This work is dedicated to her, with deepest gratitude, and to her forebears, who made our encounter possible.

1   Equality, Liberty, and Fairness in America

"All men are created equal" is the first "self-evident truth" of the Declaration of Independence. However, clearly they are equal only in their fundamental humanity, not in their physical attributes or mental talents. These natural differences create distinctions both rational and irrational. The law is called upon to regulate these distinctions, to ensure rationality while preserving liberty through the institutions of a democratic state.[1] Is distinction based on language natural and rational, or arbitrary and irrational? In the following pages we will examine the determination of legal and illegal distinctions, in national and international frameworks.

Distinction based on race and gender has been the primary focus of rights in the United States. The Fourteenth and Fifteenth Amendments, so crucial to our notions of equality, were added to the Constitution in the first years after the Emancipation, shortly after the Civil War, to address the rights of African-American former slaves. But other targets of discrimination have always been part of our history. America is the land of Manifest Destiny and a land of

---

[1] Liberty is one of the three unalienable rights according to the same Declaration of Independence; the others being life and the pursuit of happiness. As these rights are described as exemplary but not an exhaustive list, others are imaginable. Life was considered unalienable because it is our moral duty to protect a gift of God. The right to property is a means to preserve life. Liberty is unalienable because it is our moral duty to make judgments. Without the free will to do so, we cannot be moral beings. Freedom of speech is the means to making moral judgments. Liberty then is defined as "freedom from all substantial arbitrary impositions and purposeless restraints" (*Poe* v. *Ullman* 1961, Harlan dissent at 543). Paul and Pauline Poe, a married couple that had suffered through the birth of three congenitally deformed children who died shortly after birth, asked the court to rule unconstitutional Connecticut's ban on contraceptives. Justice Harlan defined liberty in the context of this intrusion into the intimacy of marriage.

The pursuit of happiness is not individual license but rather the framework for constitutional government, the goal of the social contract. As James Wilson put it at the Pennsylvania Convention, the state of nature provides happiness only to a small minority of people, so constitutional government was necessary to promote the greatest happiness for the greatest number: "each gains more by the limitation of the freedom of every other member, than he loses by the limitation of his own. The result is, that civil government is necessary to the perfection and happiness of man" (cited in Charles 2011, 484). John Adams (1781) explained that "happiness did not embody an individual natural right, but a democratic principle of representation" (cited in Charles 2011, 496). For further discussion of these questions, see Haakonssen (1991).

immigrants. The history of discrimination against speakers of other languages, against speakers of other varieties of English, and of restrictions on certain types of English is as old as European settlement of the continent.

The percentage of Americans born on foreign soil is today at its highest level in over a century.[2] Today, 60 million Americans – more than 20 percent of the population – speak a language other than English at home, and more than 13 million speak English "less than well" (in self-reported census responses).[3]

The triumph of English has been taken for granted, even though English speakers were not dominant in the earliest period of colonization. Even when English became dominant in the thirteen colonies, the rest of the territory that would become the United States was populated mainly by Native Americans and by speakers of French and Spanish. The expansion of the United States was accompanied by anglicization or marginalization of non-English speakers. Territorial expansion favored policies encouraging immigration, while at the same time fanning the xenophobia of the already established English-speaking populations. Each new wave of immigration is subjected to the same prejudices that the older waves endured, often by those whose grandparents suffered the same indignities, and inter-ethnic tensions sometimes work against their general interest:[4] the first lessons learned by victims are how to victimize and how to exploit victimhood.[5] Victimhood conflicts with the American ideology of recreating oneself, of overcoming all odds to succeed, of making no excuses.

---

[2] The United States Census Bureau estimated (2011) a Limited English Proficient population of 25.3 million (9.2 percent of the population). Those who self-identify as "Hispanic or Latino" constitute 17.2 percent of the population. Of course, not all who self-identify as Hispanic or Latino speak Spanish. No accurate statistics of (or indeed definitions of) speakers of non-standard English are available.

[3] Almost 21 percent of the population, 60.5 million, spoke a language other than English at home. A broad array of language statistics can be found in "Language Use in the United States: 2011," a Bureau of the Census report by Camille Ryan (August 2013). This number reflects only those over five years of age. The full report can be consulted at www.census.gov/prod/2013pubs/acs-22.pdf. The history of immigration and language use will be discussed in much more detail in subsequent chapters.

[4] See, for example, Zimmerman (2002), who documents how other ethnic groups sometimes cooperated to stop German-language teaching, even to the detriment of the teaching of their own native languages. Similarly, Germans in Buffalo blocked efforts by Poles to have Polish taught in the public schools, though the German community had successfully lobbied for the teaching of German a couple generations earlier (Seller 1979, 52).

[5] James R. Barrett (2012) has demonstrated how the Irish, as one of the first mass immigrant groups, showed subsequent immigrant groups how to navigate the American system. One way is to victimize the newer arrivals: Zimmerman (2002, 1389) cites the Irish tactics to block instruction in German, starting in the 1870s, by demanding equal opportunity for Gaelic, despite the widely different sociolinguistic status of the two languages. Another of those means is to encourage a sense of group solidarity through an ideology of victimhood, a status that certainly has real roots in history and in contemporary America. It can also serve tactical purposes. See, for example, Jensen (2002) on the history of "No Irish Need Apply." For a more general study of how prior experience does not translate into empathy, see Ruttan, McDonnell, and Nordgren (2015), who conclude that "previously enduring an emotionally distressing event led to more

This ideology of mutability is an essential part of the American dream, the ability to make a fresh start in the New World. No aspect of our being is less mutable than our appearance, commonly interpreted as race. No aspect of our being is more mutable than our language. Therefore, it is not surprising that language per se has been the least protected aspect of discrimination law in the United States.

Race is the most common ground for protection because it combines immutability[6] with the harsh history of enslavement and Jim Crow. The initial measures taken against discrimination aimed specifically to protect African-Americans and to remediate the continuing effects of slavery in the former states of the Confederacy. However, these legal instruments have had repercussions far beyond that geographic and historic focus. The official protections enumerated in constitutional amendments and in Civil Rights Acts from Reconstruction to the present have grown to include race, color, sex, religion, and national origin. At the state level, in other parts of the world, and in universal declarations of rights, a number of other classifications, including language, are given equal consideration. But at the federal level in the United States pluralism fatigue has set in (see Yoshino 2011), the list of protected groups remains unchanged, and white English-speaking males are claiming victim status.

Language has proven to be a significant barrier to ideals of equality, fairness, and justice. The plaintiffs in the cases we will study were not always successful, but their efforts bear witness to the range of issues where language intersects with these fundamental notions. These principles require rational distinctions rather than irrational discrimination.

Discrimination

Discrimination is irrational because it does not depend on the qualities of the individual but rather on prejudice against the individual as a member of a group. Individuals have to be associated with a group to qualify for protection, but their rights are individual. Illegal discrimination supposes an adverse effect against an individual motivated by an irrational criterion related to that individual's membership in a protected group. An adverse effect must be proven, along with the existence of the protected group, and then discriminatory intent or discriminatory impact that demonstrates the relationship of that irrational basis to a protected group. Not all adverse effects constitute illegal discrimination. Some rights can and do conflict with others. Legitimate state

negative evaluations of those who failed to endure a similar emotionally distressing event" (2015, 619).

[6] We set aside for the moment the extensive scholarly literature on physical and social definitions of race.

interests and *bona fide* business needs might justify actions that appear discriminatory. Subsequently, the definition of rational and irrational groupings has taken center stage.

The foundations of antidiscrimination law in the United States are the Fifth, Fourteenth, and Fifteenth Amendments to the Constitution, the Civil Rights Acts of the Reconstruction Era and again after World War II, and the Voting Rights Act of 1965. Since the 1970s, prevailing majoritarian social attitudes, reflected in court decisions, have turned antidiscrimination law on its head: now it frequently serves to protect the privileges of white English-speaking males. Proving discrimination has grown more and more difficult, while the legal grounds for rejecting positive antidiscriminatory programs such as affirmative action have grown easier and easier.

Language can be a discrimination issue: one irrational basis among many for exclusion or adverse action. Language can only exist as a group dynamic (you need to speak your language with someone who understands it), so language rights are inherently group rights. However, language groupings are not coextensive with those traditionally recognized as eligible for protection in the United States: religion, race, color, sex, or national origin. Therein lies the complexity of protecting against discrimination based on language.

A Short History of Rights

The development of antidiscrimination rights was essentially a recognition of an inability to agree and a product of modern conceptions of the relationship between the individual and society. The first human right so conceived was freedom to practice one's religion, a mutable characteristic to be sure, but one which had to be protected from forcible change in order to maintain the peace. Freedom of religion came into being because Christendom, in the second half of the sixteenth century, was in the throes of an irreconcilable divorce. It is not irrelevant that the modernist insistence on the ability of the individual to interpret the Bible was a key point of dispute. After more than thirty years of reciprocated massacres in France, the Edict of Nantes was proclaimed in 1598. Through this limited decree Protestants were to be tolerated, in a paternalistic sense, but did not have equal rights with Catholics, and other religions had no protection at all.

When seventeenth-century philosophers, such as Spinoza and Locke, took up the question, true reciprocity was envisioned, and from reciprocity emerged the universality of certain freedoms. This reciprocity, and the universality of its application, was the result of a new way of conceiving the state. Political structures were no longer seen as a matter of divine authority and providence, but rather as dependent on human reason and free will under a social contract between the individual and the state.

Starting from this conception the state is both the guarantor of individual freedom of action and the biggest threat to that freedom. The state is the servant of the individual; in return, the individual recognizes certain responsibilities toward the state. The French Declaration of the Rights of Man and of the Citizen holds that the goal of political structures is the "conservation of the natural and imprescriptible rights of man."[7]

Under this formulation, the state is minimalist, so as not to interfere with the freedom of individuals, except where there is a conflict between these freedoms. By limiting the essential freedoms to liberty, property, and safety, or, in the American formulation, "the pursuit of happiness," the state does not have to involve itself in other domains.

Another formulation is possible, in which the state is given more obligations – education, feeding the hungry, providing shelter, clothing the poor, and protecting minorities from forced assimilation to the majority. If the basic material and spiritual needs of human existence are a concern of the state, the state has authoritarian, or even totalitarian, potential.[8] The proliferation of those needs ends only with death, as Hobbes recognized some 350 years ago.[9] We are a greedy species.[10]

If the state is the guarantor of rights, then citizens of the state have the first claim on such protections. Citizens have more rights than foreign residents, indigenous peoples more rights than immigrants. Not everyone benefits in the same way, creating a hierarchy of rights. Theoretically, at least, the equal protection of the law does not vary according to such status, but other types of equality do.

This division of rights is crucial for understanding the issues peculiar to language and the law. Indigenous-language speakers, subsumed into a state more or less against their will, have certain claims for using their languages that immigrants do not, having voluntarily chosen to move to their new home. Some rights supersede such classifications – the right to understand criminal

---

[7] "Le but de toute association politique est la conservation des droits naturels et imprescriptibles de l'homme. Ces droits sont la liberté, la propriété, la sureté et la résistance à l'oppression."

[8] See Mourgeon (2003, 27–30).

[9] Hobbes, *Leviathan* (1651, 47), Ch. 11:

BY MANNERS, I mean ... those qualities of man-kind, that concern their living together in Peace and Unity. To which end we are to consider, that the Felicity of this life consisteth not in the repose of a mind satisfied. For there is no such *Finis ultimus* (utmost ayme) nor *Summum Bonum* (greatest Good) as is spoken of in the Books of the old Morall Philosophers. Nor can a man any more live, whose Desires are at an end, than he, whose Senses and Imaginations are at a stand. Felicity is a continuall progresse of the desire from one object to another, the attaining of the former being still but the way to the latter ... I put for a general inclination of all man-kind, a perpetuall and restlesse desire for Power after power, that ceaseth onely in Death.

[10] Friedman (2011) describes the expansion of these rights. His fundamental position is that talk of rights is the product of modern individualism, itself a product of economic liberalism (in the European sense), and that human rights promises have not been matched by performance.

proceedings, for example. Voting and education in immigrant languages are not necessarily protected: enforcement depends on, among other things, a certain established population density of speakers of the immigrant language.

The protection of a group can be approached in two ways: through the provision of a list of protected classes or as a general prohibition against irrational discrimination. The United Nations Charter (1945) followed the first route: it limited the classifications to race, sex, language, and religion. The United Nations' Universal Declaration of Human Rights (1948) then took the second route, treating the list as exemplary, not exhaustive. The initial wording of Article 2 of the Universal Declaration of Human Rights (1947) read

Everyone is entitled to all the rights and freedoms set forth in this Declaration, without distinction as to race, colour, sex, language, religion, political or other opinion, national or social origin, property, birth or other status.

It was revised by the drafting subcommittee to "without *distinction* of any kind, such as race."[11]

The effect, in the final document (1948), was to de-emphasize the importance of the individual classifications, in favor of a general prohibition of irrational discrimination.

Discrimination itself has been defined by the UN Human Rights Committee in the following manner:

Discrimination as used in the Covenant [*The International Covenant on Civil and Political Rights,* 1966] should be understood to imply any distinction, exclusion, restriction or preference which is based on any ground such as race, colour, sex, language, religion, political or other opinion, national or social origin, property, birth or other status, and which has the purpose or effect of nullifying or impairing the recognition, enjoyment or exercise by all persons, on an equal footing, of all rights and freedoms.[12]

The different types of adverse treatment (distinction, exclusion, restriction, or preference) are viewed both in their intent and in their impact, a distinction that will be crucial in the American context.

Universality. As a fundamental right, protection from discrimination is to be enforced (to the extent that any UN resolution is enforced) in all countries. Previous international treaties concerning rights had not applied universally. The League of Nations' "minority treaties," which focused heavily on language rights, were imposed on the new states created from the Russian, Austro-Hungarian, and Ottoman empires of Eastern Europe, but quite hypocritically they did not apply to the allied victors in World War I.[13]

---

[11] Skogly (1992, 62). The drafting subcommittee included Eleanor Roosevelt.
[12] This is included in General Comment no. 18 from UN document HRI/GEN/1/Rev. 3, p. 26, attached to the Covenant and cited in Alfredsson and Ferrer (1998, 8).
[13] For example, Eugène Muller, an Alsatian deputy in the National Assembly, cited the minority treaties in the hope of restoring German-language education in his region (speech

In his "four freedoms" speech of 1941, Franklin D. Roosevelt promoted the universality of rights by reiterating the phrase "everywhere in the world," seeking universal guarantees – the freedom of speech, the freedom of religion, the freedom from want, and the freedom from fear.[14] The proliferation of categories in the Universal Declaration of Human Rights was accompanied by the change in wording cited above that made the classifications indicative but not exhaustive.

Language as a Right in the International Tradition

To participate in the social contract, the parties must agree on the definition of essential terms. This is why Hobbes included a chapter on language early in the *Leviathan* (chapter 4)[15] and returned to the subject on many occasions. He acknowledged that the meaning of key terms such as "good" and "evil" can be twisted for self-centered purposes, looked to the sovereign to regulate meaning, and decried the adversarial common law approach to justice as a temptation to stretch or deform meanings.[16]

Agreeing on the definition of essential terms is hard enough if all speak the same language.[17] It becomes even more difficult if those supposedly participating in the social contract do not speak the same language. Some terms simply

---

delivered December 2, 1924). Similar complaints were coming from Breton, Flemish, Basque, and Occitan regions of France.

[14] Speech to Congress, January 6, 1941:

In the future days, which we seek to make secure, we look forward to a world founded upon four essential human freedoms. The first is freedom of speech and expression – everywhere in the world. The second is freedom of every person to worship God in his own way – everywhere in the world. The third is freedom from want – which, translated into world terms, means economic understandings which will secure to every nation a healthy peacetime life for its inhabitants – everywhere in the world. The fourth is freedom from fear – which, translated into world terms, means a world-wide reduction of armaments to such a point and in such a thorough fashion that no nation will be in a position to commit an act of physical aggression against any neighbor – anywhere in the world ... Freedom means the supremacy of human rights everywhere.

From the FDR library site: www.fdrlibrary.marist.edu/pdfs/fftext.pdf. The evolution of this part of Roosevelt's text can be followed at www.fdrlibrary.marist.edu/pdfs/ffdrafts.pdf.

[15] "In the right definition of names lies the first use of speech; which is the acquisition of science" (*Leviathan* 8, 22). This right definition is subject to human power relations, which also calls into question the traditional assertion of linguists that terms are "conventional." This is not to say that power is necessarily abused in imposing names, but it certainly can be. The naming of bills in the US Congress is a typical example, for example "The Defense of Marriage Act," which would deny the possibility of marriage to same-sex couples. Convention and the social contract are convenient fictions for those who already possess power.

[16] "A Pleader commonly thinks he ought to say all he can for the Benefit of his Client, and therefore has need of a faculty to wrest the sense of words from their true meaning" (Hobbes 1681, 6). For a discussion of Hobbes' view of the abuse of language, see Whelan (1981).

[17] See, for example, how Marine Le Pen, the leader of the Front National in France, has appropriated the terminology of the secular post-revolutionary state to her own xenophobic vision, documented in Alduy and Wahnich (2015). Thus, *laïcité* "secularism" is transformed from

do not translate,[18] and others are situated within different cultural contexts.[19] The historical references of different groups within the same nation oppose positive and negative interpretations of shared history and shared terms. One side's defining victory is the starting point for another's victimization, as demonstrated in Anglo and Hispanic perceptions of the Mexican–American War.

The social contract requires at least a pretense of mutual respect. The first sign of mutual respect is meeting linguistic difference halfway. The fatal failures of such respect inspired the "minority treaties" following World War I. Even though the minority treaties ultimately failed,[20] the recognition of the destabilizing effect of linguistic minorities led, after World War II, to a series of international treaties supporting the rights of linguistic minorities. The International Covenant on Civil and Political Rights and the International Covenant on Economic, Social, and Cultural Rights (both passed in 1966 and put into effect in 1976) protected the right of criminal defendants to an interpreter, gave parents the right to choose the language of instruction for their children, and prohibited laws or practices that would prevent linguistic minorities from using their language. In Europe, the Council of Europe, the European Union, and the Organization for Security and Cooperation in Europe (OSCE) have approved international instruments promoting the rights of linguistic minorities, culminating in the Charter for Regional or Minority Languages (Council of Europe 1992).

The Charter requires signatory countries to identify languages they will protect and to specify at least 35 areas and levels of protection from a menu of over 100 options. In 1994, the United Nations issued a Declaration on the Rights of Persons Belonging to National or Ethnic, Religious and Linguistic Minorities and another draft declaration on the Rights of Indigenous Peoples.

---

a neutral term against all religion in government to a weapon against one religion, Islam, and *racisme* "racism" is invoked only to evoke anti-white racism.

[18] The *Dictionary of Untranslatables* (Cassin 2014) provides many examples of incommensurable terms. Consider, for example, the notion of "free will," so essential to the political philosophy of democracy. The original Greek term (*eleutheria*) meant the ability to grow according to one's true nature, and importantly, surrounded by one's own people (i.e., within a homogenous group). The Latin translation, *liberum arbitrium*, emphasized freedom of choice. In the American context, it has been confused with lack of constraint, liberty in the sense of license to act, even to act irrationally.

[19] For cultural context contrast the difference between terms used in common law (the Anglo-American tradition) and those in civil law drawing on Justinian's code, but frequently combined with local customary law, as in Grotius' *Inleydinge tot de Hollandsche recht-geleertheyt* (1631) and the *Code Civil* in France (1804).

[20] The vast majority of the complaints submitted to the League of Nations were by German-speaking minorities in the newly formed states of Eastern Europe. The former oppressors became the oppressed. The inability of the League to enforce its rulings within the new nations was one of the factors used by Hitler to justify the annexation of the Sudetenland in 1938 and the invasion of Poland in 1939.

These efforts are frequently symbolic,[21] as no enforcement method exists, but have had some effect even in countries that have refused to ratify these treaties.[22] Some countries have created semi-autonomous zones for linguistic minorities, where government services can be provided in languages not recognized as official in the state as a whole (e.g., Basque and Catalan in Spain).

Even if the concrete results fall short of the rhetoric, the proliferation of such treaties, covenants, and conventions recognizes that inequality in the linguistic definition of fundamental terms – essential to the social contract – subverts equal participation in civil society. Is equality best served by a single standard language based on the majority culture, or by equal consideration for other languages and language varieties? The former conception offers a unifying goal but perpetuates historical inequalities, while the latter offers immediate participation but perpetuates division.

The American Tradition

In the United States, the Lockean conception of natural rights, divinely given to each individual, rights that transcended the power of the state, inspired the overthrow of British control of the colonies. After the Revolution, faced with creating a government, the successful rebels formulated a much more limited conception of rights.[23] The enumeration of rights in the Bill of Rights took responsibility for the granting of rights and their protection from God and gave it to the state.

Subsequently, in the American tradition, the promise of equality has been pursued through protected classification status granted to religion, race,[24]

---

[21] Often the expectation is that unspecified "measures" will be taken to "promote" the language rights of minorities. Typical is the Convention Concerning Indigenous and Tribal Peoples in Independent Countries (1989, entering into force in 1991), which provides the escape of "wherever practical" to signatory countries.

[22] The passage of the European Charter inspired France to amend its constitution to include the statement "The language of the Republic is French" (1992). France has not signed the Charter, but it has created the Délégation Générale à la Langue Française et aux Langues de France (DGLFLF) which, while insisting on the primacy of French, seeks to support indigenous minority languages (Basque, Breton, etc.) as part of the cultural heritage of the French nation.

[23] See Breen (2001) for an interesting discussion of this transition. The Declaration of Independence states that all men "are endowed by their Creator with certain unalienable Rights." The white male colonists quickly realized the dangers, for their own privilege, of God-given rights. John Adams feared that "new claims will arise, women will demand a vote; lads from twelve to twenty-one will think their claims not closely attended to; and every man who has not a farthing will demand an equal vote with any other, in all the acts of the state" (cited in Breen 2001, 20–21, from a letter to James Sullivan, May 26, 1776).

[24] The definition of race has been an ongoing controversy, sometimes extended to national (e.g., Mexican-Americans in *Manzanares* v. *Safeway Stores* 1979) or religious groups (e.g., Jews in *Shaare Tefila* v. *Cobb* 1986), sometimes not (*Anooya* v. *Hilton Hotels* 1984). For further discussion, see Evren (1986).

color,[25] national origin,[26] and gender. The attempt to protect ever more classes is one of the contributing factors to what Kenji Yoshino (2011) has described as "pluralism anxiety." This anxiety pervades every country in the developed world – and many in the developing world – as they take in immigrants of diverse backgrounds and confront more openly than ever in the past the issues of diverse sexual identities. Language groups have never been a protected class in the American tradition.

The United States is, in this respect, in stark contrast to the evolution of rights, human and civil, in the Western tradition. Instead, in the United States, legislation and constitutional amendments have promoted equality through English-language uniformity,[27] the type of convergence Lawrence Friedman celebrates in his consideration of "human rights culture" (2011, especially pp. 120–130). However, what some consider the triumph of English-language uniformity perpetuates and reproduces inequalities in

---

[25] Color is often considered equivalent to race, but there is a distinction: lighter skin within a racial classification has often been preferred, but one of the few cases based on color alone considers the opposite situation. In *Walker* v. *IRS* (1990), the plaintiff alleged discrimination by a darker African-American against a lighter African-American. The court recognized that color was different from race and that intra-racial color discrimination claims could be pursued under Title VII of the Civil Rights Act of 1964. Nonetheless, color on its own has rarely been considered within legal history, and even more rarely has such an approach succeeded. In *Walker*, the court concluded that this case was simply a matter of personality conflict, not one of color discrimination.

[26] "Nationality" is protected in *Yick Wo* v. *Hopkins* (1886, at 369): "The Fourteenth Amendment to the Constitution is not confined to the protection of citizens ... These provisions are universal in their application, to all persons within the territorial jurisdiction, without regard to any differences of race, of color, or of nationality." Nationality refers to citizenship, however, not the national origin of citizens. "National origin" was a legal form of discrimination in immigration quotas established in 1924, applying to non-citizens who wished to enter the country. National origin of US citizens was not an issue in readmission to the country (*U.S.* v. *Wong Kim Ark* 1898). The expression "national origin" was first inserted into federal protections in the run-up to World War II, slightly earlier than in Perea's account (1994, 811–812), primarily in reaction to the exclusion of Italian-Americans from jobs in the defense industry. Steele (1991) outlines this development at the federal level, and Higbee (1966) at the state level (for New York).

[27] Even before independence Benjamin Franklin insisted on the pre-eminence of English: "Why should Pennsylvania, founded by the English, become a colony of aliens who will shortly be so numerous as to Germanize us instead of our Anglifying them?" (*Observations Concerning the Increase of Mankind, Peopling of Countries, &c.*, first circulated in 1751, first published in 1755); in later editions of this essay, Franklin deleted the final two paragraphs, which contained his most virulently ethnocentric and racist comments. The full text of the essay is available at https://ia801405.us.archive.org/29/items/increasemankind00franrich/increasemankind00franrich.pdf.

DeWitt Clinton (1815, 8), himself of mixed Dutch-English descent, noted approvingly that four languages (English, Dutch, German, and French) had been widely used in New York, but at the time of his writing "[t]he triumph and general adoption of the english language have been the principal means of melting us down into one people, and of extinguishing those stubborn prejudices and violent animosities which formed a wall of partition between the inhabitants of the same land."

a country of indigenous peoples, of immigrants, and of speakers of disfavored dialects of the dominant language.

The assumption that English is the official language of the United States, even though no federal law grants it that status, has important consequences for the ways in which equality, fairness, and justice are applied in the American legal system and in the actions of the government. As we have seen, the application of those principles has depended on the ability to distinguish rational from irrational groupings, but language has not been one of the broad categories deemed worthy of protection.

The United States thus lists today five such categories. Any classification is a recognition of inequality.[28] Legislation that affects a specified group can only be justified by appealing to a greater good for the society as a whole. Classification is a necessary part of preventing irrational discrimination in private as well as public dealings, as justified by §1981 and §1982 of the Civil Rights Act of 1866.

As the country was founded in the period of the Enlightenment, initial concerns were about religious prejudice, but race has, since the Civil War era, more often been the primary focus of American rights.[29] Even before the

---

[28] Tussman and tenBroek (1949, 344) lay out paradox in this manner: "The equal protection of the laws is a 'pledge of the protection of equal laws.' But laws may classify. And 'the very idea of classification is that of inequality'" (citing *Atchison, Topeka & Sante Fe R.R.* v. *Matthews* 1899, at 106).

[29] Race is, of course, a hotly debated concept. It has the illusion of being a physical characteristic, or set of characteristics, but the definition of those characteristics is a social construction. While the courts have, for the most part, considered race a social rather than a biological construct, in the area of Title VII discrimination race means visible features (skin color) and national origin means invisible features (such as language and accent) (Bridges 2013).

Racial categories were treated as scientific realities by eighteenth-century biologists (Linnaeus, Cuvier, Blumenbach) and served to justify eugenics, enslavement, and extermination of "inferior" races. Racism produces the concept of race; it is the essentialization of difference (Bridges 2013, 38). *Ozawa* v. *U.S.* (1922) and *US* v. *Thind* (1923) are the immigration court cases that shaped the court's vision of race as a social construct, in part because the experts (biologists and anthropologists) could not agree on racial categories. According to Bridges (2013, 43), the court did not reject the possibility of racial categories; it just questioned its own ability to reconcile the conflicting schemata of the experts. If "white" were essentialized as privilege, both Ozawa and Thind would have been declared white. *Korematsu* v. *U.S.* (1944) treated the Japanese as a "race" in that there is an assumption of shared birth equating to shared behavior. In *Hernandez* v. *Texas* (1954, concerning jury selection), Spanish surname was the distinguishing characteristic. Because Americanness and whiteness are associated with specific varieties of English, "Latinos are a racial group because they are imagined as such – and are treated as such" (Bridges 2013, 75).

In *St. Francis College* v. *Al-Khazraji* (1987), the court understood the category of "Arab," though "Caucasian," to be a victim of discrimination. The statute (§1981 of the Civil Rights Act, see below) bans discrimination because an individual "is genetically part of an ethnically and physiognomically distinctive group of *homo sapiens*" (Bridges 2013, 54, see note 148); the emphasis is still on genetic origin and thus biological. In Powell's opinion on *Bakke* (*Regents of the U. of California* v. *Bakke* (1978)), he distinguishes *scientific races* and *ethnicities*, with the assumption that biological race exists and that discrimination against the advantaged (white)

Civil War, the rights of free blacks challenged the Comity Clause of the Constitution.[30] After the Civil War, the rights of newly freed slaves forced a focus on racial prejudice. From the mid-nineteenth century the women's rights movement gradually gained recognition of sex as a protected classification. "National origin" was the last classification generally received, a response to the mass immigrations of the nineteenth and early twentieth centuries. Other classes of victims of discrimination have had to demonstrate how their groups could reasonably be associated with the five basic categories (four if color and race are conflated).

Groups, Classes, and Classifications

The appeal to a general sense of rationality would undoubtedly expand protection efforts that have become bogged down in quibbling about suspect classes and suspect classifications.[31] Indeed, some legal opinions have moved in this direction: *LaFore* v. *Emblem Tape and Label Co.* (1978) interpreted the phrase "white citizens" in §1981 of the Civil Rights Act of 1866 "to prohibit the maintenance of a favored class":

> Historically a class called "white citizens" received more favorable treatment than other classes. If we understand the term "white citizen" in the statute to mean that group which was most favored, the rule becomes understandable. All persons are entitled to the same rights and benefits as the most favored class. (*LaFore* 1978, at 826)

But classifications are hard to avoid, and the quibbling shows no sign of abating. The equation of equal rights with the rights enjoyed by a "most favored class" does not solve the issue, as it requires definition of the most favored class. Favored in what? Membership in that class is determined by rights and benefits that exceed those of others in the society. Through this interpretation, if others, not "white citizens," have more rights or benefits in some particular domain, white English-speaking citizens could pursue a case based on anti-discrimination law.

And this, of course, has happened. Under the Burger, Rehnquist, and Roberts Supreme Court (1969–), the heightened scrutiny of laws affecting suspect

---

race is racial discrimination. The court thus follows the unscientific prejudices of the general population, reaffirming a biological conception of race.

[30] Article IV, Section 2, Clause 1 of the Constitution: "The Citizens of each State shall be entitled to all Privileges and Immunities of Citizens in the several States." Originally, in the Articles of Confederation, this clause included wording excluding paupers, vagabonds, and fugitives from justice. In 1947, President Truman signed a law expressly extending these protections to Puerto Ricans, which served as a legal basis for challenges to voting rights for non-English-speakers (see below, p. 40 sqq.).

[31] See, for example, Pollvogt (2014).

classes (e.g., African-Americans, women, non-English speakers) has been superseded by heightened scrutiny based on classifications (race, sex, national origin).[32] This transition allows politically and economically dominant classes to claim victim status, and thus to receive protection originally intended to counteract majoritarian discrimination.[33]

In the American legal tradition the classes and classifications are incorporated within a system of judicial review, in which courts can rule on the constitutionality of laws approved through the legislative process. The groups affected by laws can be defined as non-suspect and suspect, with greater level of scrutiny applied to laws that might have a bigger impact on suspect classes, particularly when those laws touch on some fundamental right.

Defining Groups

How does one define a group for legal protection? The federal courts do not have a consistent approach for distinguishing who should be protected. Some groupings are perceived to be rational, such as the class of convicted felons, frequently denied voting rights; others are perceived to be irrational, such as race. Irrational classifications are considered automatically suspect. The distinction between rational and irrational is not clear and has depended heavily on identity-based social movements, such as the Civil Rights movement, the Women's Rights movement, and the Gay Rights movement. The social effect of these movements has changed public opinion so that behaviors that were once deemed (by the majority) morally wrong or distasteful circa 1950 came to be acceptable (miscegenation, contraception, homosexuality).[34] The court has acceded to these changes in public opinion, essentially specifying protected groups according to moral normativity. Thus,

---

[32] *Bakke* (1978 at 291): "Racial and ethnic distinctions of any sort are inherently suspect and thus call for the most exacting judicial examination." This line of thought was pursued in *City of Richmond* v. *Croson* (1989) and *Adarand Construction* v. *Pena* (1995), both dealing with minority business set-aside plans in public construction projects. For a discussion of this transition from classes to classifications, see Oh (2004), and for the Latino classification in these two cases, Rivera (2007). In *Hilber* v. *International Lining Technology* (2012), the court rejected the adjective "reverse" in the expression "reverse discrimination": "The adjective 'reverse' is unnecessary ... it has no place in the legal analysis of the alleged governmental action before us. Discrimination is discrimination no matter what the race, color, religion, sex or national origin of the victim" (at 3–4).

[33] As Fraser (1990, 73) noted, "any consensus that purports to represent the common good in this social context should be regarded with suspicion, since this consensus will have been reached through deliberative processes tainted by the effects of dominance and subordination."

[34] Eskridge (2001) outlines the history of this transformation, which is exemplified by the court's divisions in the cases discussed in Note 35.

gays and lesbians,[35] hippies,[36] and the disabled[37] are socially salient groups that merit recognition under the Fourteenth Amendment, while felons[38] and nude dancers[39] are not (McGowan 2004, 1313–1314).

The protected groups trigger closer scrutiny of laws whose constitutionality is questioned. Federal courts have applied multiple tiers of scrutiny: strict, heightened, intermediate, rigorous rational basis, ordinary rational basis, and

[35] See *Romer* v. *Evans* (1996) and *Lawrence* v. *Texas* (2003). *Romer* concerned a constitutional amendment in Colorado prohibiting homosexuals from having or claiming "any minority status, quota preferences, protected status, or claim of discrimination" (1996 at 625). It was a reaction against antidiscrimination laws passed in Boulder and Denver. The majority found that this amendment served no legitimate governmental interest and that "the disadvantage imposed is born of animosity toward the class of persons affected" (1996 at 634). Justice Scalia, joined by Thomas and Rehnquist, dissented, arguing that the amendment was a modest attempt "to preserve traditional sexual mores against the efforts of a politically powerful minority" (1996 at 636). *Lawrence* reversed an earlier decision, *Bowers* v. *Hardwick* (1986), which had upheld a Georgia law banning homosexual sex. Lawrence and his partner were surprised by Houston police, in their home, while engaging in homosexual sex. The *Lawrence* court, citing the Due Process Clause, concluded that "the Texas statute furthers no legitimate state interest which can justify its intrusion into the personal and private life of the individual" (2003 at 578). Justice O'Connor concurred, but did not feel the case needed to overturn *Bowers*, and based her decision on the Equal Protection Clause. Justices Scalia and Thomas dissented, attributing the majority's position to its acceptance of the "agenda promoted by some homosexual activists" (2003 at 602).

[36] See *U.S. Dept. of Agriculture* v. *Moreno* (1973) in which the state tried to prevent distribution of food stamps to unmarried couples as a way to restrict such government support for "hippy communes." Similarly, *Parr* v. *Municipal Court* (1971) reversed a Carmel, CA, ordinance to limit use of public spaces by "hippies."

[37] Notably, *City of Cleburne* v. *Cleburne Living Center, Inc.* (1985), a case concerning zoning laws meant to exclude the possibility of a group home for the developmentally disabled.

[38] For example, *Richardson* v. *Ramirez* (1974). Three men convicted of felonies (robbery, heroin possession, forgery) who had served their time and probation periods tried to register to vote in California and were denied. The majority acknowledged conflicting opinions about what crimes were included in the Fourteenth Amendment's phrase banning restrictions on voting for adult male citizens "except for participation in rebellion, or other crime." Even though the California Secretary of State could find no "compelling or rational policy interest in denying former felons the right to vote," the rights of ex-felons as a class were not recognized, and the case was treated as regarding three individuals. One of the justifications for excluding ex-felons is the fear that they would vote to change laws regarding crime. Justice Marshall, in his dissent, remarked on the danger of excluding people on the basis of their potential for trying to effect change in a particular area of the law: "Our laws are not frozen into immutable form, they are constantly in the process of revision in response to the needs of a changing society ... A temporal majority could use such a power to preserve inviolate its view of the social order simply by disenfranchising those with different views" (1974 at 82).

[39] *City of Erie* v. *Pap's A.M.* (2000) and *Barnes* v. *Glen Theatre, Inc.* (1991). Both of these cases involved statutes outlawing nude dancing. The question was whether freedom of speech was involved in the prohibition. The Supreme Court, in sharply divided decisions, ruled that the states had a compelling interest in regulating nude dancing, citing regulations against public nudity in general. But the performance areas involved in these cases were not public spaces but rather private establishments that charged admission. Ultimately, the decisions were based on moral distaste for the proscribed performances.

rational basis "with bite."[40] Scaperlanda (2005, 8) perceives a move away from categorical applications of scrutiny to a more ad hoc approach, giving "primacy of consideration to governmental interests above those of the individual, locating ultimate power and authority in the 'non-political' branch of the federal government," that is, the judiciary.

Any scrutiny beyond "ordinary rational basis" puts the burden on the state to show that the law targets a compelling state interest and is not based on irrational prejudice; under such scrutiny the state rarely wins. The heightened scrutiny of laws that appear to affect essential rights of a particular group of people is determined by a five-part test, each part with its own problems.[41] Furthermore, different courts assign different weights to different parts, some stressing immutability, others the history of discrimination.

The group constitutes a discrete and insular minority.[42] At issue is how such minorities, lacking political power, need to be protected from the tyranny of the majority. *Discreteness* is defined by the ability to identify a person as a member of the minority, and thus it relates to immutability (see the following). To a certain extent individuals have the freedom, and must have the freedom, to decide if they wish to be considered part of a minority group. In terms of language, there are many people with Hispanic surnames (one way of grouping together Latinos) who do not speak Spanish, and many whose first language is Spanish, without having a Spanish surname.[43] *Insularity* addresses the cohesiveness of the group – the traits shared by members of the group that distinguish them from the members of the majority group. In some circumstances, the group might not be a statistical minority, but through the history of discrimination and political powerlessness has suffered in a manner similar to true minorities, as in the case of French speakers in Québec before the *Révolution tranquille* of the 1960s (which in fact was not so "tranquil"). The importance ascribed to Justice Stone's phrase in *Carolene Products* generally excludes economic categories, such as the poor.

---

[40] These terms reflect a realization that the scrutiny/no scrutiny distinction was not nuanced enough, but the replacement range of terms overlap and are not clearly defined. For a recent summary of rational basis and rational basis with bite, see Holoszyc-Pimental (2015).

[41] For an extensive discussion of these criteria, see Strauss (2011).

[42] This phrase first appears in Justice Stone's footnote 4 in the decision *U.S.* v. *Carolene Products Co.* (1938). The court opinion suggested that prejudice against such groups might be a "special condition" which, when combined with a curtailment of an essential right (voting, freedom of religion), "may call for a correspondingly more searching judicial inquiry" (1938 at 153).

[43] The complexities of group membership, voluntary (by the choice of the individual to self-identify as a member of the group) or involuntary (by others' identification of the individual as a member of the group), are glossed over in Tussman and tenBroek's analysis (1949, 345): "It is elementary that membership in a class is determined by the possession of traits which define that class. Individual X is a member of class A if, and only if, X possesses the traits which define class A."

The group has suffered a history of discrimination: Measuring discrimination is difficult, and "history" requires the establishment of a time frame. Some groups' history of discrimination might be relatively short and recent (HIV positive) while that of others dates back to the history of Europeans' arrival in the new world (Native Americans, certain religious groups). The metric for discrimination has proceeded from the worst-case scenario (enslavement), through various forms of legal restriction (e.g., women's inability to vote or to own property, gays and lesbians' inability to marry), to the linguistic minorities' specific issues: the difficulty of voting effectively, inequality of services provided by the government, including education, and various forms of prejudice in employment.

The group is politically powerless: Powerlessness has been defined by the ability to vote, the number of voters, the enactment of laws favoring the group, and the representation of the group in positions of power. The right to vote does not guarantee political power, as voting power can be diluted in many ways. Raw numbers can also be misleading, as women have constituted 50 percent of the population but lacked, until the twentieth century, basic rights of property and voting. Similarly, adequate representation is hard to define: does the presence of three women on the Supreme Court constitute adequate representation, or inadequate since it does not reach the 50 percent of the general population?

The group is defined by an immutable trait: In *Frontiero* v. *Richardson* (1973), immutable traits are those "determined solely by the accident of birth."[44] An immutable trait that is highly visible is more likely to render a group politically powerless, or make it subject to discrimination.[45] Therefore, "the imposition of special disabilities upon the members of a particular sex because of their sex would seem to violate 'the basic concept of our system that legal burdens should bear some relationship to individual responsibility'" (citing *Weber* v. *Aetna Casualty and Surety Co.* 1972, at 175).

However, defining biological traits is not obvious; so a second test is whether the trait can be easily changed – or whether it "would be abhorrent for

---

[44] This case concerns equality of benefits for male and female members of the armed services (housing allowances for dependents). "Appellants contend that classifications based upon race, alienage, and national origin are inherently suspect and must therefore be subjected to close judicial scrutiny. We agree" (1973 at 682). The Supreme Court referred to *Reed* v. *Reed* (1971), in which the court found unconstitutional a law granting automatic preference for men over women as administrators of an estate. Idaho argued that in general men knew more about business affairs than do women. The Supreme Court noted that "our Nation has had a long and unfortunate history of sex discrimination. Traditionally, such discrimination was rationalized by an attitude of 'romantic paternalism' which, in practical effect, put women, not on a pedestal, but in a cage" (*Frontiero* 1973 at 684).

[45] "Justice is pictured blind, and her daughter, the Law, ought at least to be color-blind," argued Albion Tourgée, the attorney for the African-American plaintiffs in *Plessy* v. *Ferguson* (1896), cited in Fiss (1976, 119).

government to penalize a person for refusing to change" (such as religion). The Ninth Circuit rejected immutability of sexual orientation in *High Tech Gays* v. *Defense Industrial Security Clearance Office* (1990, at 573): "homosexuality is not an immutable characteristic; it is behavioral and hence is fundamentally different from a trait such as race." Visibility and personal choice have combined in a number of cases: is hair style an esthetic choice or an intrinsic part of a racial or ethnic identity? In the case of language, immutability has been conflated with the notions of "voluntary" versus "involuntary" action: does a bilingual person choose to use one language or another? Voluntarism has another aspect with respect to language rights: immigrants who have chosen to come to the country are assumed responsible for learning the majority language; indigenous peoples who have been forcibly incorporated into the country have a stronger claim to retaining their own language. This did not stop aggressive attempts to eradicate Native American languages, as we shall see in Chapter 4.

The group is defined by a trait that is generally irrelevant to one's ability to function in society: In a case involving a city's exclusion of group housing for the developmentally disabled (*City of Cleburne* v. *Cleburne Living Center, Inc.*, 1985), the Supreme Court reviewed classifications such as gender and illegitimacy to explain why some have "no sensible ground for differential treatment" and therefore deserve heightened scrutiny. Context is crucial: what is relevant in one situation may be irrelevant in another. As Supreme Court Justice Thurgood Marshall observed in his opinion in this case, "A sign that says 'men only' looks very different on a bathroom door than a courthouse door" (at 468–469). Whether one is black or white has no bearing on the ability to drive a car: does the ability to understand English? In some states the driver's license examination may be taken in multiple languages; in others only in English. Relevance might be argued on the basis of English-language road signs; irrelevance on the widespread use of language-independent signage. The relevance of language is hotly contested, as we shall see in the chapters that follow.

Symmetry is sometimes considered, giving laws that affect whites and men heightened scrutiny even though these are generally powerful and over-represented groups: suspect classes (e.g., African-Americans) and suspect classifications (race) are not equivalent (Strauss 2011, 169–170). The principle of symmetry is one way in which legislative attempts to correct a history of discrimination can perpetuate the dominance of the privileged.

The original impetus of the Fourteenth Amendment was to guarantee that states would not enact laws that would deny equal protection to recently freed African-Americans. Since then the suspect classes have been established by comparison to that history of enslavement – a history that no other group matches exactly (women, sexual orientation, language). Strauss (2011, 152) asks, "How should a court analyze such similarities and differences? Without more guidance, judges are free to indulge their own stereotypes and biases about a particular group." All racial groups are considered suspect, but non-racial groups are considered quite differently.

Language has most frequently been considered under the rubric of national origin, rather than of race. Jurisprudence concerning this type of discrimination originally defined national origin as "the country from which you or your forebears came,"[46] but discrimination is more likely to be against traits that relate to the country of origin. Only one Supreme Court case has interpreted the expression "national origin," to reject an appeal against discrimination based on citizenship.[47]

The emphasis on national boundaries and more generally on geography has important ramifications for language-based discrimination. Subnational groups of foreign origin could, for instance, be linguistic minorities within their own country. Consider, for example, Mayan-language speakers in Central America: if Spanish speakers of Guatemalan origin were given preferential treatment and Kanjobal speakers of Guatemalan origin were excluded, there would be no basis for claims invoking national origin discrimination – an employer could point to the number of Guatemalans hired as proof of good intentions.[48]

---

[46] From Representative James Roosevelt's commentary during debate of the 1964 Civil Rights Act, 110 *Congressional Record* 2549 (1964). Diaz (2014) calls for the recognition of subnational origins, so that regional accents in the United States could be protected, as well as foreign accents.

[47] In *Espinoza* v. *Farah Manufacturing Co.* (1973), the Supreme Court ruled that the refusal of a company to hire a legal resident who was not a citizen did not constitute national origin discrimination. Citing Roosevelt's definition at the time of passage of the Civil Rights Act of 1964, the Court found national origin to mean "the country from which you or your forebears came." Citizenship was not an issue, as demonstrated by regulations requiring that federal employees be citizens. Even though Farah refused to hire non-citizens, 96 percent of its workforce was, at that time, of Mexican origin, so no discriminatory animus can be attached to their citizens-only policy. The sole dissenter in the case, Justice William O. Douglas, objected that any "barriers to employment when the barriers operate invidiously to discriminate on the basis of racial or other impermissible classification" are illegal (1973, 96–97).

[48] *Pejic* v. *Hughes Helicopters* (1988) recognizes this difficulty, though not on a linguistic basis. Vojislav Pejic worked as a machinist for Hughes Helicopters. He claimed that he was discriminated against for being Serbian, by a supervisor who had family ties to Croatia, both ethnic groups being at that time part of the country of Yugoslavia. The company argued that Serbia was no longer a country, and therefore Serbian origin could not be protected in a Title VII framework. The court ruled that Serbians were a protected class, finding that "given world history, Title VII cannot be read to limit 'countries' to those with modern boundaries, or to require their existence for a certain time length before it will prohibit discrimination. Animus based on national origin can persist long after new political structures and boundaries are established" (1988 at 673). Pejic lost his case on other grounds. The same principle applied in the recognition of Acadians as a protected class, even though Acadia had never been a sovereign nation (*Roach* v. *Dresser* 1980 at 218): "Distinctions between citizens solely because of their ancestors are odious to a free people whose institutions are founded upon the doctrine of equality, and we decline to accept the argument that litigation of this sort should be governed by principles of sovereignty."

Supranational groups could be Spanish speakers as a whole (rather than, for instance, people of Mexican descent), or non-English speakers of whatever national origin, or nomadic groups like the Roma.[49] Regional origins within the United States might be the victims of discrimination on the basis of their language (e.g., speakers of southern dialects of American English), but they have no recourse based on the Civil Rights Act.[50]

Initially, national origin law focused on a geopolitical definition of discrimination, even though the discrimination was more frequently based on cultural factors. The identification of protected classes with sovereign countries was soon rejected by court decisions. To resolve these issues the Congress passed amendments in 1991 that added the wording mentioning discrimination based on traits associated with a non-US national origin ("the physical, cultural or linguistic characteristics of a national origin group"). This extension confirmed the Supreme Court's interpretation of the Civil Rights Act of 1870 in *Saint Francis College* v. *Al-Khazraji* (1987), which confounds national origin and race:

Congress intended to protect from discrimination identifiable classes of people who are subjected to intentional discrimination solely because of their ancestry or ethnic characteristics. Such discrimination is racial discrimination that Congress intended section 1981 to forbid, whether or not it would be classified as racial in terms of modern scientific theory. (at 613)

Justice Brennan, in a concurring opinion, noted that "the line between discrimination based on 'ancestry or ethnic characteristics' ... and discrimination based on 'place or nation of ... origin' is not a bright one" (at 614) and concluded that birthplace alone is not sufficient to claim protection. The characteristics, including linguistic characteristics, of people from that place of origin are the crucial factor.

This leads naturally to the arguments presented by Abellera Cruz (1998, 164) that ethnic traits associated with a given geographic origin are the perceptible instigators of discriminatory behavior. To him, national origin is a "shallow, if not meaningless, construct." However, national origin has the advantage of

---

[49] In *Janko* v. *Illinois State Toll Highway Authority* (1989), the employer argued that "Gypsy" could not be ascribed to a specific country and therefore was not a protected class under Title VII. Even if the court's reliance on inaccurate dictionary definitions is rather astonishing, the decision excluded a territorial imperative for national origin claims.

[50] See, for example, the rejection of a Title VI claim on behalf of Appalachian identity in *Bronson* v. *Board of Education* (1982): "There is no indication that 'national origin' was intended to include Appalachians or to include groups such as Appalachians who do not possess a national origin distinguishable from that of other citizens of the United States" (at 959). However, the city of Cincinnati's Human Rights Ordinance (1992) forbids discrimination against Appalachians. For a discussion of regional discrimination within the United States, see Diaz (2014). A Title VII case similarly rejected a national origin designation of "Confederate Southern-American" (*Storey* v. *Burns International Security Services* (2004)).

being both indisputable and immutable. One can argue whether a certain trait is representative of a given national community. Or, one can argue that certain traits, such as language, can be voluntarily changed. National origin cannot be disputed and also cannot be changed.

The national origin aspect of the Civil Rights Act of 1964 was followed shortly thereafter by the lifting of national origin quotas in immigration (1965), the source of new waves of immigrants who spoke little or no English. Thus, as the primary focus of the 1960s was on equal opportunity regardless of race, through this change in immigration policy language again entered the discussion of equality, this time equal treatment in private employment.

The application of the five criteria for scrutiny in the case of language has varied widely. Spanish speakers come from many national origins, and often the relevant category is "language other than English," which covers immigrants from vast areas of the globe, as well as indigenous peoples in the United States and its territories. In the first instance, the courts have only gradually come to view Spanish speakers as a class that has experienced roughly the same history of discrimination in American society.

Even more problematic is the classification "limited English proficient" (LEP), the category of native speakers of a language other than English whose English-language skills do not permit them to participate equally in American society. In *Olagues* v. *Russionello* (1985), Chinese and Latino groups sought to promote voter registration and to insist on bilingual voting materials. They protested the US attorney's investigation of their activities, asking the court to review the case with heightened scrutiny, because it focused on a suspect class and a fundamental right, voting, was impeded by the action of the US attorney. The Ninth Circuit, citing *Frontiero* (1973) and *Carolene Products* (1938), disagreed, stating that "No court has yet held that a language-based classification is the equivalent of one based on race or national origin requiring heightened scrutiny as a 'suspect class'" (1985, at 801):

Unlike race, place of birth, or sex, language is not one of those "immutable characteristic[s] determined solely by the accident of birth" which typically are the basis for finding a suspect class. Although our first choice of language may be initially determined to some extent "by the accident of birth," we remain free thereafter to choose another should we decide to undertake the initiative. Indeed, bilingualism or multilingualism is hardly an extreme rarity today, as Olagues' own bilingualism exemplifies. Moreover, even if a significant percentage of those speaking a particular language can be shown to be of one "discrete and insular" racial or ethnic minority, not all persons speaking that language would be so situated. The court would thus face the problem of blurred lines defining those persons entitled to heightened protection from use of the challenged classification, with the possibility of overbroad protection leading to the striking down of otherwise rationally based official action.

In general, the courts have not considered "non-English-speaking" or "limited English proficient" as a cognizable group, for example in the decision in *People v. Lesara* (1988).[51] The Ninth Circuit cited *Sugarman v. Dougall* (1973, at 637) that "it would hardly take extraordinary ingenuity for a lawyer to find 'insular and discrete' minorities at every turn in the road." Suspicion of suspect classes has limited protection against discrimination.

Groups and classes are crucial to the American way of protecting minorities against majoritarian impositions. The problems lie in defining which types of minorities are to be afforded such protection and what kind of protection is required. Individuals are not created equal in certain respects: some are taller, some are shorter; intelligence varies widely (as do the means for measuring intelligence). Some speak English well, others less well, or differently, and yet others not at all. Nonetheless, according to the Fourteenth Amendment,[52] the individual states must respect the privileges and immunities of all citizens.[53] Similarly, but for all persons (not just citizens), the states must observe due process of the law if they seek to deprive individuals of life, liberty, or property, and they must provide equal protection of the laws. To what extent does language intersect with these three fundamental principles? The motivation of the Fourteenth Amendment was a well-placed fear of local and state governments, where the prejudices and the corruption of state and local officials (and of their constituents) could trample the rights of newly freed African-Americans. The effect of jurisprudence resulting from the amendment has been to limit judicial interference with legislative decisions, a deference that has freed special interests and majoritarian politics to preserve and expand inequalities.

---

[51] Jose Lesara was convicted of rape but claimed he had an unfair trial because, by excluding a juror with "insufficient knowledge of the English language" (1988 at 1307), he was denied a jury representing a cross-section of his community. He argued that the inconvenience of providing an interpreter for a non-English-speaking juror was no greater than that for a person with visual or hearing disabilities. The court was not persuaded, though its rebuttal seems more a matter of opinion than of factual determination, and New Mexico's practice seems to disprove the court's assumptions (see Chavez 2012, 32–33; we will discuss jury issues further in Chapter 3).

[52] Section 1 of the Fourteenth Amendment: "No state shall make or enforce any law which shall abridge the privileges or immunities of citizens of the United States; nor shall any state deprive any person of life, liberty, or property, without due process of law; nor deny to any person within its jurisdiction the equal protection of the laws."

[53] For an extensive discussion of the history of the expression in the United States, see Hamburger (2011). Curtis (2000) traces the interchangeability of "right" and "privilege" in the pre-Revolutionary and Revolutionary era. However, in the context of the Fourteenth Amendment, privileges and immunities are specifically those rights accorded to *citizens*, as the *Slaughterhouse Cases* (1873) decided – much to the disgust of future judges and legal scholars – while a number of the "fundamental rights" of the Bill of Rights, the Northwest Ordinance's Articles of Compact, and in *Corfield v. Coryell* (1823) apply equally to citizens and non-citizens. Those are covered by due process and equal protection.

The first section of the amendment can be divided into three components: the Privileges and Immunities Clause, the Due Process Clause, and the Equal Protection Clause. Each of these has been used to guarantee some rights, but court decisions have restricted each of these clauses in ways that prevent an expanded vision of potential protections.

The phrase "privileges and immunities" was a standard feature of international treaties even before the writing of the Constitution. The fundamental issue was mobility, at least for white males. The question facing interpreters of this phrase through history has been the extent of privileges and immunities: do they extend to all the elements of the Bill of Rights, or is there a hierarchy even within the Bill of Rights? The Northwest Ordinance of 1787 listed articles of compact, between the people of the original thirteen states and those of the territory that would later become states. The essential rights were freedom of religion, proportionate representation in a legislature, and a number of principles relating to the legal system: *habeas corpus*, trial by jury of one's peers, bail, fines, cruel and unusual punishment, compensation for property. The Supreme Court attempted to list the privileges and immunities in *Corfield*:

Protection by the government; the enjoyment of life and liberty, with the right to acquire and possess property of every kind, and to pursue and obtain happiness and safety; subject nevertheless to such restraints as the government may justly prescribe for the general good of the whole. The right of a citizen of one state to pass through, or to reside in any other state, for purposes of trade, agriculture, professional pursuits, or otherwise; to claim the benefit of the writ of habeas corpus; to institute and maintain actions of any kind in the courts of the state; to take, hold and dispose of property, either real or personal; and an exemption from higher taxes or impositions than are paid by the other citizens of the state. (1823, at 551–552)

This list was restated in the language education case of *Meyer* v. *Nebraska*, which we will discuss in more detail in Chapter 4:

[The Fourteenth Amendment] denotes not merely freedom from bodily restraint but also the right of the individual to contract, to engage in any of the common occupations of life, to acquire useful knowledge, to marry, establish a home and bring up children, to worship God according to the dictates of his own conscience, and generally to enjoy those privileges long recognized at common law as essential to the orderly pursuit of happiness by free men. (1923, at 399)

However, any list eventually encounters problems. In the case of the Fourteenth Amendment, one was how to treat the right of suffrage, and in particular the treatment of free blacks. Until the Fourteenth Amendment, they did not enjoy such equality of privileges and immunities when they crossed state lines. The adoption of this clause in the Fourteenth Amendment was thus a way to apply the Comity Clause of the Constitution to free blacks following the Civil War, in direct reaction to the decision of the Dred Scott case (1857).

The Supreme Court ruling in the *Slaughterhouse Cases* (1873) has limited the use of the Privileges and Immunities Clause for the past 140 years, most recently in *McDonald* v. *City of Chicago* (2010).[54] The *Slaughterhouse* interpretation makes clear that naturalized citizens have all the privileges and immunities of native-born citizens, but it defines what is meant by privileges and immunities as much less than the full Bill of Rights. The subsequent *Civil Rights Cases* (1883) limited the scope of the Privileges and Immunities Clause to government action, permitting private actors to engage in discriminatory behavior.[55] These decisions have frustrated lawyers and legal scholars of all political and philosophical persuasions,[56] some thinking that the Privileges and Immunities Clause could restrict rights, especially unenumerated rights, others contending just the opposite. In the meantime, many of the "fundamental rights" have instead been guaranteed by the Due Process Clause.

The Due Process Clause of the Fourteenth Amendment has two aspects: substantive due process and procedural due process. Substantive due process determines if the government has sufficient justification to infringe on a right otherwise protected. It limits the government's ability to act in certain domains, even if the process is fair. In the first third of the twentieth century, substantive due process arguments were used to prevent state legislation that would have limited regulation of free markets.[57] The decision in the case of *Meyer* v. *Nebraska* cited earlier was based on the freedom from state interference in the pursuit of one's career, not on the merits of bilingual education.[58]

---

[54] Otis McDonald wanted to keep a handgun for self-defense, but the City of Chicago had banned unregistered firearms and stopped registering almost all handguns, effectively making handgun ownership illegal. Justice Thomas would have liked to see the Privileges and Immunities Clause applied to this case concerning gun rights, but other justices saw no reason to overturn the *Slaughterhouse* precedent, when the Due Process Clause could be invoked without opening this Pandora's box.

[55] The *Civil Rights Cases* (1883) combined several cases involving racial discrimination in lodging, theaters, and railroad transportation to test the constitutionality of the Civil Rights Act of 1875. The ruling decided that "it is State action of a particular character that is prohibited. Individual invasion of individual rights is not the subject matter of the amendment" (1883 at 11). This then served to justify the "separate but equal" fallacy of *Plessy* v. *Ferguson* (1896), finally overturned in *Brown* v. *Board of Education* (1954).

[56] See, for example, Gerhardt (1990), Chemerinsky (1992), and, for a less critical view, Jackson (2011).

[57] During the so-called *Lochner* era (after the case *Lochner* v. *NY*, 1905), state rules on child labor and minimum wage were considered an infringement on such rights. The case involved the number of hours a baker could work, both in a day and in a week. Regulating such matters was considered an unconstitutional restriction on individuals' right to make contracts. The *Lochner* era came to a close with decisions in the 1930s that refused to consider freedom to contract a fundamental right.

[58] We will discuss educational choices in much more detail in Chapter 4.

Since the 1930s, the focus has been on other types of rights, some not specifically enumerated in the Constitution or other foundational documents. In *U.S.* v. *Carolene Products, Inc.* (1938)[59] the court ruled that

regulatory legislation affecting ordinary commercial transactions is not to be pronounced unconstitutional unless in the light of the facts made known or generally assumed it is of such a character as to preclude the assumption that it rests upon some rational basis within the knowledge and experience of the legislators. (1938, at 152)

The court then went on to discuss the areas that might require "more exacting judicial scrutiny" – restrictions on political processes, such as voting and freedom of speech, and statutes directed at particular religious, national, or racial minorities (citing *Meyer* v. *Nebraska* as an example): "prejudice against discrete and insular minorities may be a special condition, which tends seriously to curtail the operation of those political processes ordinarily to be relied upon to protect minorities, and which may call for a correspondingly more searching judicial inquiry" (*Carolene Products* 1938, footnote 4).

The pains of the Depression forced the court to reverse course and take a more expansive view of rights; since the 1990s, the pendulum has swung back. The Supreme Court has been more cautious. Substantive due process has been derided as an oxymoron by some members of the court (Scalia, Thomas). The fear of conservative justices has been that substantive due process gives unelected judges too much power, power better left to elected representatives. The fear of less conservative justices is that unrestricted power in the hands of elected representatives can lead to majoritarian excesses. In the post-World War II era, substantive due process has justified some of the most important extensions of rights, including *Brown* v. *Board of Education* and the privacy rights concerning reproduction and sexuality. More recently, the Supreme Court has backtracked from some earlier applications of substantive due process, particularly in restrictions on abortion.

Language issues and substantive due process have intersected in several ways. Substantive due process has been invoked to protect the fundamental democratic process (voting) and other crucial aspects of liberty. Participation in that process and the full enjoyment of liberty can depend crucially on language, but substantive due process has not extended rights to language groups. The voting issues we will discuss in Chapter 2 have been based on legislative action (the Voting Rights Bills and their reauthorizations).

Procedural due process ensures that the government has followed its own rules in imposing its powers. It guarantees fairness and impartiality through such mechanisms as legal notice, legal representation, trial by jury, and the

---

[59] In 1923, the Congress passed the Filled Milk Act, banning the substitution of non-dairy fats in reconstituted milk products. Carolene Products was shipping "Milnut," a combination of condensed skimmed milk and coconut oil.

ability to confront witnesses. The appearance of fairness and impartiality is crucial to a civil society, but fairness and impartiality are perceived differently by different actors in the judicial process. Sivasubrahmaniam and Heuer (2007) performed a psychological study of how the authorities (judges, police officers, prosecutors) and the subordinates (litigants, civilians, disputants) of the legal process interpreted fairness in the legal process. The authorities tended to see fairness by the outcome (justice is done), while the recipients valued more the perception of respectful treatment and hearing through the process.

As we shall see in Chapter 3, fairness and impartiality have a significant linguistic component. Denton (2007) presented a study of perceptions of fairness and impartiality in the California court system, in which language issues were considered a significant barrier to fairness. Focus groups from immigrant communities expressed particular reservations about interpretation services in the legal process (Denton 2007, 46). Even among those whose native language is English, legal language can be a barrier to understanding and participation in the legal process, both essential to the perception of fairness and impartiality.

Due process is guaranteed by the Fifth Amendment,[60] essentially a guarantee against over-reaching state action. Equal protection, added in the Fourteenth Amendment, institutes a state obligation to act in defense of rights. Strauss (2011, 173) wonders if the goal of the Equal Protection Clause is "to achieve a procedural objective (to compensate for an inadequate or untrustworthy political process), a substantive one (to prevent groups from being treated differently for an immutable trait) or both." The procedural approach emphasizes the historical dimension, and issues of power, while the substantive approach emphasizes immutability and relevancy.

Equal protection depends on the notion of protected classes – people are protected from irrational and arbitrary harms, such as discrimination: "all persons similarly situated should be treated alike" (*City of Cleburne* v. *Cleburne Living Center* 1985, at 439). The application of the Equal Protection Clause is inherently comparative: The affected persons must be similarly situated with respect to the purpose of the law, in the words of Tussman and tenBroek (1949, 346), "the elimination of a public 'mischief' or the achievement of some positive public good." Equal protection attempts to match the class of affected persons to the class intended for protection. A perfect match is almost impossible: there will always be some underinclusiveness or overinclusiveness. In *Jana Rock Inc.*

---

[60] "No person shall be held to answer for a capital, or otherwise infamous crime, unless on a presentment or indictment of a grand jury, except in cases arising in the land or naval forces, or in the militia, when in actual service in time of war or public danger; nor shall any person be subject for the same offense to be twice put in jeopardy of life or limb; nor shall be compelled in any criminal case to be a witness against himself, nor be deprived of life, liberty, or property, *without due process of law*; nor shall private property be taken for public use, without just compensation" (emphasis added).

v. *New York State Department of Economic Development* (2006) business owners contested an affirmative action class of Hispanic, arguing that it was under-inclusive because it limited the term to Western Hemisphere origins, excluding Spanish and Portuguese speakers from Spain and Portugal.

To be protected from discrimination normally one must first establish one's membership in a protected class.[61] In essence, all Equal Protection claims are class actions, which makes the definition of the class crucial. Other texts from the same period as the Fourteenth Amendment, such as the Civil Rights Act of 1866, limit the definition of protected groups to race and color. The specific rights guaranteed are the ability to enter into contracts, to participate in the legal system, to purchase and inherit property, and "the equal benefit of all laws and proceedings for the security of person and property" (Green 2008, 18).

An emphasis on "equal" challenges irrational classifications, while an emphasis on "protection" has been interpreted as requiring the government to provide equal benefit of its laws. Green (2008, 44) would prefer to read the phrase as a duty to protect, restricting the meaning of protection to life and property: "The conclusion is virtually inescapable that the text expresses an entitlement to the equal fulfillment of the government's remedial and enforce-ment functions, not a generic right against improper legislative classifications." The confusion of classes and classifications is at the heart of the problem in equal protection law. The choice of terms affects the requirements for proof, the distinction between discriminatory intent and disparate impact. How does one prove irrationality in purpose or in application?

The enforcement of Equal Protection has been limited by the level of proof required to challenge discrimination. Illegal discrimination supposes an adverse effect against an individual motivated by an irrational criterion related to a protected class. Intent supposes the ability to foresee a negative effect on a particular group. The evidence for such intent is hard to come by, and frequently circumstantial rather than overt. Siegel (2013, 2–3) contrasts the type of proof necessary for minorities claiming suspect classes, as opposed to that required of majorities contesting suspect classifications:

When minorities challenge laws of general application and argue that government has segregated or profiled on the basis of race, plaintiffs must show that government acted for a discriminatory purpose, a standard that doctrine has made extraordinarily difficult

---

[61] Normally, selective application of the law – the singling out of one individual – has not qualified as an equal protection issue. However, equal protection can have a class of one if the government's actions reflect "sheer vindictiveness" (*Esmail* v. *Macrane* 1995, at 179). As early as 1918, the Supreme Court ruled that "the purpose of the equal protection clause of the Fourteenth Amendment is to secure every person within the State's jurisdiction against intentional and arbitrary discrimination, whether occasioned by express terms of a statute or by its improper application through duly constituted agents" (*Sunday Lake Iron Company* v. *Township of Wakefield* 1918, at 352).

to satisfy. .... By contrast, when members of majority groups challenge state action that classifies by race – affirmative action has become the paradigmatic example – plaintiffs do not need to demonstrate, as a predicate for judicial intervention, that government has acted for an illegitimate purpose.

The concepts of discriminatory intent and disparate impact affect the treatment of suspect classes and suspect classifications in many domains of the law – employment, education, voting, and justice, among others.

As the nature of discriminatory activity has changed, so has the law. Initially, the assumption was that discrimination was explicit or clear, currently or historically with current effects. As more subtle types of discrimination, even totally unconscious discrimination, became the more common situation, proof has become more contentious.[62] Disparate impact focuses on the consequences of actions that may at first glance seem innocuous but have a discriminatory effect upon a suspect class. Disparate treatment looks at the intent of the employer, who treats similarly situated employees differently, when the disfavored employees belong to a suspect class.

The fundamental procedures for disparate impact were laid out in the landmark cases concerning employment law, *Griggs* v. *Duke Power Co.* (1971)[63] and *Wards Cove Packing Co.* v. *Atonio* (1989). The disparate treatment framework was established in *McDonnell-Douglas* v. *Green* (1973).[64] Both approaches involve shifting burdens of proof: in disparate impact the plaintiff must first present a prima facie case establishing the disparity between the availability of members of suspect classes in the labor pool and the proportion of members of that class hired or promoted. This disparity must then be attributable to a policy that might appear neutral but in fact has a discriminatory impact. If the plaintiff succeeds in establishing this prima facie case, the defendant employer must rebut with a non-discriminatory justification for the policy, a bona fide business necessity. Is speaking English

---

[62] For a discussion of changes in discrimination focusing more on implicit bias and stereotyping, see Selmi (2014).

[63] In *Griggs*, the power company used tests that had nothing to do with actual job requirements to ensure that African-Americans were limited to the lowest-paid jobs. In *Wards Cove*, Filipino and Alaskan Natives complained that skilled non-cannery jobs were overwhelmingly filled by white employees, while they were restricted to unskilled and lower-paid cannery jobs. The Supreme Court reversed the Ninth Circuit because it felt that the statistical comparisons were improper: instead of considering the proportion of non-white workers and white workers in the community, with the proportion in skilled jobs, the appropriate comparison was between the proportion of workers in the minority groups with the necessary skills and the proportion of minority group members in skilled positions. In *McDonnell-Douglas*, an African-American who had led protests of hiring practices at the company sought re-employment and was denied by the corporation on the grounds that the employee had engaged in unlawful conduct against the company.

[64] Sperino (2011) would reject the various frameworks altogether, arguing that the frameworks exclude cases of discrimination targeted by legislation. By returning to the statutes, instead of relying on the frameworks, a broader range of discrimination cases could be considered.

a business necessity? As we shall see, where employers cite workplace peace and safety issues, limited English speakers perceive prejudice.

In the *McDonnell-Douglas* framework, the plaintiff must first establish membership in a suspect class, and qualifications equal or superior to those required for a job. The plaintiff then must demonstrate that even after s/he was rejected, the employer continued to take applications from persons with lesser qualifications. Once again the employer can rebut the plaintiff's claims by proffering a bona fide occupational qualification for its decision. This approach has subsequently been modified to allow for a "mixed-motives defense," that is, illegal discrimination as one of several factors in an employment decision.[65]

Disparate treatment once hired requires proof that the employer has a discriminatory intent, such as derogatory comments made about particular suspect classes who are then treated differently. For example, an employer who has insulted Spanish speakers and then denies a promotion to a Spanish speaker whose performance is equal to or better than another employee has demonstrated an animus against a particular class. Derogatory comments can also be the basis for claims of a hostile workplace environment. Disparate impact, disparate treatment, and hostile environment claims are pursued through the legal framework established by the Civil Rights Act of 1964 and subsequent legislative work and judicial decisions.

A hostile work environment claim requires that one prove the workplace "is permeated with discriminatory intimidation, ridicule and insult." Single incidents are not sufficient, though the statutes require only that "the terms or conditions of plaintiff's employment were affected or that the conduct did or tended to deprive a plaintiff of employment opportunities" (Sperino 2011, 97). The Supreme Court guidelines on hostility consider the frequency and severity of malicious conduct and distinguish between threatening or humiliating behavior and "merely offensive." The employer's actions or words must interfere with the employee's performance[66] (*Harris* 1993, at 23). In some courts the high standard for a hostile workplace is one that is "hellish" (*Baskerville v. Culligan International Co.* 1995, at 430), though in others a less stringent level seems to qualify (e.g., *Lolonga-Gedeon* v. *Child & Family Services*[67]) so long as it interferes with the ability to perform one's duties.

---

[65] See *Desert Palace* v. *Costa* (2003), a sexual discrimination case covered under Title VII of the Civil Rights Act. The use of the mixed-motive approach depends on the statute: Title VII, which includes language issues under national origin, outlines mixed-motive proof requirements, but the First Circuit found that the mixed-motive approach was not applicable to age discrimination cases, covered under the Age Discrimination in Employment Act 29 U.S.C.S. §§621–624 (*Diaz v. Jiten Hotel Mgmt*, 2012). Diaz was successful anyway because Massachusetts state law allowed this approach.

[66] *Harris* v. *Forklift Systems, Inc.* 1993. This is a sexual hostile environment case.

[67] *Lolonga-Gedeon* v. *Child & Family Services* 2014, 2015. This case involved a woman of Congolese origin who upon taking a job was denied the opportunity to assume the duties she

In addition to the constitutional amendments, Congress has enacted several Civil Rights Acts to specify areas of illegal discrimination. After the Civil War, Congress passed, over President Andrew Johnson's veto, a Civil Rights Act that first defined "citizen of the United States" in such a way as to include former slaves and then declared that all citizens

shall have the same right, in every State and Territory in the United States, to make and enforce contracts, to sue, be parties, and give evidence, to inherit, purchase, lease, sell hold, and convey real and personal property, as is enjoyed by white citizens, and shall be subject to like punishment, pains, and penalties, and to none other, any law, statute, ordinance, regulation, or custom, to the contrary notwithstanding.

The Reconstruction Acts of 1867 and 1868 were passed, again over presidential veto, as a means to enforce the Civil Rights Act by placing power in the hands of military commanders and requiring new state constitutions that granted full voting rights to African-Americans, in accordance with the Fifteenth Amendment. Enforcement Acts of 1870 and 1871 gave the federal government the right to intervene if local government, or extra-governmental groups like the Ku Klux Klan, was not respecting the protections of the Fourteenth and Fifteenth Amendments. The Civil Rights Act of 1875 sought to ensure equal treatment of African-Americans in public accommodation, public transportation, and jury selection. The Supreme Court declared it unconstitutional in 1883, in the *Civil Rights Cases* (see above, p. 23), limiting federal intervention to cases in which states were involved, thus allowing private discriminatory action to continue unabated.

Civil Rights Acts returned after World War II. The integration of the armed services[68] and the rejection of "separate but equal" expressed in Supreme Court decisions in *Mendez* v. *Westminster* (1946, 1947) and *Brown* v. *Board of Education* (1954) gave momentum to civil rights legislation. The first Civil Rights Act since Reconstruction was passed in 1957, despite strong opposition by senators from southern states. The Civil Rights Act of 1957 was primarily focused on voting rights, to try to improve access to voting by

---

was hired to perform because her supervisor felt her language skills were insufficient. The supervisor made numerous comments about her language. Though Ms. Lolonga-Gedeon's testimony included several language errors, only two of more than 1,000 clients mentioned any language issue. The court therefore expressed skepticism about the supervisor's evaluation and, finding that there was a reasonable suspicion of a hostile workplace, denied the agency's request for a summary judgment.

[68] President Truman issued Executive Order 9808 (1946) establishing the President's Committee on Civil Rights, which led to Executive Orders 9980, desegregating the federal workforce, 9981, desegregating the armed forces (1948), and 9988, revising the selection principles of the Selective Service (§622.21 (d): "in classifying a registrant there shall be no discrimination for or against him because of his race, creed, or color, or because of his membership or activity in any labor, political, religious, or other organization. Each such registrant shall receive equal justice").

African-Americans, whose suffrage was limited by poll taxes, literacy tests, and other means of intimidation:

No person, whether acting under color of law or otherwise, shall intimidate, threaten, coerce or attempt to intimidate, threaten or coerce any other person for the purpose of interfering with the right of such other person to vote or to vote as he may choose.

This Civil Rights Act also established the Commission on Civil Rights, and, in the Justice Department, a position of Assistant Attorney General for Civil Rights. The charge of the Commission was to investigate allegations that citizens of the United States were "being deprived of their right to vote and have that vote counted by reason of their color, race, religion or national origin" (Section 1 W. (a)). A subsequent bill, the Civil Rights Act of 1960, sought to close some loopholes in the earlier statute, requiring officials to keep accurate records of elections and voter registration and barring local officials from inconsistent application of voting laws.

Much more dramatic in its effect has been the Civil Rights Act of 1964. Title VI of this act bans discrimination on the ground of race, color, sex, or national origin by programs and activities that receive federal funding.[69] Title VII covers discrimination by employers, private as well as public, who have fifteen or more employees.

It shall be an unlawful employment practice for an employer –
(1) to fail or refuse to hire or to discharge any individual, or otherwise to discriminate against any individual with respect to his compensation, terms, conditions, or privileges of employment, because of such individual's race, color, religion, sex, or national origin; or
(2) to limit, segregate, or classify his employees or applicants for employment in any way which would deprive or tend to deprive any individual of employment opportunities or otherwise adversely affect his status as an employee, because of such individual's race, color, religion, sex, or national origin.

Title VII also created the Equal Employment Opportunity Commission (EEOC) to address compliance issues. Guidelines relating to national origin discrimination were issued by the EEOC in 1970. Subsequent acts extended the protected categories to women (Title IX of the Education Amendments of 1972), Americans with disabilities (Section 504 of the Rehabilitation Act of 1973, Education for All Handicapped Children Act of 1975, Americans with

---

[69] The wording reprises President John Kennedy's executive order 10925 (March 6, 1961): "The contractor will not discriminate against any employee or applicant for employment because of race, creed, color, or national origin. The contractor will take affirmative action to ensure that applicants are employed, and that employees are treated during employment, without regard to their race, creed, color, or national origin" (cited in www.eeoc.gov/eeoc/history/35th/thelaw/eo-10925.html). President Kennedy's Executive Order 11063 (1962, revised by Executive Order 12259 (1980)) banned discrimination in housing affected by federal funding.

Disabilities Act of 1990), limited-English-proficient students (Title I of the Elementary and Secondary Education Amendments Act of 1974), and older employees (Age Discrimination in Employment Act of 1967, amended in 1978).

The Civil Rights Act of 1991 clarified some issues that had been the subject of Supreme Court decisions in the intervening years.[70] Guidelines issued by the EEOC in 2002 further specified the Title VII distinctions between legitimate business necessity and unlawful discrimination.[71] Guidelines are not statutes, leaving courts the right to disregard them, as in *Garcia v. Spun Steak* (1993), which we will consider in Chapter 6, p. 171). The Civil Rights Acts have been further supplemented by executive orders, most notably Executive Order 13166 (August 11, 2000), "Improving Access to Services for People with Limited English Proficiency."

We are constantly called on to discriminate: to determine the best, the most efficient, the most advantageous. In a meritocracy we seek rational bases for decisions that affect participation in the political, educational, and economic life of the country. The range of the irrational is broad, perhaps infinite, as those who benefit from some historical advantage fight to maintain that privilege. The slate is never clean. Even if one could imagine an ahistorical society, the demarcation line between rational and irrational is not clear. Physical standards for fire fighters, police officers, and combat military might or might not discriminate against women or certain ethnic groups.

Participation in society is crucially dependent on the most social of our human characteristics, language. Language brings us together, and linguistic divisions pull us apart. The divisions can be between clearly distinct languages – English and Chinese, for example – or between versions of the same dominant language – different accents or dialects of English.

The law, in its attempt to distinguish rational from irrational discrimination, forces us to reconsider prejudices so embedded as to have become ideologies.

---

[70] President Reagan vetoed the Civil Rights Restoration Act in 1988, but Congress overrode his veto. This bill extended antidiscrimination law to all entities receiving federal funding in any manner, a reaction to the Supreme Court's narrow reading of the Title VI obligations in *Grove City College v. Bell* (1984). President George H. W. Bush vetoed a Civil Rights bill in 1990, citing concern about quotas, but signed the 1991 act. See "President Vetoes Bill on Job Rights; Showdown Is Set," a *New York Times* article by Steven A. Holmes (October 23, 1990). The Civil Rights Act of 1991 was passed partly in reaction to Supreme Court rulings in *Griggs* and *Wards Cove* (see above, p. 27), codifying the concepts of "business necessity" and "job-related" in discrimination suits. For a different reading of *Griggs*, see Barry (2001, 100–102). In addition, it countered the narrow reading of "making and enforcing contracts" in the majority decision *Patterson v. McLean Credit Union* (1989) and *Price Waterhouse v. Hopkins* (1989) concerning burden-of-proof issues in discrimination suits.

[71] The full text of these guidelines is found at www.eeoc.gov/policy/docs/national-origin.html. For a discussion of the growth of administrative guidelines, which generally lack the force of law, see Chen (2014).

Some bases for discrimination and some discriminatory historical practices are clearly irrational – Jim Crow laws and the exclusion of women from voting. Decisions based on immutable characteristics such as race and gender, combined with a historical record of oppression, contradict the fundamental principles of a meritocracy. Other factors are mutable (language) and other practices are more subtle (supposedly neutral testing systems).

Language discrimination is construed as national origin discrimination when associated with immigrants but as racial discrimination when associated with African-American English. Dialectal differences of native English speakers have been an issue, primarily but not exclusively in the role of African-American English in the schools (see Chapter 4). English learners' accents and several native dialects are the targets of negative stereotypes that can lead to illegal discriminatory behavior (see Chapter 5).

Language is thus a particularly challenging aspect of a meritocracy. English was the dominant language, but not the only language, in the thirteen colonies. At the time of the Revolution, English was not the dominant language in 90 percent of the territory that would ultimately become the United States. It was imposed on the peoples who inhabited the rest of the land, never without some tension. It has also been imposed on and embraced by newer arrivals, the waves of immigrants, again with inevitable tensions. The incorporation of non-English speakers into American society never has happened instantaneously, and never will. For full and fair participation in American society language remains a barrier, the object of constant negotiation and accommodation. The demands of equality conflict often with those of efficiency, the social costs of exclusion with the financial costs of inclusion.[72]

---

[72] See, for example, the "fact sheet" prepared by the anti-bilingual organization US English, www .usenglish.org/view/301. This site has apparently not been updated since 2003. This is not a new argument. A decision to publish a German-language version of a federal report on agriculture in 1862 was reversed the following day when the cost of special fonts and typesetters was invoked (Kloss 1998, 33–34). We will treat questions of the language of government services in more detail in Chapter 5.

2   Language and Democracy

One of the rallying cries of the American Revolution was "No taxation without representation."[1] The fundamental promise of a democracy is the opportunity to participate in the direction of the society one lives in. As Western democracies developed from the eighteenth century on, this promise has been realized through the election of representative government, and sometimes through direct voting on specific issues in referenda. The extension of that opportunity to an ever-expanding number of adults, the methods of delivery on that promise, and the ultimate effectiveness of democracy for representing common interests all intersect with considerations of the language of potential participants in self-government. The expansion of the right to vote focuses on individuals' input, while effectiveness stresses outcomes relating to group membership.[2] Both individual and group claims thus present issues linking language and the law.

Even before voters get their say, the choices open to them can be limited by language. Arizona had an English literacy test for voters from the time of its entry into the Union as a state (1912), a law overthrown by the Voting Rights Act of 1970. The Voting Rights Act says nothing about candidacy for election. Even before Arizona was a state, the territorial code declared ineligible for office anyone who "cannot write and read in the English language,"[3] and the Enabling Act of 1910 requires of all state officers "the ability to read, write, speak and understand the English language sufficiently well to conduct the duties of the office without the aid of an interpreter."[4] Arizona's version of an English-only law, in 1988, included a provision in the state constitution requiring English fluency of all public office holders.[5]

---

[1] J. L. Bell has explored the origins of this phrase in the American colonies in three blog entries, http://boston1775.blogspot.com/2009/04/looking-for-taxation-without.html.

[2] For further discussion of how this division of concerns is expressed in the Voting Rights Act of 1965, see Karlan (1995, 84).

[3] Cited in *Escamilla* v. *Cuello* (2012, at 204).

[4] This is the fifth provision of Section 20, but not the only mention of English. The fourth provision requires that public schools "shall always be conducted in English," www.azleg.state.az.us/con st/enabling.pdf.

[5] Article 28 of the Arizona Constitution.

In San Luis, a small town on the Mexican border, Alejandrina Cabrera wanted to be a candidate for the city council; the sitting mayor, Juan Carlos Escamilla challenged her right to be on the ballot, given her lack of proficiency in English.[6] The Arizona Supreme Court ruled in favor of the mayor, after admitting testimony of an expert who evaluated the English proficiency required to function in the position and Ms. Cabrera's level. As to the general principle of excluding those who do not speak English from public office, the court found that "there is no general constitutional right to seek or hold public office" (2012, at 207). No alternative solutions were suggested, such as using interpreters or conducting public business in both of the town's languages.

Once the candidates have been determined, the next step is voter registration. The criteria for participating in an election are only tangentially mentioned in the US Constitution. Article 1, Section 2, states only that members of the House of Representatives will be elected every second year "by the People of the several States." The definition of "people" was left vague and in the hands of the individual states: "the Electors in each State shall have the Qualifications requisite for Electors of the most numerous Branch of the State Legislature." For some states, particularly those trying to attract new immigrants, extending suffrage to the newly arrived was an important strategy of enticement.

The history of voting has seen the progressive implementation of national standards requiring states to permit more and more people to participate in elections. African-Americans were guaranteed the right to vote through the Fifteenth Amendment to the Constitution (1870),[7] though terrorist tactics by the Ku Klux Klan and a variety of provisions adopted by states were used to severely restrict their access to the ballot. Suffrage was extended to women by the Nineteenth Amendment (1920).[8] The expansion of the right to vote for these categories came at the same time as voting rights for immigrant non-citizens were being eliminated. The proponents for such restrictions frequently cited language issues and the potential for fraud.

Before independence, suffrage for those who were not British citizens was widely recognized, allowing French Huguenots in South Carolina and Germans in Pennsylvania to vote (Raskin 1993, 1399–1400). In the early years of the Republic, the selection of the representatives in legislatures was limited to a relatively small percentage of the population, but gender, race, wealth, and religion were considered more important qualifications than citizenship. Only white males over 21 years of age who owned a certain amount of property had the right to vote. With the confirmation of the Northwest Ordinance in 1789, the

---

[6] For a fuller discussion of this case, see Callagy (2013).
[7] "The right of citizens of the United States to vote shall not be denied or abridged by the United States or by any State on account of race, color, or previous condition of servitude."
[8] "The right of citizens of the United States to vote shall not be denied or abridged by the United States or by any State on account of sex."

first Congress specifically provided voting rights to non-citizens with more than two years' residency in the concerned territories (Ohio, Michigan, Wisconsin, Indiana, Illinois, and part of Minnesota).

From the founding of the Republic, the extension of suffrage has been a point of tension. Suspicion of foreigners during the War of 1812 led several states to exclude non-citizens from voting (Louisiana, Indiana, Mississippi, Alabama, Maine, and Missouri). Ironically, the suppression or reduction of the property requirement to extend suffrage was used as an argument to restrict suffrage to citizens. Illinois was a notable exception, its commitment to suffrage for resident non-citizens confirmed in *Spragins* v. *Houghton* (1840).[9] Abraham Lincoln rejected lengthy residency requirements for new immigrants, defending the rights of new German-Americans to participate in elections, and specifically mentioning language difference as a non-issue:

> I am against its adoption in Illinois, or in any other place, where I have a right to oppose it. Understanding the spirit of our institutions to aim at the elevation of men, I am opposed to whatever tends to degrade them. I have some little notoriety for commiser-ating with the oppressed condition of the negro; and I should be strangely inconsistent if I could favor any project for curtailing the existing rights of white men, even though born in different lands, and speaking different languages from myself. (Cited in Keyssar 2000, 87)

The legal process of naturalization was invoked by Wisconsin to establish a compromise between the two positions. In its 1848 constitution, the state granted voting rights to immigrants who had formally declared their intention to become citizens, the first step in the naturalization process outlined in federal law in 1795. Other Midwestern and Western states quickly followed the Wisconsin example (e.g., Minnesota (1849), Michigan (1850)), with the result that by 1880 seventeen states allowed non-citizens to vote, and most of those non-citizens were immigrants speaking languages other than English. With mass immigration in the period 1880–1920 and the anti-foreign sentiments aroused by World War I, all of these provisions were repealed by 1926.

A number of justifications for extension and restriction of suffrage have been proposed over the years. Perhaps the least compelling reason to extend voting rights has been the most philosophical: the Declaration of Independence's statement that "all men are created equal." Supporters of the expansion of the right to vote have been somewhat more successful in citing the taxation argument, although taxation is of course not the only agenda item for elected officials. The most successful argument has been military service. How can

---

[9] Spragins was an election judge who permitted Jeremiah Kyle, an Irish national not yet natur-alized, to vote in the 1838 election. Foreign nationals in the state at the time voted overwhel-mingly Democratic, which led the Whigs to challenge their vote.

veterans who have put their lives on the line for the country be denied the right to vote for those who decide to put them in harm's way?

Those who would constrain voting emphasize the stake the voter has in the community and the ability to cast a knowledgeable vote. Why should a person – for instance, a university student or an immigrant – have a voice in local affairs when that person is newly arrived and possibly transient? Can a person who has no knowledge of the issues, perhaps because of a language barrier, cast a meaningful ballot?

Foreigners coming to this country to become citizens, who are educated in their own language, should acquire the requisite knowledge of ours during the necessary residence to obtain naturalization. If they did not take interest enough in our language to acquire sufficient knowledge of it to enable them to study the institutions and laws of the country intelligently, I would not confer upon them the right to make such laws nor to select those who do. (Ulysses Grant, Eighth annual message, December 5, 1876. *Messages and Papers of the Presidents* (Richardson 1902, Vol. 7, 411))

Concern about election fraud through manipulation of immigrants ignorant of the English language is a constant refrain, as exemplified by a history book popular early in the twentieth century:

The process of making citizens out of foreigners was frequently turned into a farce. People unable to read or write, ignorant of the principles of free government, and in many instances still loyal in spirit to the land of their birth, were massed by hundreds on the eve of an election and run through the mill of citizenship with little or no regard for legal requirements. It was simply a matter of political influence, and the politician who could round up the largest number of men willing to become citizens stood the best shot of winning at the polls. (Jackman *et al.* 1911, Vol. 6, 1815–1816)

Knowledge of the majority language is certainly no guarantee against voting in ignorance, or against manipulation by demagoguery, or direct voter fraud. One way to try to overcome these concerns is the literacy test, an added qualification for voting that has frequently been used to deny the vote to linguistic minorities, as well as to African-Americans.

Literacy tests as a qualification for voting were first instituted in Connecticut in 1855, a reaction to the rapid increase in immigration during the 1840s. Three million immigrants, constituting more than 15 percent of the population, arrived during the period 1845–1854 (Tucker 2009, 4), primarily from Ireland and Germany. Voters were expected to be able to read a passage from the state's constitution, but could do so in any language. New York, however, rejected such tests at that time, in constitutional conventions both before and after the Civil War. Horace Greeley chaired a commission that studied the question in 1867, concluding that excluding illiterates from the vote was not fair and prone to political manipulation:

men's relative capacity is not absolutely measured by their literacy acquirements; and the State requires the illiterate, equally with others, to be taxed for their support, and to shed their blood in her defense. . . . inspectors of election are fallible and swayed by like passions with other men . . . they might be tempted, in an exciting and closely contested election, to regard with a partial fondness, almost parental, the literacy acquirements of those claimants of the franchise who were notoriously desirous of voting the ticket of those inspectors' own party, while applying a far sterner and more critical rule to those who should proffer the opposite ballots. (Gellman & Quigley 2003, 284)

Greeley's concerns about the abuse of the literacy test for political purposes were well founded. In a Wyoming case from 1897 the loser in a race for county treasurer sought to have the votes of Finnish voters disqualified because they could not read the state constitution in English, though they could read it in Finnish translation.[10]

In the former states of the Confederacy, the laws provided loopholes to permit white, native-born illiterates to vote without passing the test, excluding only African-Americans and recent immigrants. North Carolina's constitution effective in 1902 was typical:

Every person presenting himself for registration shall be able to read and write any section of the Constitution in the English language. But no male person, who was, on January 1, 1867, or at any time prior thereto entitled to vote under the laws of any State in the United States wherein he then resided, and no lineal descendant of any such person shall be denied the right to register and vote at any election in this State by reason of his failure to possess the educational qualifications herein described. (N.C. Constitution of 1902, Article VI, § 4 cited in Tucker 2009, 8)

The date was meant to ensure that African-Americans enfranchised under Reconstruction would not be exempted from the literacy test.

The Fifteenth Amendment, enacted in 1870, confirmed Reconstruction Era voting rights, providing that voting privileges could not be denied or abridged on account of "race, color or previous condition of servitude." During the congressional debates on this amendment, protection from discrimination based on "nativity" and on "education" was also considered (Keyssar 2000, 95). Senator Simon Cameron of Pennsylvania spoke in favor of this version "because it invites into our country everybody: the negro, the Irishman, the German, the Frenchman, the Scotchman, the Englishman, and the Chinaman. I will welcome every man, whatever may be the country from which he comes, who by his industry can add to our national wealth" (cited in Keyssar 2000, 97).

---

[10] *Rasmussen* v. *Baker* (1897). The Wyoming Constitution Art. VI §2 provided that "No person shall have the right to vote who shall not be able to read the constitution of the state." The court ruled that a translation is not the same as the original, and "no person is able to read the constitution of this State who can not read it in the English language; and consequently is not entitled to vote" (at 148–149).

Opposition, in part from northeastern Republicans who feared the immigrant vote, led to a more narrowly constructed amendment limited to African-Americans.

As mass immigration from Southern and Eastern Europe increased in the 1880s, fears of the immigrant vote grew stronger. The literacy test took on an "English-only" aspect. An 1897 amendment to the Connecticut constitution required that the prospective voter be literate in English. Between 1889 and 1924 sixteen states adopted literacy tests, eight southern states in order to keep African-Americans from voting, and eight northeastern and western states to prevent voting by immigrants.

These literacy tests remained in effect as the civil rights era dawned in the 1950s. In 1956, Louise Lassiter, a 41-year-old African-American in North Carolina, a "farm wife" with one year of high school education, started a test case against the state's literacy test. In Northampton County, whites constituted 36 percent of the population but 84 percent of the registered voters. Ms. Lassiter was denied the right to register to vote because she allegedly mispronounced three words, including the word "indictment" during her literacy test.[11] At the time her case reached the United States Supreme Court in 1959, nineteen states had literacy tests in effect, with widely disparate standards applied for political purposes. The Supreme Court rejected the claim that all literacy tests were invalid, but allowed that they could be unconstitutional if used as devices for racial discrimination (*Lassiter* v. *Northhampton County Board of Elections* 1959).

The fact that such tests were being used for discriminatory purposes led to the Voting Rights Act of 1965. Again the primary target was discrimination against African-Americans, but language issues were included, particularly in response to the growing Puerto Rican population on the mainland. After failed experiments in English-only education in Puerto Rico the schools were, by federal decision, conducted in Spanish. When Puerto Ricans moved to the mainland, they were excluded from voting by English-only literacy tests. Thus, provision was made for those who were literate in other languages:

(1) Congress hereby declares that to secure the rights under the Fourteenth Amendment of persons educated in American-flag schools in which the predominant classroom language was other than English, it is necessary to prohibit the States from conditioning the right to vote of such persons on ability to read, write, understand, or interpret any matter in the English language.

(2) No person who demonstrates that he has successfully completed the sixth primary grade in a public school in, or a private school accredited by, any

---

[11] For a full account of the evolution of this case, see Wertheimer (2009), especially Chapter 7, "Reading and the Right to Vote: James R. Walker Jr. and North Carolina's Literacy Test."

State or territory, the District of Columbia, or the Commonwealth of Puerto Rico in which the predominant classroom language was other than English, shall be denied the right to vote in any Federal, State, or local election because of his inability to read, write, understand or interpret any matter in the English language, except that in States in which State law provides that a different level of education is presumptive of literacy, he shall demonstrate that he has successfully completed an equivalent level of education in a public school in, or a private school accredited by, any State or Territory, the District of Columbia, or the Commonwealth of Puerto Rico in which the predominant classroom language was other than English. (Voting Rights Act of 1965 (42 U.S.C. § 1973b(e), Section 4(e))

The provisions for Puerto Ricans reflected a growing campaign against the literacy test for voting in New York State. New York State had tried to protect itself from political uses of the literacy test by placing the authority for the test in the hands of the Board of Regents, the state board of education. However, for Puerto Rican citizens this was no protection, as their education was in Spanish and the test was in English.

The Puerto Rican population in New York City alone grew from 7,364 in 1920 to 612,574 in 1960 (Tucker 2009, 31), making the potential Puerto Rican vote an important political question. Indeed, while 150,000 Puerto Ricans were registered to vote in New York in 1965, some 330,000 potential voters were being excluded (Cartagena 2004, 206).

Jose Camacho unsuccessfully challenged the English-language limitations of the literacy test in the late 1950s (*Camacho* v. *Doe* (1958; affirmed 1959), *Camacho* v. *Rogers* (1961)). He claimed that the Fourteenth Amendment[12] prohibited the state of New York from denying him the privileges of a citizen, while the Fifteenth Amendment (see note 7, above) protected him on racial grounds. He further claimed that Article IX of the Treaty of Paris, giving the United States control over Puerto Rico at the conclusion of the Spanish–American War (1898), gave the US Congress alone the power to determine the political status and civil rights of Puerto Ricans. Finally, he invoked the United Nations Charter granting protection from discrimination on the basis of language. Along lines similar to the *Lassiter* decision, the court found the literacy in English requirement reasonable and dismissed the Fifteenth Amendment claims because language is not equivalent to race.

---

[12] Section 1 reads:

All persons born or naturalized in the United States, and subject to the jurisdiction thereof, are citizens of the United States and of the State wherein they reside. No State shall make or enforce any law which shall abridge the privileges or immunities of citizens of the United States; nor shall any State deprive any person of life, liberty, or property, without due process of law; nor deny to any person within its jurisdiction the equal protection of the laws.

The arguments based on the Treaty of Paris were rejected because they were held to apply only to those living on the island of Puerto Rico, not those of Puerto Rican descent who lived on the mainland. Finally, the court ruled that the provisions of the United Nations Charter did not supersede domestic legislation.

As the courts provided no relief, the Latino community turned to federal legislation, pressing for insertion of protections for Puerto Ricans in the Voting Rights Act of 1965, as seen in the text above. Section 4(e) of the Voting Rights Act was proposed by the two senators from New York (Jacob Javits and Robert Kennedy). Representative Jacob Gilbert (D., NY) promoted the section in the House version, protesting that it was an "anomaly for [Congress] to encourage the perpetuation of Puerto Rico's Spanish language culture and at the same time do nothing to protect the rights of citizenship of Puerto Ricans who move to other sections of the country" (111 *Cong. Rec.* 15666 (Daily Ed.), cited in *US* v. *County Board of Elections of Monroe County* 1965, at 321). The bill passed overwhelmingly in the House and Senate; President Lyndon Johnson signed the bill on August 6, 1965.

A few weeks later, Maria Lopez tried to register to vote in Rochester, New York. She was a 21-year-old hotel service worker in Rochester who had completed 9th grade schooling in Puerto Rico. When her request was denied because of her inability to read English, it presented a test case for the power of Congress to restrict states' rights to determine the qualifications for voting. In a ruling issued December 8, 1965, the court in *US* v. *County Board of Elections* ruled that "[i]nherent in its power to enforce the Fourteenth Amendment, Congress must be considered as having some latitude to determine for itself what patterns of activity contravene Fourteenth Amendment rights" (1965, at 322). The enforcement of the Fourteenth Amendment trumped Article 1, Section 2, of the Constitution, resulting in the extension of the right to vote to Puerto Ricans who do not know English and the protection of the rights of all potential voters who speak a language other than that of the majority.

As we have seen, the Voting Rights Act focused initially on the effect of literacy tests on African-American and Puerto Rican voters. The initial court cases, such as *Katzenbach* v. *Morgan* (1966), upheld the right of Congress to take action against the states yet insisted on this narrow application of the law:

The Solicitor General informs us in his brief to this Court, that in all probability the practical effect of § 4 (e) will be limited to enfranchising those educated in Puerto Rican schools. He advises us that, aside from the schools in the Commonwealth of Puerto Rico, there are no public or parochial schools in the territorial limits of the United States in which the predominant language of instruction is other than English and which would have generally been attended by persons who are otherwise qualified to vote save for their lack of literacy in English. (*Katzenbach* 1966, at 647)

Katzenbach was brought by registered voters in New York who favored the English-only literacy test. The US Supreme Court was asked to decide not if the English literacy test was constitutional but rather whether the Voting Rights Act's prohibition of literacy tests was appropriate legislation to enforce the Equal Protection Clause of the Fourteenth Amendment in this particular situation:

We hold only that the limitation on relief effected in § 4 (e) does not constitute a forbidden discrimination since these factors might well have been the basis for the decision of Congress to go "no farther than it did." (*Katzenbach* 1966, at 658)

With the registration issue mostly solved for Puerto Ricans, the attention of that community moved on to voter assistance (see the following).

Other linguistic minorities clamored for equal treatment. In *Reynolds* v. *Sims* (1964), a reapportionment case that we will return to in the following, the Supreme Court stressed the importance of voting as a basic right of people in a democratic society:

the right of suffrage is a fundamental matter in a free and democratic society. Especially since the right to exercise the franchise in a free and unimpaired manner is preservative of other basic civil and political rights, any alleged infringement of the right of citizens to vote must be carefully and meticulously scrutinized. (*Reynolds,* at 561–562)

In keeping with this policy of "strict scrutiny," *Oregon* v. *Mitchell* (1970) prohibited all states from using literacy tests, at the same time casting aside the requirement for a sixth-grade education and extending consideration to two other linguistic minorities, Mexican Americans and Native Americans.

When the Voting Rights Act came up for reauthorization in 1975, these two groups along with Asian-Americans and Alaskan Natives were protected, as the Congress settled for this middle ground between granting protection to all language minorities (as proposed by Mario Biaggi and Stephen Solarz (D., NY)), and restricting the protections to Spanish speakers and Native Americans (as proposed by Charles Wiggins (R., Calif.)). The rationale for limiting protection to these four groups was based on evidence of pervasive discrimination that had significantly affected voter registration.[13] The negative

---

[13] Alaska protested its inclusion on this list, as its "literacy test" required only that potential voters be able to say "hello" and their name. Prior to 1924, Alaskan Natives had been subject to extremely difficult tests for citizenship, which were vacated by the congressional act to extend citizenship to all native peoples in the United States (Landreth & Smith 2007, 90). The Alaskan literacy test provisions were written by a Native Alaskan to avoid the more restrictive tests proposed by others. The Department of Justice agreed that literacy tests were not used to discriminate against Alaskan Natives, and in 1970, Alaskans voted to remove the English literacy test from the list of voter qualifications (see Harrison (2007)).

consequence has been that members of other ethnic minorities who arrived in greater numbers after 1975, such as Haitians and Arabs, have been unable to benefit from these protections.

The Voting Rights Act came up for reauthorization in 2006, at which time Arab-Americans in Michigan and Haitian-Americans in South Florida asked to be included in the list of protected linguistic minorities. Congress has been unwilling to expand the list of specifically targeted linguistic minorities, though the more general provisions of Section 2 offer some relief.

Furthermore, states have found new ways to discriminate against minority voters, most notably through strict voter identification laws.[14] These measures are said to target fraud, but consciously or inadvertently they serve to exclude the poor and linguistic minorities. State after state has enacted voter identification requirements (state-issued identification) that make it harder for the poor to vote, and especially poor eligible voters with a limited command of English. When the state of Texas passed Senate Bill 14 (2011), limiting far more stringently than before the types of identification voters could use, the US Assistant Attorney General objected. He found that 10.8 percent of Hispanic voters did not have the necessary identification, as opposed to 4.9 percent of the non-Hispanic population. One-third of Texas counties do not have a Department of Public Safety office, where a voter could obtain the required identification. A three-judge panel from the US District Court in Washington, DC, ruled that "SB 14, if implemented, would in fact have a retrogressive effect on Hispanic and African American voters."[15] Nonetheless, as long as states have not charged for identification cards, the courts have not considered the other expenses involved (time off work, travel to a site to obtain an identification card, fees for obtaining a birth certificate, or other required documents) as a "poll tax," which would be outlawed by the Twenty-Fourth Amendment.

The enforcement of voter identification laws is indicative of discriminatory impact, whatever the intent. A study of the 2012 election showed that African-Americans and Latinos were far more likely to be required to show identification than their white counterparts.[16] Just as voter identification laws were establishing a new means of discriminating against minority voters, in

---

[14] According to the Center for Media and Democracy, the new voter identification laws follow closely the model for vote suppression legislation written by the American Legislative Exchange Council in 2009, http://alecexposed.org/w/images/d/d9/7G16-VOTER_ID_ACT_E xposed.pdf.

[15] *Texas v. Holder* (2012, at 138), August 30, 2012, cited in a complaint filed in the US District Court, S.D. Texas, Corpus Christi Division, August 22, 2013.

[16] A survey of young voters (18–29) found that 64.5 percent of African-American voters were asked for photo IDs, 57 percent of Latino voters, but only 42.2 percent of white non-Hispanic voters.

Shelby County v. *Holder* (June 25, 2013) the US Supreme Court held, in a 5–4 ruling, that pervasive discrimination in voting was a thing of the past.[17]

Even before the Supreme Court ruling, President Obama issued an executive order establishing a Presidential Commission on Election Administration (Executive Order 13639, March 28, 2013) "to ensure that all eligible voters have the opportunity to cast their ballots without undue delay, and to improve the experience of voters facing other obstacles in casting their ballots." The Commission's charge specifically targets, among others, "voters with limited English proficiency." The Commission's report[18] did not directly address the registration issues specific to LEP voters but did suggest the use of non-English media to inform potential voters and the creation of community advisory groups to help address accessibility issues (2014, 50).

There is a stark disparity between the encouragement of community organizations to increase accessibility and the passage of state laws to restrict such organizations from conducting voter registration drives. Florida HB 1355 (2012) requires that any individual or group engaging in voter registration must have state approval before they can approach unregistered potential voters, must submit daily reports on every registration form (blank or complete) and on all voter registrations completed, and must submit the completed forms to county officials within forty-eight hours. The law had the effect of forcing several groups, including Democracia USA and the League of Women Voters, to abandon their efforts for voter registration (Levitt 2012, 100). Levitt notes that Latinos and other minority groups are twice as likely as non-Hispanic whites to be registered (or re-registered after changing residences) through voter registration drives.

Registration is only the first step. Access to the polling place is the next. Frequently, in American history registered voters' right to cast their votes has been challenged for political motives in the name of fraud prevention. This is a technique known as "vote caging":

a three-stage process designed to identify persons in another party or faction whose names are on a voter registration list, but whose legal qualification to vote is dubious, and then to challenge their qualification either before or on Election Day. Ostensibly, caging is an attempt to prevent voter fraud. In practice, it may have the effect of

---

[17] Tokaji (2014, 71–72) argues that the Voting Rights Act is more effective at preventing discriminatory uses of redistricting than it has been in preventing suppression of voting through voter ID laws. Table 1 (2014, 79) shows that sixty-two of seventy-six objections between 2000 and 2012 concerned vote dilution; only three involved bilingual issues. Fraga and Ocampo (2007) studied "More Information Requests" over the period 1982–2005, in which the Department of Justice did not immediately object but rather asked for clarification. Again, issues relating to the dilution of minority votes were far more frequent than issues of voter participation.

[18] The full report is found at www.supportthevoter.gov/files/2014/01/Amer-Voting-Exper-final-draft-01–09-14–508.pdf.

disenfranchising voters who are legitimately registered. (Davidson *et al.* 2008, 537–538)

In 1918, Texas established a "Loyalty Ranger Force" to challenge Mexican-American voters (Cartagena 2004, 2112). In the late 1950s and early 1960s, when he was a young politician in Arizona, the future Chief Justice of the Supreme Court William Rehnquist was accused of involvement in the same practice (Davidson *et al.* 2008, 549–559). Complaints about such practices persist to the present.[19]

Once the barriers to registration were addressed, and problems of access recognized if not solved, the focus for linguistic minorities turned to helping voters through the voting process. Again the Constitution gives the states wide latitude in deciding how to conduct elections:

Article 1, Section 4, clause 1: The Times, Places and Manner of holding Elections for Senators and Representatives, shall be prescribed in each State by the Legislature thereof; but the Congress may at any time by Law make or alter such Regulations, except as to the Places of chusing Senators.

Voting rights are not limited to access to the ballot box; the voter must have the ability to use the ballot box in an effective manner. Voter assistance includes bilingual ballots, bilingual voting information, bilingual poll workers, and other aids. Once in the polling place, a voter needs to know how to cast an informed ballot.

Discrimination in voting in some areas was deemed so pervasive, and the tactics employed to maintain discriminatory practices so difficult to keep up with, that Congress required certain political districts to request "preclearance" for any changes to their voting laws. Initially, such preclearance requirements targeted areas that had used some "test or device" to restrict registration. In 1972, Congress extended the definition of "test or device" to include

any practice or requirement by which any State or political subdivision provided any registration or voting notices, forms, instructions, assistance, or other materials or information relating to the electoral process, including ballots, only in the English language, where the Director of the Census determines that more than five per centum of the citizens of voting age residing in such State or political subdivision are members of a single language minority. (§ 4(f)4)

Voter assistance has thus depended on the concentration of minority language voters. In the 1975 reauthorization, Section 203 established other criteria, expanding the number of targeted jurisdictions. Current law, extended in 2006 for another twenty-five years, requires voter assistance in a language other than English if

---

[19] See above p. 42–43 concerning voter ID enforcement.

(a) 5 percent of all citizens of voting age are in a single language group
(b) or there are 10,000 citizens of voting age in a single language group
(c) and the illiteracy rate of the limited-English-proficient community must be greater than the national illiteracy rate. (Those who have five years or fewer of primary education are considered illiterate.)

Thirty-one states are partially or fully under the provisions of this section of the law. In Florida, the number of counties covered has gradually expanded from four in 1975 to seven in 1984, nine in 1994, and today thirty-seven counties (Newman 2007, 345–346). The language groups protected are still those mentioned above, limited to Spanish speakers, Asian-American, Native American, and Alaskan Native voters.[20] Some of the fastest-growing language minorities in the United States are thus excluded from these rights, including Arab-Americans and Haitian-Americans.[21]

The requirements for bi- or multilingual voting materials have been a continuing source of controversy. A staple of "English-only" movements is the demand that all ballot material be prepared in English and no other language. Typical is the American Elections Act of 2009 (H.R. 764, 111th Congress) proposed by Congressman Dean Heller (R., Nev.), which would eliminate protections for all groups except Native Americans and Native Alaskans. The arguments in favor of such bills are that immigrants are required to prove competence in English as part of naturalization and non-immigrants have been educated in English-language schools in the United States. Therefore, all adult citizens are in principle English speakers requiring no such assistance.

If they are not English speakers, then – opponents of voter assistance have argued – the desire to participate in an election would be a means of encouraging them to learn English. Furthermore, bilingual ballots add expense at a time when governments at the local, state, and national levels are having trouble balancing their budgets. Typical is this complaint by Congresswoman Ginny Brown-Waite (R., Florida), in her remarks concerning the extension of the Voting Rights Act in 2006: "the bilingual ballot provision has long kept new citizens from increasing their knowledge of our language and from fully integrating into our society. Not only is it expensive to print ballots in a variety of different dialects and tongues, but it reinforces a fractious society" (*Congressional Record* June 27, 2006, p. H4563).

Finally, it is claimed that voter assistance facilitates election fraud, fears summarized in *Garza* v. *Smith* (1970), a case we shall return to below: "the dangers are that the person rendering assistance will mark the ballot in

---

[20] 52 USCS § 10310 (c) (3): "The term 'language minorities' or 'language minority group' means persons who are American Indian, Asian American, Alaskan Natives or of Spanish heritage."

[21] For further discussion of the inequities resulting from these limitations, see Abdelall (2005) and Barbas (2009).

accordance with his own purpose instead of that of the voter, falsely represent to the voter that a given mark will record his political choice, take advantage of his presence in the voting booth to influence the choice of those voters who are vulnerable to pressure, or otherwise substitute his will for that of the voter" (1970, at 138).

The courts, however, felt that the risks of fraud were just as great if the will of the voters was not heard through participation in elections and that the societal cost of low voter participation from specific language groups was greater than the financial burden of providing assistance for such voters.

Since the early 1970s the courts have been consistently affirming the need for informed participation of the greatest number of voters: "the 'right to vote' additionally includes the right to be informed as to which mark on the ballot, or lever on the voting machine, will effectuate the voter's political choice" (*Garza* 1970, at 136). Protections provided to illiterate voters in the *Garza* case would soon be extended to LEP voters.

The provisions of the Voting Rights Act reauthorization of 1975 standardized the expectations established by several court cases in the preceding years. The Illinois case *PROPA (Puerto Rican Organization for Political Action)* v. *Kusper* (1972; affirmed 1973) extended the *Garza* protections to qualified voters who could not read English texts:

Section 4(e) requires that persons in the plaintiff class, notwithstanding their "inability to read, write, understand, or interpret" English, be permitted to vote, *i.e.*, to effectively register their political choice. If voting instructions and ballots or ballot labels on voting machines are printed only in English, the ability of the citizen who understands only Spanish to vote effectively is seriously impaired. It follows that the members of the plaintiff class are entitled to such assistance as may be required to enable them to vote effectively. (1972, at 610)

A preliminary injunction granted by the District Court required the State of Illinois to provide Spanish-language versions of instruction cards, to display posters informing voters of the availability of assistance, and to appoint bilingual election judges.

Torres v. *Sachs* (1974) in New York and *Arroyo* v. *Tucker* (1974) in Philadelphia affirmed the *PROPA* guidelines. *Arroyo* v. *Tucker* required the city of Philadelphia to provide all written materials relating to registration and voting in both Spanish and English, to post translations of all propositions, questions, and amendments in each voting booth, and to have available bilingual assistance for voters in all voting precincts where Puerto Ricans constitute 5 percent or more of the local population (as determined by the most recent census).[22]

---

[22] The provision of bilingual materials can be compromised in various ways. Mandarin ballots can be provided for Cantonese speakers, or mistranslated ballots can lead to the disqualification of ballots. See Benson (2007, 290).

While Alaska received a declaratory judgment that its literacy test for voter registration was not discriminatory, it did not receive such favorable reception to its record in voter assistance. In a 1995 referendum on a ban of alcohol sales in the village of Barrow, voters complained that bilingual materials were not available and that poll workers misled voters about the meaning of a "yes" or "no" vote (Landreth & Smith 2007, 117–118).

Efforts since 1975 have tried to extend such assistance to language groups beyond the four specified in the 1975, especially for Haitian-Americans and for Arab-Americans. Neither of these groups was large in the mid-1970s, but their numbers have been growing quickly. The US Census estimated the number of Arab-Americans at 1.2 million in 2000, double the number for 1980. There were 290,000 Haitian-Americans in 1990, but an estimated 830,000 in 2009.[23] Arab-Americans have an especially large presence in southeastern Michigan, while Haitian-Americans are most concentrated in South Florida and in the New York City metropolitan area. Accordingly, these areas have been targeted in voting assistance legal cases, often resulting in Department of Justice consent decrees with states or smaller jurisdictions.

In 1999, a Hamtramck, Michigan, group called "Citizens for a Better Hamtramck" challenged voters with "dark-skin and distinctly Arab names" to prove their citizenship.[24] The consent decree required an immediate end to potentially discriminatory use of challenges and the training of bilingual English-Arabic and English-Bengali election inspectors for each precinct where challenges took place and to post in public places and in the local newspapers bilingual notices about fair election practices, including recourse for voters when challenged. A 2002 decree in Miami-Dade County had similar provisions for Haitian-Americans (*US* v. *Miami-Dade County*, Civil Action 02–21698); Palm Beach County and Broward County have since instituted the same policies for Creole speakers (Ancheta 2010, 186).

Under these consent decrees the defendants are obligated to hire a bilingual coordinator and an advisory group to that coordinator. Additionally, every polling place with a set number of probable non-English-speaking voters is required to have bilingual election officials. An example is the 2010 Memorandum of Agreement between the Department of Justice and Riverside County (California). One formula requires one bilingual election

---

[23] For Haitian-Americans, www.census.gov/prod/2010pubs/acsbr09-18.pdf. For Arab-Americans, www.census.gov/prod/2003pubs/c2kbr-23.pdf.

[24] All the information about this incident is from the consent decree entered August 7, 2000, between the Department of Justice and the City of Hamtramck: www.justice.gov/crt/voting/sec_2/hamtramck_cd.pdf.

worker at each polling place where there are 100–249 voters with Spanish surnames; two if there are 250–499; and three if there are 500 or more.[25]

The use of Spanish surnames as a surrogate for Spanish-speaking is easy but highly inaccurate. The Department of Justice's use of Spanish surnames as an equivalent for "limited English proficient" earned a stern rebuke from a federal court in the case of *U.S.* v. *City of Philadelphia* in 2006: "[The Department of Justice's] analysis makes several assumptions regarding Spanish-speaking voters that are too attenuated to actual English language ability to support a finding regarding the distribution of limited-English-proficient voters throughout the City" (*U.S.* v. *City of Philadelphia* 2:06cv-4592, p. 8).

The DOJ also used an alternate method: self-reported census data. In the census data, the government claimed that all who described themselves as speaking English less than "very well" were LEP. The other choices are "well," "not well," and "not at all." The use of Spanish surnames as a proxy for LEP had already been discarded by federal courts (*US* v. *Alamosa County* 2004; *Rodriguez* v. *Bexar County* 2004), both cases involving apportionment, to which we now turn our attention.

Once voters have been able to make informed use of the ballot to express their desires, their votes are *effective* only if they have some chance of electing the representatives they favor. Apportionment, reapportionment, and malapportionment have been issues since the founding of the Republic. In general, the political process assumes geographic representation is required for fairness – people from the same region will have similar interests that deserve representation in an elected body. Similarity of interest based on other grounds, particularly those of race and national origin, has also been considered, which is why language and apportionment issues are intertwined.

Elections ranging from those for city council to those for the US House of Representatives in most states divide the polity into a number of districts, usually based on equivalent population. The city of Chicago has fifty legislative wards, for example, and the state of Illinois has nineteen congressional districts (in 2010). Today the number of seats in the House of Representatives is fixed at 435, a number that dates only to 1910. Each congressional district is supposed to have roughly the same population in each district, averaging 710,767 after the 2010 Census. After each census, the district boundaries are redrawn in the reapportionment process. Even under the best of circumstances, the principle of one person one vote is not realized.[26] The relationship of voting to real power is further weakened by reapportionment politics. The temptation for those in

---

[25] Sometimes the threshold is lower, as in the Settlement Agreement between the Department of Justice and Salem County (New Jersey) in 2008. For a description of state and local accommodations to minority language groups, see Sutherland (2009).

[26] The lone House member from Montana represents 994,416 people, while the representative from Rhode Island District 1 represents only 526,283. In the Senate, Wyoming's two Senators,

power is to draw the district map in such a way as to maximize the chances for staying in power. The political manipulation of the electoral district map is commonly referred to as "gerrymandering," a term invented when, in 1812, the Governor of Massachusetts Elbridge Gerry created a district in the shape of a salamander to further his political goals (see Griffith (1907) for the early history of this practice).

The effectiveness of the vote can be thwarted by apportionment practices known colloquially as "vote packing" and "vote cracking." In "vote packing" the districts are drawn so that one district pulls all the votes of a given group, with the result that the party in power wins all of the other districts. The interests of the group may have one vote, but they will never have the majority. In "vote cracking" the map is divided so that the voters of a particular group are split among several districts, with the result that they never succeed in electing a person to represent their views. Their voices may never even be heard.

Rulings against gerrymandering have been based on the Equal Protection Clause of the Fourteenth Amendment. In the second half of the nineteenth century Congress repeatedly addressed the abuse of redistricting for political purposes, eventually settling on requirements that districts be compact, contiguous, and roughly equal in population. In 1929, this formula was not repeated, leaving the door open for a variety of political shenanigans. Fairness has proven a difficult, if not impossible, standard.

The argument against biased maps is based on the disparity between the votes cast and the composition of the elected body. For example, in *Davis* v. *Bandemer* (1986), Democrats protested that they received 51.9 percent of the votes for the Indiana House of Representatives but won only 43 of the 100 seats. The claim, successful in the lower courts but reversed by the US Supreme Court, was that these results were obtained by political gerrymandering of a Republican majority.

the mere lack of proportional representation will not be sufficient to prove unconstitutional discrimination. .... without specific supporting evidence, a court cannot presume in such a case that those who are elected will disregard the disproportionally underrepresented group. Rather, unconstitutional discrimination occurs only when the electoral system is arranged in a manner that will consistently degrade a voter's or a group of voters' influence on the political process as a whole. (at 132)

In this case, the alleged discrimination was purely political, and the court reasoned that long-term systematic discrimination needed to be proved. Though the judges in *Bandemer* proffered varying ideas about how one could make a legal case for a malapportionment claim, these were all dismissed in

representing 563,626 people, have equal voting rights with California's two Senators, representing 37,253,956 (2010 Census figures).

Vieth v. *Jubelirer* (2004), and the courts have essentially given up on regulating political manipulation of reapportionment, though some continue to try to establish a "scientific" standard.[27] The courts have been more sympathetic to claims that reapportionment discrimination on the basis of protected classes – notably race and national origin – needs to be addressed.

According to the estimates of the 2010 Census, African-Americans constitute about 12.8 percent of the US population and Latinos 15.5 percent. In the 112th Congress, of 435 total members of the US House of Representatives there are 42 African-American voting members (9.66 percent) and 26 Latinos (5.98 percent). In 2010, there were two Latinos and no African-Americans in the Senate (of 100 members). As striking as these numbers may seem, the disparities alone are not enough; court cases involving low representation of linguistic minorities have been based, as the *Davis* case suggests, on long-term systematic discrimination.

Section §5 of the Voting Rights Act of 1965 placed certain regions of the country, with a long history of discrimination, under special reapportionment scrutiny. Most of the southern states, Alaska, and Arizona are covered in their entirety, with a sprinkling of smaller jurisdictions, usually counties, in other parts of the country. In these regions, any change to the boundaries of political jurisdictions must obtain preclearance from the Attorney General of the United States.

In *White* v. *Regester* (1973) the Supreme Court ruled that a Texas House of Representatives' reapportionment plan that included multi-member districts was an intentional and impermissible attempt to dilute the votes of minority communities. One part of this decision was based on the lack of representation for Mexican-Americans living in San Antonio (Bexar County). Noting that only five Mexican-Americans had been elected from Bexar County in almost a century, though the population in 1973 was 29 percent Mexican-American, the court concluded that "the multimember district, as designed and operated in Bexar County, invidiously excluded Mexican-Americans from effective participation in political life" (1973, at 769).

The 1982 amendments to Section 2 of the Voting Rights Act focused on results, outlawing any electoral practices that lead to reduced opportunity for minority groups "to participate in the political process and to elect representatives of their choice" (U.S.C. § 1973(b), *as amended by* Voting Rights Act Amendment of 1982, 96 Stat. 131). The best method to assure the representation of linguistic or racial minorities' perspectives depends on local circumstances; no single solution is prescribed. In *Georgia* v. *Ashcroft* (2003), the court held that different approaches are possible and reasonable: creating "safe" districts in which voters of a given racial or national origin minority

---

[27] See, for instance, Grofman and King (2006), promoting the idea of "partisan symmetry."

are in fact the majority, and therefore the election of a minority candidate is all but assured. Alternatively, one could create multiple districts where the concentration of minority voters is high enough to ensure minority influence on the outcome, though less certainty of election of a minority candidate.

An example of the creation of safe districts is the 4th Congressional district created in Chicago to ensure that a Latino candidate will be elected. In some places no more than a block wide, the 4th is shaped like the pincers of a crab in order to combine two Hispanic neighborhoods separated by Oak Park and a large African-American community on Chicago's West Side. Explicit limits on strangely shaped districts were attempted in *Shaw* v. *Barr* (1992), which went to the US Supreme Court as *Shaw* v. *Reno* (1993), a North Carolina case involving a district some 160 miles long and sometimes only a few feet wide.

At the same time, at-large election systems, in which some or all representatives are elected by an entire jurisdiction rather than by particular districts, have been the subject of scrutiny. While such systems give a broader constituency for those elected, they make it easier for the majority community to have a monopoly on power. In *Thornburg* v. *Gingles* (1986), the Supreme Court found a North Carolina system for at-large voting unconstitutional because it led to "vote dilution," that is, the dispersal of minority voting in such a way as to render unlikely the election of a minority candidate. The *Gingles* decision notes not only that the Supreme Court "has long recognized that multimember districts and at-large voting schemes may 'operate to minimize or cancel out the voting strength of racial [minorities in] the voting population'" (1986, at 47) but also that multi-member and at-large voting schemes "are not *per se* violative of minority voters' rights" (*ibid.*). This decision sets out a three-prong approach for determining if a violation has occurred:

1. The minority group is "sufficiently large and geographically compact to constitute a majority of a district"
2. The minority group is politically cohesive
3. The minority group votes as a block.

In applying these preconditions the court considers the "totality of the circumstances," including the history of discrimination, polarized voting along ethnic or racial lines, and the election of minority candidates. In *Bartlett* v. *Strickland* (2009) a narrow majority of the Supreme Court considered the 50 percent rule of the first prong as decisive in dismissing a vote dilution claim based on the Voting Rights Act, while the dissenting justices argued for a more flexible interpretation of the intent of the statute. In general, the effect of at-large or multi-member district voting has been found to be more pronounced in racial divisions than in linguistic divisions (Welch 1990), in part because patterns of residential segregation were stronger on the basis of race than on language.

The apportionment disputes rest on the conviction that language (as represented by national origin) or race is the most salient feature determining how a voter will vote and what constitutes proper representation. Other factors such as gender, level of education, or socio-economic status are not given the same consideration. For proponents of protection, the equivalence of race or linguistic heritage to voting preference is a fact; overcoming discrimination by ensuring representation for minority voices is necessary to have minority voters feel part of the system. For opponents, this equivalence is an ideology that emphasizes difference and supports continued segregation.

The ability to select officials who represent our collective will is fundamental to the functioning of a democracy. To the extent that linguistic minorities have a shared interest, representation of those interests is a normal expectation of this constituency. Adequate representation first requires registration to vote and uninhibited access to the polling place. Once that is secured, potential voters need access to knowledge of what the choices are and how to make their wishes known through the ballot. Finally, the configuration of districts can determine the likelihood that their voices will be heard.

Each of these issues has a long history in American politics. Access of immigrant and indigenous linguistic minorities to the ballot box has been restricted by the connections made between citizenship and voting and inhibited by organized challenges to their right to vote. The ability to make an informed choice and to represent that choice properly on the ballot has been hampered by language barriers and at least partially overcome by measures to provide bilingual or multilingual ballots, election materials, and election assistance. The opportunity to elect an official of their linguistic group has been slowed or blocked by the apportionment of political boundaries to manipulate the outcome of elections in favor of those in power.

The primary weapons of the linguistic minorities are the Equal Protection Clause of the Fourteenth Amendment to the Constitution and the Voting Rights Act of 1965. The interplay between court decisions and amendments to that act continues to be a battleground between those who wish to preserve rights while maintaining linguistic difference and those who see the elimination of linguistic difference as a prerequisite for equal rights.

3   Linguistic Inequality in the Legal System

The justice system requires both fairness and impartiality, a matter of perception as well as reality. The right to a fair trial or hearing applies to all, regardless of their citizenship, their social status, or their knowledge of the English language. The potential of the government to abuse its power was of great concern for the framers of the Constitution. The Bill of Rights was designed to constrain the power of government through equity and due process, which, for those who speak English as a second language – or not at all – requires special services that are negotiated at every stage of the legal process.

The Fifth Amendment to the Constitution provides a number of protections against self-incrimination and for due process: "No person shall ... be compelled in any criminal case to be a witness against himself, nor be deprived of life, liberty, or property, without due process of law."

The Fifth Amendment applies to the federal courts; Section 1 of the Fourteenth Amendment explicitly extends the due process protections to the states and further guarantees equal protection of the laws: "nor shall any state deprive any person of life, liberty, or property, without due process of law; nor deny to any person within its jurisdiction the equal protection of the laws."

The procedures that constitute due process are further elaborated in the Sixth Amendment, which adds the right to assistance by counsel, to confrontation of witnesses, and to an impartial jury:

In all criminal prosecutions, the accused shall enjoy the right to a speedy and public trial, by an impartial jury of the state and district wherein the crime shall have been committed, which district shall have been previously ascertained by law, and to be informed of the nature and cause of the accusation; to be confronted with the witnesses against him; to have compulsory process for obtaining witnesses in his favor, and to have the assistance of counsel for his defense.

The nature of due process is fairly well defined in criminal cases, less so in others such as immigration hearings, welfare eligibility cases, and civil suits.[1]

---

[1] The principles were described by Judge Henry Friendly in his article "Some Kind of Hearing" (1975). The extension of the hearing principle to administrative judgments was effected through the *Interstate Commerce Commission* v. *Louisville & Nashville Railroad* decision (1913), cited

In addition to the constitutional guarantees, the Civil Rights Act of 1964 includes Title VI regulations that provide "No person in the United States shall on the ground of race, color or national origin, be excluded from participation in, be denied the benefits of, or be subjected to discrimination under any program or activity receiving Federal financial assistance" (42 U.S. C. §2000d).

As national origin is often closely related to language, linguistic minorities have been protected by these provisions. The antidiscrimination protections are explicitly extended to language through Executive Order 13166 (2000), "Improving Access to Services for Persons with Limited English Proficiency." As part of these requirements, the Department of Justice developed a "Language Access Plan," and many states have done so as well.[2] In general, the constitution, the amendments, the statutes, and the executive order combine to promise an impartial hearing after the person involved has been notified of a proposed action and the reasons for it. Persons affected have the opportunity to contest those reasons.

Each of these protections has implications for minority language speakers. A first consideration is fairness to all parties, guaranteed by communication through the use of interpreters. The second consideration is impartiality, as reflected by the composition of a jury once a case has come to trial.

Fairness requires the ability to understand the legal procedure as it unfolds, and, in the case of the accused, the capacity to defend oneself. From the beginning, a determination of the necessity of an interpreter, and for which language, is a first concern. In pre-trial stages, the issue is often the choice of interpreter, frequently not a certified professional. As the case proceeds through the judicial process, the courts pay closer and closer attention to the need for and the choice of interpreter and the quality and type of interpretation provided.[3]

In criminal cases the procedures are becoming more standardized, but for civil cases the requirements vary from state to state, and even from munici-pality to municipality.[4] The federal Court Interpreters Act (1978) provides for

---

in Friendly (1975, 1271). He notes, with some trepidation, the rapid increase of required hearings, particularly following the Supreme Court's decision in *Goldberg* v. *Kelly* (1970).

[2] See, for example, Wisconsin's Language Access Plan developed by the Wisconsin Director of State Courts, outlining statutory requirements, funding, certification programs, etc. www.wico urts.gov/services/interpreter/docs/laplan.pdf.

[3] For a general introduction to the issues relating to legal interpretation, see Berk-Seligson (1990).

[4] In *Jara* v. *Municipal Court* (1978), the Supreme Court of California considered an appeal of a municipal court ruling in a property damage claim after a car accident. Jara, who did not speak English, asked the municipal court to provide an interpreter at its expense, but the court refused. Justice Tobriner dissented from the denial of this appeal, finding that without providing access to an interpreter to an LEP litigant, the court reduces the proceedings to "an empty and meaningless ritual" (1978 at 97). In Texas, the litigant in a civil suit has a statutory right to an interpreter (Texas Government Code section 57.002), but the right has not necessarily been applied (see

interpreters in civil cases only when the suit targets the federal government. The underlying assumption is that civil cases are voluntary whereas criminal cases are involuntary, though this distinction is questionable: Are legal responses to eviction really voluntary?

An essential component of fairness is understanding what is going on when interacting with the police or other administrative and legal agencies. The concept of fairness has most often been applied only to the accused, not to witnesses or victims, with sometimes disastrous results (see the following). Understanding legal proceedings is complicated enough for native speakers of English who have lived in the United States since birth.[5] For those who have limited or no understanding of English, much less the Anglo-American legal system, the language of the courts is a significant barrier. A number of state and national commissions have recognized the issue: "Without communication and understanding, individuals are unable to participate in, to benefit from, to access the protection of the courts or otherwise to obtain a fair and impartial hearing from the legal system."[6]

Assistance by counsel requires either counsel that speaks both English and the language of the suspect or the presence of an interpreter. An interpreter may also be necessary during trial to assure the right to confront witnesses. A continuing matter of controversy is how the court determines if the accused needs an interpreter. A second issue is the selection of an appropriate interpreter, at each stage of the process, and third the determination of the quality of interpretation provided.

The duties of the interpreter are "to ensure that the proceedings in English reflect precisely what was said by a non-English-speaking person" and "to place the non-English-speaking person on an equal footing with those who understand English."[7] Interpretation in a trial is expected to be simultaneous, but other styles of translation have not led appeals courts to reject earlier decisions. The assumption of the courts is that something close to

Cochrane 2009, 80–82). In *Gardiana* v. *Small Claims Court* (1976), the appeals court held that the court was obliged to appoint and pay for interpretation only if the litigant was both non-English-speaking and indigent. The draft of the Language Access Plan for California (consulted August 19, 2014) recommends eliminating the exception for small claims proceedings (2014, 82).

[5] The Director of the Administrative Office of the federal courts estimated that "because of the sophisticated language level used in courts, it is necessary to have a minimum of fourteen years of education to understand what goes on in a criminal trial" (cited in Del Valle 2003, 169).

[6] Commission to Study Racial & Ethnic Bias in the Courts, Mass. Supreme Judicial Court, Final Report: *Eliminating the Barriers: Equal Justice* (1994, 34), cited in Salimbene (1997, footnote 9).

[7] Oklahoma Code of Professional Responsibility for Interpreters in the Oklahoma Courts, Supreme Court of Oklahoma, 2014 OK 46.

word-for-word translation is possible and in fact desirable. The interpreter is to be simply a "conduit."[8]

A further weakness of interpretation protections is that they guarantee interpreting services only to the accused, and not to the accuser. The Illinois Criminal Proceeding Interpreter Act requires an assessment of the accused's English-language skills, but it denies the right of victims and witnesses to request an interpreter.[9] A 2013 case in Chicago illustrates the problem: A woman testified in a preliminary hearing concerning an alleged sexual assault. She had trouble understanding and asked for an interpreter. The judge instead asked the attorney to rephrase the question. The confusion in her responses led to the release of the suspect, who already had charges of sexual battery in his file and would be arrested again for a similar attack a few months later.[10]

While interpretation of some sort has been used since the earliest years of the Republic, the formal requirements for such services date only to the 1970s. In the 1920s, for example, the state of Florida relied on two high school students "familiar with the Spanish or Cuban language" to translate for a defendant who, it turned out, was not a Spanish speaker at all.[11] A study of Mexican-American prisoners in Illinois, conducted in 1930, found that 78 percent of those charged with felonies were not provided with an interpreter.[12] Legal decisions relating to interpretation led to the passage of

---

[8] This metaphor for the role of the interpreter is coming under increased scrutiny, as we shall examine in the following (p. 65). Influenced by modern technologies (telegraph, telephone, and computers), it assumes the equivalence of input and output.

[9] Section 1 reads:

Whenever any person accused of committing a felony or misdemeanor is to be tried in any court of this State, the court shall upon its own motion or that of defense or prosecution determine whether the accused is capable of understanding the English language and is capable of expressing himself in the English language so as to be understood directly by counsel, court or jury.

Section 4 guarantees the right to a qualified court-appointed interpreter only to victims and witnesses with disabilities who require sign-language interpretation. Illinois Compiled Statutes 725 ILCS 140.

[10] See *Chicago Sun-Times*, January 7, 2014, "Prosecutors, alleged victim differ on language-barrier issue in dismissed rape case," www.suntimes.com/news/24817562–761/language-barrier-led-to-confusion-in-dismissed-rape-case-woman-says.html#.U9f17Vap3fM. The released man was subsequently arrested again, three months later, for a brutal sexual assault on a 15-year-old honor student that left her with severe brain injuries. See the letter from the president of the National Association for Judiciary Interpreters and Translators, Rob Cruz: www.najit.org/chicago%20rape%20case%20pdf.pdf.

[11] *Kelly* v. *State* (1928). The conviction was overturned on this basis.

[12] Warnshuis report included in Abbott (1931, 292). Paul Warnshuis was a graduate student at the University of Chicago when Abbott asked him to study "Crime and Criminal Justice among the Mexicans of Illinois." He had spent considerable time with Presbyterian missions in the Southwest and spoke Spanish fluently. He interviewed ninety-eight prisoners at four different correctional facilities. His report, pp. 265–329, of the Abbott volume, described a system in which non-English-speaking defendants understood little to nothing of the legal procedures against them.

the Court Interpreters Act (1978) and to the professionalization of court interpreting. Certification of interpreters is available in a limited number of languages (three in the federal system (Spanish, Haitian Creole, and Navajo), and a number of others in programs developed by individual states). New Jersey, for example, offers certification in twenty languages.[13]

U.S. ex. rel. Negrón v. *New York* (1970) was the landmark case that inspired the first Court Interpreters Act. Negrón came to Suffolk County (New York) from his native Puerto Rico, working primarily as a potato picker. He was charged with murder following the stabbing death of his housemate, Juan Del Valle. Negrón had a sixth-grade education, all in Spanish, and spoke no English. Before the trial, an interpreter was available for attorney–client consultation for only twenty minutes. During the trial, testimony of Spanish speakers was translated into English, but no interpretation of English speakers' testimony was provided for Negrón. Twelve of the fourteen witnesses testified in English. The appeals court found that without such interpretation Negrón was "not present at his own trial," and thus denied the effective assistance of counsel and the opportunity to confront witnesses.

Who Decides If an Interpreter Is Needed?

At first contact, the determination is most often an informal decision on the part of the police or other government representative. A person in custody[14] being questioned by the police must be told of their rights in a language he or she understands. Hundreds of languages are spoken in the United States. A first challenge for law enforcement is to determine the preferred language of the person questioned and to be sure that advice concerning rights is clearly explained in that language.

"I speak" cards are widely used to help determine which language is involved,[15] sometimes accompanied by the use of language services available by telephone. This is not a foolproof method, as some people are illiterate, and their real native language might not appear as an option. Many Central Americans are native speakers of a (frequently unwritten) indigenous language and second-language speakers of Spanish with little formal education in that language. A Spanish-language interpreter was of little avail to Ventura

---

[13] National Center for State Courts, www.ncsc.org/~/media/Files/PDF/Services%20and%20Exp erts/Areas%20of%20expertise/Language%20Access/Written%20and%20Oral/Oral_Exam_Re ady_for_Administration_rev_April2014.ashx.

[14] Custody does not mean arrest but implies a similar curtailment of freedom of action. See Einesman (1999, 10–17). The crucial element is the sense of coercion implied when one is held, a sense that might be exacerbated by language issues: "when a suspect's knowledge of English is clearly inadequate, it may be appropriate to refine the standard to account for this characteristic" (*U.S.* v. *Joe* 1991 at 611).

[15] For example, www.lep.gov/ISpeakCards2004.pdf.

Morales, who spoke only Mixtec and spent four years in prison before the courts recognized that he had not understood a word of his trial (cited in De Jongh 2008, 33).

Assistance from an interpreter may be available from the very earliest point of contact with law enforcement agencies. A person with limited proficiency in English may not understand police instructions, as in the case of German Marquez, a Spanish monolingual accused of refusing a breathalyzer test when he had no idea what the police were asking him to do (cited in Miller *et al.* 2011, 118).

In this period of initial inquiries, the issue is legal interpreting rather than court interpreting, a much less formal process with fewer guarantees of quality. For those who are more comfortable in a language other than English, this first encounter might involve the use of an interpreter, but not necessarily a certified interpreter. A number of cases have turned on the use of inappropriate interpreters, which might be members of the community, even children, or police officers who are already looking to establish a suspect.[16]

Executive Order 13166 issued by President Clinton in 2000 ("Improving Access to Services by Persons with Limited English Proficiency") led to a Stakeholder Conference that included a wide variety of federal agencies with law enforcement responsibilities, resulting in guidelines to ensure "uniform language assistance initiatives." Subsequently, the Department of Justice (DOJ) has provided tips to law enforcement agencies, follow-up interagency conferences in 2007 and 2008, and numerous memoranda on proper enforcement.[17]

In April of 2014, the DOJ reached agreements with Rhode Island and New Jersey to ensure compliance throughout the court systems in those states.[18] Such agreements have three components: assistance of interpreters should be appropriate, comprehensive, and free.

Police interviews with suspects, witnesses, and victims are in theory a truth-finding exercise, but particularly in interviews with suspects, the interview assumes guilt, and the goal is to elicit a confession. To protect a suspect from self-incrimination, suspects in the United States are given a version of the "Miranda warning" before questioning can continue.[19] The warning has slight variations in different jurisdictions, but in general it includes

---

[16] Berk-Seligson (2009) discusses the distinction between informal legal interpreting and court interpreting in Chapter 3 and describes a variety of circumstances in which less than optimum interpreter choices have been the object of later appeals, usually unsuccessful.

[17] See www.lep.gov/guidance/guidance_DOJ_Guidance.html for an extensive list of these documents. A summary of those documents through 2008 is provided in Berk-Seligson (2009, 11–13).

[18] The Rhode Island complaint was first filed in 2004 (DOJ Number 171–66-2). Similar measures have been taken with other states, counties, and cities. Language assistance was one of many requirements in the consent decree signed with the Orleans Parish in Louisiana (2012, 34–37).

[19] Ernesto Miranda was arrested on charges of kidnapping and rape. He signed a confession but had not been apprised of his right against self-incrimination and his right to counsel (1966). The

- You have the right to remain silent.
- Anything you say or do may be used against you in a court of law.
- You have the right to consult an attorney, and to have an attorney present.
- If you cannot afford an attorney, one will be appointed for you if you request one.
- If you answer questions without an attorney, you can stop answering questions at any time and wait for advice from an attorney.
- Do you understand these rights?

This warning requires some linguistic sophistication to be understood completely – according to some studies, a high school education (Brière 1978).[20] In addition to the linguistic features of the texts of the warning, other factors influence the interviewees' understanding, such as the attitudes and bearing of the police officer and the attitudes of the community toward figures of authority.

These protections apply also to requests for searches. A person must understand that a request to search is a request, not an order. The warnings typically conclude with a question, "Do you understand?" An overwhelming percentage of interviewees respond in the affirmative, even if in fact their understanding is only partial. This self-evaluation, even for native speakers of English, depends on many social factors that have nothing to do with knowledge of the law. Those who have limited exposure to the American justice system are even less likely to have understood fully the import of the warning, even if presented with a warning in a language they understand.

A problem for LEP suspects at this early stage of the criminal investigation is waiving the Miranda rights. The natural inclination, strongly encouraged by the interrogating officers, is to forego the protections against self-incrimination guaranteed by the Constitution and by the *Miranda* ruling and subsequent case law. Assertion of these rights must be given in an unequivocal manner; any weakness in the demand is perceived as a waiver. This is once again particularly problematic for the LEP suspect, who may not know that a strong formulation of the request to remain silent and for assistance by an attorney is required, or whose unambiguous request in another language might be translated otherwise in English by an interpreter. In *Davis* v. *U.S.* (1994), the US Supreme Court ruled that a suspect must "unambiguously request counsel" (at 459), a standard

---

warning is specific to custodial interrogation, that is, to interrogation at a point in which the suspect is held in police custody and thus deprived of freedom of action.

[20] See also the testimony of Dr. William Eggington in *U.S.* v. *Dutchie* (2008), a case involving a Ute defendant. Eggington described the standard Miranda warning as requiring 11.6 years of schooling; Dutchie had a third-grade education. Ultimately, this testimony was dismissed: "the court does not find Dr. Eggington's testimony particularly persuasive," and instead relied on case law which has accepted as legitimate Miranda warnings given to persons with "mild to borderline mental retardation."

that other courts have extended to the right to remain silent. Justice Souter concurred with the decision, but added a caveat that criminal suspects "would seem an odd group to single out for the Court's demand of heightened linguistic care." As he observed, "A substantial percentage of them lack anything like a confident command of the English language; many are 'woefully ignorant', and many more will be sufficiently intimidated by the interrogation process or overwhelmed by the uncertainty of their predicament that the ability to speak assertively will abandon them" (at 469–470).

Furthermore, speaking assertively is culturally conditioned and represented in diverse manners in different languages. Ainsworth (1993) explores the difference in the use of indirect or hedging speech patterns between women and men, between lower-class and professional witnesses, and between African-Americans and European-Americans in English. Many other languages similarly favor speech patterns that are perceived as non-assertive by the legal standards that have been established by legal precedents.

Three standards have been used to determine if a right has been invoked:

1. "threshold of clarity," which sets a fixed linguistic standard for invocation of the right to counsel;
2. "*per se*," in which any post-warning statement suggesting a desire for legal representation is considered an invocation of the right to counsel;
3. "clarification," which requires the police to follow up on any invocation of right to counsel, to be sure of the suspect's intent. (Ainsworth 1993, 301–302, citing *Smith* v. *Illinois* 1984)

The first of these has been the most commonly used and poses the greatest difficulty for the LEP suspect.

Following the *Smith* ruling, the issue has come up a number of times. A suspect's observation "maybe I should talk to a lawyer" was not considered assertive enough (*Davis*, at 462). The courts have generally rejected the idea that a question about being represented by an attorney is a kind of request: "Can I have my attorney present now?" (*Gutierrez* v. *State* 2004) was considered a request for information rather than a request for an attorney. However, "You mind if I not say no more and just talk to an attorney about this?" was considered to meet the "clarity" standard, as an "unequivocal invocation of the right to counsel" in *Ballard* v. *State* (2011).[21] Common non-standard

---

[21] Similarly, in *State* v. *Avila-Nava* (2013), the right to remain silent was considered invoked by a Spanish-speaking suspect who responded to the detective's explanation of the Miranda warning: "Anything you say may be used against you in a court of law," with "I won't answer any questions." The detective skipped ahead to the next points of the Miranda list and then came back to the right to remain silent, convincing the suspect to talk. Once a right has been invoked, the court ruled, all further discussion should stop. See also Berk-Seligson (2002, 137), describing a case in which a policeman serving as interpreter, and speaking very poor Spanish,

English was the issue in *State* v. *Gobert* (2009), where the suspect stated "I don't want to give up any right, though, if I don't got no lawyer." The appeals court observed that

Common experience counsels that, in the context of this particular dialogue with the police, the appellee's use of the double negative should be disregarded. We reasonably construe the appellee's phrase, "if I don't got no lawyer", to be functionally equivalent to the phrase in standard English, "If I don't have lawyer" or "unless I have a lawyer." (at 893)

In *State* v. *Martinez* (2010), a conflict between the state's translation and the defense's translation of the Miranda conversation with the suspect led to an appeal. After having the right to counsel explained to him, the suspect, who seemed confused about whether he would have to pay legal fees, said

if you have an attorney available ... it's that I want ... I know that I am going to pay ... I want ... well that he [inaudible] me. (defense's translation)

or

if you have an attorney ... well, what I want ... I know I will pay ... but I want ... well (prosecution's translation)

The appeals court considered the defense's translation more accurate and a clear enough request for counsel that any statement made after that should have been suppressed.

Once formal charges are considered, the discretion of the judge is broad, and it has been the basis for numerous appeals. Judges have frequently used simple questions to determine competency in English, or relied on assumptions based on the amount of time the person concerned has spent in the United States. Neither approach is a very accurate measure of the ability to understand legal proceedings, but appeals courts have been extremely reluctant to second-guess the decision of the trial court judge.

A 2014 Maryland case, *Kusi* v. *State*, illustrates the issues and the difficulties. Maryland law, typical of many states, establishes when an interpreter is necessary and how the court should determine if that standard is met.[22] George

---

continued interrogation after the suspect stated "No quiero hablar más. No quiero hablar más de nada [I don't want to talk more. I don't want to talk more about anything]."

[22] Section 1–202 of the Criminal Procedure Article: "The court shall appoint a qualified interpreter to help a defendant in a criminal proceeding throughout any criminal proceeding when the defendant ... (2) cannot readily understand or communicate the English language and cannot understand a charge made against the defendant or help present the defense." Rule 16–819 of the Maryland Rules specifies how the need for an interpreter shall be determined:

(2) Spoken language interpreter. (A) Examination of party or witness. To determine whether a spoken language interpreter is needed, the court, on request or on its own initiative, shall examine a party or witness on the record. The court shall appoint a spoken language interpreter if the court determines that (i) the party does not understand English well enough to participate

Kusi, a native of Ghana, was charged with a variety of sexual offenses. He had lived in the United States for four years prior to the arrest, working on construction jobs for a Ghanaian contractor. Before the trial he requested an interpreter from his native Ashanti. His attorney tried to find an interpreter using telephonic services, but the judge decided to interview the defendant himself to determine his linguistic abilities. The questions were generally short-answer ("How old are you?") or yes–no questions to which the defendant always responded "yes."[23] A crucial exchange was more open-ended:

COURT: And have you had any difficulty understanding what he's telling you [the defense attorney]?
KUSI: Sometimes, but I put some words at, words down to ask some inmate in the [unintelligible]
COURT: So sometimes there's an idiom he uses that's not clear, right?
KUSI: Yeah.

The defense attorney objected:

Judge, I know you've been asking him . . . several questions, and he's . . . been acknowledging by saying yes. Because of their leading nature . . . I'm suggesting maybe a little alternating or something, because it's just the routine of saying yes . . . to Your Honor, the authority, so I just want to make sure, because he's expressed to me not always understanding me, even the second or third time that I've met with him by not understanding what we talked about before.

The judge tried some other questions, with varying success, and then decided to proceed without an interpreter. After conviction, Kusi appealed, partly on the basis of this denial.

At the appeals court level, the standard for overturning a factual finding is "clear error," a very difficult standard to reach for it requires that the judge's decision be "so contrary to unexplained, unimpeached, unambiguous documentary evidence as to be inherently incredible and unreliable" (*Kusi*, at 384, citing another case). The appeals court could find no clear error in the factual finding and then assessed the judge's ruling by another standard, "abuse of discretion," defined as "discretion manifestly unreasonable, or exercised on untenable grounds, or for untenable reasons" (*Kusi* 2014, at 385, citing other cases). Again the appeals court could not overturn based on that standard, as it is very unclear what Kusi understood, and what he did not. Trial judges have no

---

fully in the proceedings and to assist counsel, or (ii) the party or a witness does not speak English well enough to be understood by counsel, the court, and the jury. (cited in *Kusi v. State* 2014 at 366)

[23] Ainsworth (1993) focuses on women's language and the sense of powerlessness in an interrogation setting. The same principles apply to differences in assertiveness between cultures and languages (Einesman 1999, 32–33).

training to determine the linguistic capabilities of the defendant and of the witnesses and have both financial and logistical reasons to proceed without interpreters. Those at higher levels of review have even less basis to make such determinations and so defer to the trial court.

Some have called for a standardized approach to determining the necessity of using an interpreter, such as the use of the Oral Proficiency Interview (OPI) developed by the American Council of the Teaching of Foreign Languages (ACTFL) or the Elicited Oral Response (EOR) tests.[24] The OPI requires an interview followed by evaluation by at least two certified raters for each test, which takes time and adds expense. The EOR is shorter, easier to assess, and can focus more easily on complex structures that might never occur in an open-ended interview.[25] Such tests are very rarely used by the courts. The judge's opinion, based on unarticulated and perhaps unarticulable premises, remains the usual practice.

Once an interpreter is deemed necessary, the second issue is the choice of interpreter. Certified interpreters are preferred, even required in criminal trials, but not necessarily in other contexts. With less common languages, the choices are sometimes not good, especially in first-contact situations. Some appeals are based on interpreter bias, one of several ways the interpreter can violate the ethical principles of the profession.

Following the passage of the federal Court Interpreters Act in 1978, the use of professional interpreters has been increasingly regulated. Most states have statutory guidelines for interpreters, and interpreter certification exams are offered in twenty languages, though only in Spanish, Haitian Creole, and Navajo at the federal level. Today, according to a survey conducted by the National Center for State Courts, 82 percent of the responding jurisdictions require interpreters with professional credentials.[26] For less frequently needed languages, courts try a variety of options, including borrowing interpreters from neighboring jurisdictions, employing non-certified but qualified bilinguals, and using telephone interpreting.

---

[24] See, for example, Eggington and Cox (2013). Radmann (2005) surveyed judges in several states and at several levels to study how they determined the ability to stand trial without an interpreter.

[25] Eggington and Cox foresee rapid scoring of EOR tests using automatic speech recognition and provide one example in which it worked with seeming efficiency. At its current state of development, automatic speech recognition is of limited reliability despite their claim that "a combination of the Elicited Oral Response testing protocol using Automatic Speech Recognition software provides a valid, reliable, and practical solution for the need to provide accurate language assessment" (2013, 145). This skepticism about ASR does not preclude improved reliability through future software, or by the use of other means to score the EOR tests.

[26] *A National Call for Action*, p. 6.

Interpretation by a law enforcement officer or by family members may involve conflicts of interest or inadequate translations. The Department of Justice advises that "absent exigent circumstances, the Department of Justice should avoid using family members (including children), neighbors, friends, acquaintances, and bystanders to provide language assistance circumstances," as well as "individual opposing parties, adverse witnesses, or victims to a dispute."[27] Informal interpreters have not taken an interpreter's oath and usually have not had formal training in the profession. A worst-case scenario is cited by Cochrane (2009, 48–51), in a child custody battle. The Spanish-speaking father's presentation was interpreted by the wife he had divorced. Her interpretation was both incomplete and strongly biased, leading to the father's loss of all custodial rights.

Interpreters are supposed to be without bias, "an individual who has no interest in the outcome of the case."[28] A police officer as an interpreter is perceived as having a vested interest in the outcome. In *State* v. *Mitjans* (1986),[29] a police officer served as the translator and led Mitjans to sign a statement that the defendant could not read. As the appeals court noted:

Because of the close relationship and natural empathy between a translator and a defendant dependent on that translator to communicate his thoughts and feelings, a translator should be someone a defendant can place trust in and rely on to protect his interests. This is an unnatural burden to place on the shoulders of a peace officer actively working to gather evidence to help convict a defendant. (at 225)

Even an independent interpreter can cross the line of neutrality required by the interpreter's oath. In *People* v. *Mejia-Mendoza* (1998), the interpreter advised the defendant to cooperate with the police, thus violating his role as a neutral conduit of information.

The quality of interpretation is judged on the ability to render not just the basic meaning of testimony but also register of language and dialectal variation. It is the duty of the court to ensure that the interpreter is able "to accurately communicate with and translate information to and from the communication-impaired person involved."[30] Appeals based on the quality of interpretation are hindered by the lack of records of the original testimony, as the official court

---

[27] Department of Justice Language Access Plan, March 2012, pp. 8–9, www.justice.gov/open/la nguage-access-plan.pdf.

[28] *State in the Interest of R.R. Jr.* (1979).

[29] Luis Candelario Mitjans shot and killed Michael Chapman in a Minneapolis bar, both the defendant and the victim having consumed enough alcohol to be legally intoxicated. The defendant claimed that he pulled out his gun only after the victim had insulted him and then fired when Chapman lunged at him.

[30] District of Columbia Interpreter Act, D.C. Code §§ 31–2701, quoted in *Gonzalez* v. *US* (1997, at 822).

records are kept only in English. As video recording of legal proceedings has become more common, the basis for such appeals has increased.

Even with certified interpreters, issues arise concerning the quality of translation, all the more so when the interpreter lacks formal training. Defendants must object to errors immediately or lose the opportunity to challenge them later. The standard for overturning verdicts on any of these bases is "plain" or "clear" error, which turns out to be a very difficult hurdle.

As we have noted, the interpreter is considered simply a "language conduit." This perception of how an interpreter functions is coming under increased scrutiny, as the impossibility of rendering all the levels of meaning is better understood by legal authorities. If interpreters are considered a mere conduit, they are generally not subject to confrontation in the same way as a witness.[31] The interpreter in a police interrogation is perceived as merely passing along the defendant's own statements, and the defendant cannot confront his own testimony. How realistic is this conception of how the interpreter functions?

U.S. v. *Charles*, a 2013 case, concerns a Haitian woman who was accused of trying to enter the United States with false documents. The Customs and Border Patrol officer, according to the Eleventh Circuit, could only testify to the English-language statements made by the interpreter: "the statements of the language interpreter and Charles are not one and the same" (*Charles* 2013, at 1324). The appeals court found that the trial court should have allowed confrontation of the interpreter: "because Charles has the right, under the Confrontation Clause, to confront the 'declarant', that is the person who made the out-of-court statement, she has the right to confront the Creole language interpreter about the statements to which the CBP officer testified to [*sic*] in court" (at 1325).[32] The court cited research and explanations by the National Association of Judiciary Interpreters and Translators (NAJIT) and the Occupational Outlook Handbook of the US Department of Labor to conclude, citing Ahmad (2007, 1036), that the interpreter has to understand paralinguistic cues and supply contextual and pragmatic information that is not necessarily present in the words of the speaker. The listener-interpreter does not just transfer the meaning of the words and grammatical structures used in the source language, but s/he also supplies the cultural meaning of the statement in the target language.

---

[31] See Kracum (2014) for an extended discussion of confrontation rights with respect to interpreters. The *Nazemian* court provided a four-prong test to determine if the interpreter was a conduit (no confrontation rights) or a declarant (confrontation rights) (*U.S.* v. *Nazemian* 1991). Essentially, this test attempts to determine if the interpreter has any reason to misrepresent the defendant's statements, or has, intentionally or not, misrepresented them.

[32] Nonetheless, the court ruled that the error was not "plain" because there was no prior binding precedent that would have required the trial court to consider the interpreter the "declarant" of statements attributed to the defendant. In spite of the perceived error, the judgment was therefore affirmed.

Given the complexity of task, even with an experienced certified interpreter mistakes can and will happen. Most of these mistakes will never be discovered, because few of the participants in the trial have adequate knowledge of both languages in question. *Washington Post* reporter Ruth Hammond reviewed the original and the interpreted versions of a Minneapolis rape trial, in which some of the testimony was in Hmong. She concluded:

At times, the interpreters usurped the role of the witness, providing explanations that had not been offered in Hmong, or changing details to conform with other witnesses' testimony. At other times, they usurped the roles of the prosecuting and defense attorneys, independently asking questions the attorneys had never posed in order to help the witness formulate a more detailed response. They also usurped the role of the judge when they struck answers they apparently deemed nonresponsive by not interpreting them. None of this was apparent to the lawyers, the judge or the jury, of course; nor does any of it appear in the trial transcripts. (Originally published in 1993; cited in Hsieh (2001), at 1191)

It is the duty of the trial court to ensure that the interpretation during the police investigation was accurate, as well as the interpretation in the trial itself, but the means to do so are limited. For an appeal based on quality of interpretation to be successful, the mistakes must be significant enough to change the outcome of the trial. Because the trial record is kept only in English, it is very difficult later to establish a case of "clear error" in interpretation. Therefore, the defense must recognize and object immediately to the interpretation,[33] or, alternatively, a bilingual juror can inform the court of a perceived error.[34]

In *Mitjans* cited earlier, two court interpreters were used. Luis Borges, an experienced interpreter of Puerto Rican origin, was appointed to translate the testimony to the court, and Daniela Savino, more familiar with the defendant's Cuban dialect, translated the court proceedings to the defendant. At issue was Borges' translation of crucial testimony when the defendant took the stand. Mitjans' claim was self-defense – that he pulled his gun simply to warn the victim and pulled the trigger only when Chapman charged at him. To express the idea of warning, Mitjans used the term *causionarlo*, which Borges

---

[33] The timeliness of the objection is crucial. As the *Valladares* court noted: "Only if the defendant makes any difficulty with the interpreter known to the court can the judge take corrective measures. To allow a defendant to remain silent throughout the trial and then, upon being found guilty, to assert a claim of inadequate translation would be an open invitation to abuse" (1989 at 1566).

[34] Jurors are not supposed to make a public objection, but rather they can send a note to the judge. As we shall see below, frequently bilingual jurors who might understand non-English testimony directly and differently are dismissed from the jury pool. In *Guevara and Lopez* v. *US* (2013), the court recognized the difficulties the interpreters were having and addressed them in several ways: (1) replacing the original two interpreters; (2) inviting Spanish-speaking members of the jury to notify the court of difficulties; and (3) conferencing with attorneys and interpreters when a question arose. Angela Guevara and Demecio Lopez were accused of kidnapping and stabbing Silvano Lopez (*Guevara & Lopez* v. *U.S.* 2013).

translated as "I want to coerce him." Savino, the second interpreter, testified that the word more properly should be translated as "to caution somebody." After the trial Borges suggested a third alternative, "to advise him." The difference in the defendant's intent suggested by these alternative translations was deemed significant on appeal. Conflicting translation of the term *embestir*, "to tackle" according to Borges, "to charge like a bull" according to Savino, suggested a different type of action on the part of the victim. Borges also omitted or summarized some testimony that described the victim's attack on the defendant. Even with these significant discrepancies, the appeals court concluded that "the alleged errors in translation do not in isolation warrant a new trial," but combined with other mistakes ruled in favor of the defendant.

A similar conflict between interpreters is seen in *State* v. *Ahmed* (2012), a case that required translation from the Ethiopian language Oromo. There are no certification standards for this language. Tajuden Ali Ahmed was accused of domestic assault and disorderly conduct for allegedly striking his wife when she served him a meal he found displeasing. Two Oromo interpreters were assigned, Theophilos and Aedu. The defense objected to a number of translations by Aedu, who seemed to be paraphrasing rather than directly translating the testimony. The key exchange concerned Ahmed's response to the purportedly substandard meal. He claims, as did the interpreter Theophilos, that he stated simply that if she were too tired, she could leave off preparing the meal and he would do it himself. The other interpreter, Aedu, translated this as, "if you don't want to prepare the meal, you can leave." The conflict was immediately addressed and resolved in the trial court.

Even within the same language, dialectal variation[35] can lead to communication problems. Ahmad (2007, 1039–1040) notes the confusion when Los Angeles garment workers were asked about which labels they sewed into the clothes. The interpreter used the standard Spanish term *etiquetas*, which for those workers meant "price tags." In their Spanglish, labels were *los labels*. De Jongh (2008) offers numerous examples, such as this one in which Cuban slang meanings were not understood by the interpreter:

DEFENDANT: yo era marimbero pero ahora soy tumbador porque es mas facil.
INTERPRETER: I was a marimba player but now I play the conga drums because it's easier
REAL MEANING: I was a marijuana dealer but now I do rip-offs because it is easier. (2008, 22–23)

---

[35] The distinction between dialect and language is fuzzy. While linguists would make such a determination based on the concept of mutual intelligibility (e.g., Cuban Spanish and Argentinian Spanish are dialects of one language, while Spanish and English are distinct languages), legal opinions tend to refer to unwritten languages as dialects (Mixtec, Quiche, Peul, etc.).

Rendering rapidly changing underworld slang from one language to another is an extreme challenge for any interpreter, even without dialectal variation.

Register is equally difficult to assess. In a Minnesota rape trial,[36] the appeal was partially based on alleged misrepresentation of the register of the Hmong word *txiag*, properly translated as "fuck" according to the defense but translated as "have sex" by the court interpreter. Did the use of the softer expression unfairly reinforce the stereotypical image of the naïve submissive Hmong woman, when the harsher term would have cast her in a different light? The court found this and the other conflicting translations unimportant for the outcome of the case and rejected the appeal.

Interpretation is crucial to fairness in the court system. The adversarial system of arriving at justice depends on mutual comprehension. Interpreters face at best an extremely difficult challenge. The "conduit" model is realistic only for the simplest exchanges, and even then its accuracy is tempered by a variety of paralinguistic cultural factors. The professionalization of court interpreting, the establishment of more rigorous standards for interpreting, an increase in audio and video recording of interrogations and court proceedings, and a better understanding of the complexity of interpretation are all combining to improve this rapidly growing aspect of the American judicial system. Still, appeals courts are extremely reluctant to find fault with the trial courts' decisions, even when the interpretation is clearly erroneous. Good enough interpretation is considered fair enough in the administration of justice.

The jury is a means of protecting the citizen from the power of the state, an impartial assessor of the case presented. Tradition (though not the Constitution) guarantees trial by a jury of one's peers, a concept that in the Anglo-American legal tradition is traced back to Magna Carta (1215). The barons, in their dispute with King John, insisted on the right to be tried by those of their own social rank. Impartiality is perceived as enhanced by a diverse jury. Impartiality or the perception of impartiality thus raises two issues with respect to language: (1) the exclusion of linguistic minorities from the jury pool or the empanelled jury and (2) the ability of a juror to understand non-English testimony. Often these are intertwined, as one reason to exclude linguistic minorities from juries is the possibility that they might interpret on their own non-English testimony delivered in a language they know, rather than depend on the official court record as delivered in English by the professional interpreter. Even if all the testimony is to be in English, their presence on a jury might make the trial more impartial by providing alternative perspectives.

---

[36] The case is *State v. New Chue Her* (1992), discussed extensively in Dunnigan and Downing (1995).

Impartiality has been increasingly identified with diversity in the jury pool. As the *Grigsby* court (1983, at 1311) concluded:

evidence demonstrates, and common sense confirms, that the quality of the delibera-tions, the recall of the trial evidence, the likelihood of care and concern in understanding and applying the instructions of the Court as to the applicable law are all enhanced when there is a broad diversity and heterogeneity in the jury's makeup.

The list of "cognizable groups" that might constitute a diverse jury has grown from race to include other types of distinguishable communities, including gender,[37] sexual orientation,[38] national origin, and, ultimately, language. The *Rubio* court detailed the ways in which other segments of the population might be considered cognizable groups:

(1) members must share a common perspective arising from their life experi-ence in the group, i.e., a perspective gained precisely because they are members of that group;

(2) no other members of the community are capable of adequately representing the perspective of the group assertedly excluded (*Rubio v. Superior Court* 1979, at 99).[39]

The *Fields* court expanded upon the notion of cognizable group, stating that they "are generally relatively large and well-defined groups in the community whose members may, because of common background or experience, share a distinctive viewpoint on matters of current concern" (*People v. Fields* 1983, at 349). The *Fields* court goes on to state that an "otherwise heterogeneous group" is not a cognizable group merely because it agrees on one particular matter,

---

[37] *J.E.B* v. *Alabama ex. rel. T.B.* (1994) prohibited the exclusion of potential jurors on the basis of gender. In this case involving child support payments, the court found impermissible the exclusion of almost all male members of the jury pool. Similarly, in *Hilton* v. *Cate* (2011; 2012; affirmed 2013), a case involving multiple sexual offenses against women, the defense claimed that "Caucasian males" were a cognizable protected class and should not be stricken from the jury. While accepting that white males could be a cognizable protected group, the specific jurors were found to have been excluded for permissible reasons, and the inclusion of three other men on the jury was found proof enough of lack of discriminatory intent.

[38] *People* v. *Garcia* (2000) established gays and lesbians as a cognizable group, stressing that the representation of cognizable groups "assures that as many different life views as possible will be represented in the important decisions of the judicial process" (at 1277). "Our only issue is whether lesbians – and presumably gay males – constitute a cognizable class whose exclusion resulted in a jury that failed to represent a cross section of the community and thereby violated Garcia's constitutional rights. For reasons we explain here, we are convinced they do. We are convinced they *must*" (at 1272). "Lesbians and gay men qualify under this standard. It cannot seriously be argued in this era of 'don't ask; don't tell' that homosexuals do not have a common perspective – 'a common social or psychological outlook on human events' – based upon their membership in that community. They share a history of persecution comparable to that of Blacks and women."

[39] The class claimed in *Rubio* was that of ex-felons, a claim the court rejected, along with that of "resident aliens" (claiming that naturalized citizens who had once been resident aliens ade-quately represented this perspective).

such as belief in capital punishment, but notes a contrary opinion in *Grigsby*. Discrimination against one or more of these cognizable groups through peremptory challenges is not permissible.[40]

Diversity of the jury pool is necessary not only for the quality of the jury's deliberations but also for the community's confidence in the verdict once reached. The perception of unfairness can have serious consequences, as evidenced by unrest after the verdict in the Rodney King case (1992). Rodney King was an African-American who was stopped after a high-speed chase and then beaten by four white police officers. When an all-white jury acquitted the officers in the state trial, riots broke out in Los Angeles, which spurred a federal trial for civil rights' violations.[41] Jury participation can also be considered a citizen's right, and exclusion from jury duty an affront to one's participation in the community.

Jury composition is regulated both by statute and by strategies employed by lawyers on both sides. Criminal jury trials require a panel of between six and twelve people. The jury pool, the *venire*, is often drawn from voter or driver's license registrations, or similar seemingly random cross-sections of the community. Grand juries, in those jurisdictions that use them,[42] are frequently criticized as being unrepresentative, but because they do not actually determine guilt or innocence, they have not been subject to the same kind of scrutiny as trial juries (known as *petit* or *petty* juries).[43] The cross-section principle at both levels is crucial in establishing public confidence in the judicial system.[44] The actual cross-section is skewed by the use of these selection methods, as both tend to reduce the presence of minority jurors.

The American preoccupation with race, and the perception of race as limited to black and white, has complicated efforts to have linguistic minorities considered in debates about impartiality. The Supreme Court has consistently

---

[40] Age, however, has not been recognized as a cognizable class. *Zimmerer* v. *Netgear* (2012) rejected a claim based on the peremptory challenges to several jurors over 40 years of age. *U.S.* v. *Olson* (1973) rejected a claim of 18- to 20-year-olds as a distinct group.

[41] The initial jury pool in the state trial included only six African-Americans (of 260), five of whom were dismissed for cause, and the last on a peremptory challenge. With a mixed-race jury in the federal trial, two of the four officers were found guilty and served prison time.

[42] Grand juries are used in the federal courts, and in about half of the states. In general, they serve to decide if there is probable cause to send a case to trial.

[43] Language has never been recognized as a cohesive group identifier for the purposes of creating a representative grand jury. The inherent unfairness of excluding those who do not speak English may already be the case in the grand jury. In the *Mirabal Carrion* case (1956), the court indicated that language was less relevant to a broadly representative jury than economic, social, racial, and religious groupings. The defendant claimed that the exclusion of non-English speakers in Puerto Rico created an unrepresentative jury pool. The judge, though claiming to "venture no opinion as to the percentage of Puerto Ricans within the age group qualified for jury service who understand the English language" went on to conclude that "I strongly suspect that it is much greater than the defendants would have this court believe" (1956 at 231).

[44] See Fukurai (1999) for details of several such cases in Miami.

rejected discriminatory practices in jury selection, but it has also rejected the notion that "peers" means necessarily the inclusion of jurors from the defendant's racial, ethnic, or linguistic group. Mixed juries are acknowledged to consider a wider range of arguments, as Supreme Court Justice Thurgood Marshall explained in *Peters* v. *Kiff* (1992, at 503–504):

When any large and identifiable segment of the community is excluded from jury service, the effect is to remove from the jury room qualities of human nature and varieties of human experience, the range of which is unknown and perhaps unknowable. It is not necessary to assume that the excluded group will consistently vote as a class in order to conclude, as we do, that its exclusion deprives the jury of a perspective on human events that may have unsuspected importance in any case that may be presented.[45]

For well over a century, the courts have recognized the dangers of the exclusion of minorities from juries, whether by statute (*Strauder* v. *West Virginia* 1879), by administrative practice (*Hernandez* v. *Texas* 1954), or by local tradition (*Swain* v. *Alabama* 1965). The exclusion could be at the stage of the *venire* (the constitution of the jury pool), at the *voir dire* (the selection of the jurors from the jury pool), or in the use of peremptory challenges to fashion the jury ultimately empanelled. Lawyers can dismiss prospective jurors from a panel using "for cause challenges" if there is reason to believe that the juror is unsuitable, or "peremptory challenges," for which no explicit reason is required. The use of statutes or challenges to exclude "cognizable groups" has come under increased scrutiny since the Civil Rights Act of 1964.

By a statute enacted in 1873 the state of West Virginia limited jury duty to "white male persons who are twenty-one years of age and who are citizens of this State." Taylor Strauder, an African-American carpenter from Wheeling, was convicted of killing his wife Anna[46] but throughout the proceedings objected that the state's law contravened the Equal Protection Clause of the

---

[45] In this case the petitioner, a white man, claimed that the grand jury that indicted him as well as the petit jury that convicted him were illegally constituted because no African-Americans were on either jury. The respondent claimed that such complaints were only valid if the petitioner were of the excluded race. The US Supreme Court disagreed, on the grounds that the exclusion of minorities from juries has a broader impact than simple racial prejudice.

[46] The *Wheeling Daily Intelligencer*'s breathless account of the murder (April 19, 1872) can be found at www.wvculture.org/history/africanamericans/strauder01.html. Strauder was represented by a former Union Army officer, Blackburn Barrett Dovener, who would later represent his district in the US House of Representatives. At the time of the first trial he had just been admitted to the bar. The first objections to the conviction had nothing to do with the composition of the jury, as the West Virginia statute limiting jury duty to white males had not yet been enacted. Rather, a first conviction was overturned by the West Virginia Supreme Court of Appeals because of a jurisdictional objection (circuit court vs county court; *State* v. *Strauder*, July 20, 1874; www.wvculture.org/history/africanamericans/strauder02.html). The retrial in the county court gave rise to the conviction that led to the Supreme Court case. Even after the decision, the state was reluctant to grant *habeas corpus* and Strauder remained in jail. On September 8, 1880, he was moved from state to federal custody (*Wheeling Daily Intelligencer*

Fourteenth Amendment: "No state ... shall deny to any person within its jurisdiction the equal protection of the laws." Though the *Strauder* decision is riddled with paternalistic attitudes toward African-Americans, the US Supreme Court did ultimately find impermissible the statutory exclusion of any segment of the population from jury duty.

The decision was reaffirmed several times in the subsequent years, with gradual extension of the rulings from statutes to other forms of discrimination, and from African-Americans to other groups. In the *Slaughterhouse* cases (1873), the Supreme Court warned that "a strong case would be necessary" for the application of the Fourteenth Amendment protections to any class other than African-Americans (at 83). However, the Fourteenth Amendment came to be seen as a protection against any irrational discrimination. As early as 1900, in *American Sugar Refining* v. *State of Louisiana*, a case involving taxation, Justice Brown gave a broad interpretation to protections against discrimination: "if such discrimination was purely arbitrary, oppressive, or capricious, and made to depend upon differences of color, race, nativity, religious opinions, political affiliation, such exemption would be pure favoritism, and a denial of the equal protection of the laws to the less favored classes" (1900, at 92). Such a broad view of protected classes was not immediately applied to jury selection issues, though *Juarez* v. *Texas* (1925) did condemn the exclusion of Roman Catholics from a jury trying a case about illegal alcohol sales during Prohibition.

In the 1930s, the definition of "race" became the focus of several jury exclusion cases involving Mexican-Americans. When the defendant in *Ramirez* v. *State* (1931) protested the lack of Mexican-Americans on his Texas jury, the County Attorney claimed that no Mexican-Americans in Menard County spoke English well enough to serve as jurors, and even if they did they were deemed "otherwise ignorant," while the County Sheriff testified that beyond a lack of intelligence, the Mexican-Americans had different "customs and ways" that made them a poor choice for jury duty. Because Mexican-Americans were considered legally "white,"[47] both officials claimed that there was no racial animus to their decision, and the courts accepted their rationale.

September 9, 1880). Strauder was ordered to be released from prison in 1880, only to be immediately rearrested, leading to a flurry of legal wrangling. The newspaper judged that "during his long life behind the bars Strauder has improved his mind in ordinary studies and is now a very intelligent colored man. The strong probabilities are that he will soon be at liberty and if he puts his acquired talents to good use he may yet become a valuable citizen" (*Wheeling Daily Intelligencer* May 2, 1881). A year later the same newspaper worried that he might be "guilty of many questionable transactions" following his release, surprising his Wheeling friends "who were wont to think that his former troubles and confinement had worked a wonderful reformation in his character" (May 16, 1882).

[47] For an extended history of the racial classification system in Texas, see Gross (2007).

This application of a binary categorization of race was manipulated by Texas authorities to deny prejudice in such cases, so that Serapio Sanchez' appeal was denied in 1944, because there was no holding that "nationality and race bear the same relation" (*Sanchez* v. *State*, 1944). While race is a protected class, the court ruled "We have discovered no case wherein that court [the US Supreme Court in the case of *Norris* v. *Alabama*, 1935] has applied the same rule [protection under the Fourteenth Amendment to the Federal Constitution] to members of different nationalities." Even if Mexican-Americans were in practice discriminated against in ways similar to discrimination against African-Americans – forced to attend separate schools, barred from restaurants and theaters[48] – they had no Equal Protection remedy because that amendment was found to apply only to racial categories, and Mexican-Americans were classified as "white."[49]

The limitation of jury selection protection to African-Americans began to slip in the 1940s. *Hernandez* v. *Texas* (1954) extended the Equal Protection Clause to cases of national origin as well as race, focusing on unofficial but traditional patterns of discrimination. A similar ruling in the case of *Castaneda* v. *Partida* (1977), involving grand jury selection, outlined the route to a successful appeal: first, a group must be recognized as a "distinct class, singled out for different treatment"; second, the degree of underrepresentation in the jury pool over a "significant period of time" must be demonstrated; third, the selection procedure used must be shown to be "susceptible of abuse or . . . not racially neutral."[50] The distinct class in this case was "Mexican-Americans." The *Castaneda* court did not distinguish between "Mexican-Americans" and "persons of Spanish language" (1977, at 486).[51] The majority of Spanish speakers in Texas are immigrants or children of immigrants from Mexico (more than 80 percent in the 2010 Census), thus explaining though not

---

[48] In California, a public swimming pool designated Mondays "Mexican days" and drained and changed the water before "whites" came back to the pool on Tuesdays (Arriola 1995). Restroom signs in Texas designated one set as "white" and the other as "colored" and "hombres aqui" (Gross 2007, 385).

[49] The League of United Latin American Citizens (LULAC), founded in 1927, sought to use the "white" classification as a means of breaking down barriers by passing a state statute that would guarantee equal privileges to "all persons of the Caucasian Race" (Gross 2007, 362). In 1930, the Census Bureau introduced the category "Mexican" among the racial options, applied to those who were born, or whose parents were born, in Mexico. In 1940, it reverted to counting Mexican-Americans as white, but at the same time introduced a question about the language spoken at home. For further discussion of whiteness and the Mexican-American population, in the context of school desegregation, see Rochmes (2007).

[50] Justice Powell dissented from the *Castaneda* ruling, noting that the jury commissioners in Hidalgo County, Texas, were themselves Mexican-Americans.

[51] "For our purposes, the terms 'Spanish-surnamed' and 'Mexican-American' are used as synonyms for the census designation 'Persons of Spanish language or Spanish surname'" (*Castaneda* 1977 footnote 5).

justifying the confusion of the categories "Mexican" and "Latino/Hispanic/ Spanish-speaking/Spanish-surname."

The national origin focus did not extend protection to the entire class of persons of Latin American origin, or to language per se. The *U.S.* v. *Rodriguez* decision (1979), a drug-trafficking case from Florida, rejected the notion of Latin American origin or "Spanish-speaking" as a cognizable class and denied that the failure to adjust the jury pool to reflect the rapid growth of this segment of the population constituted proof of treatment as second-class citizens. The court in *Valle* v. *Crosby* (2005), following *Rodriguez,* explicitly rejected the notion of "Latino" as a cognizable minority group, instead recognizing only specific national origin groups, such as Mexican-Americans or Cuban-Americans. The judge in *Rodriguez* stated "there (is) simply no evidence upon which this Court could base a finding that persons of such diverse national origins as Cubans, Mexicans and Puerto Ricans possess such similar interests that they constitute a cognizable group" (*U.S.* v. *Rodriguez* 1979, at 1007).

The *Hernandez* and *Castaneda* cases were situated in a very different socio-linguistic context than that of *Rodriguez*. In South Florida, the site of the *Rodriguez* trial, the Spanish speakers are from more diverse national origins (roughly equal numbers of Cuban-Americans and Puerto Ricans but also about 45 percent from other national origins). Regardless of their national origin, *Rodriguez* claimed that these groups share an experience based on language and a history of discrimination, but the court did not find this argument persuasive.[52]

However, other courts have allowed such globalizing judgments to affect juror selection. In *U.S.* v. *Burton* (1999), a Latino potential juror was stricken by peremptory challenge even though nothing in the record showed that the person did not understand English. The prosecuting attorney applied its objection to all Spanish speakers regardless of national origin: "people who are Spanish-speakers or Hispanic no matter how clear they are, they generally don't understand legal concepts of the law" (1999, at 5).

The case *Duren* v. *Missouri* (1979) established the guidelines for proving that "the group alleged to be excluded is a distinctive group in the community."[53]

---

[52] In *Valle* v. *Crosby* (2005), the appellant's claims of "Latins" as a cognizable group were similarly rejected. Manuel Valle, convicted of killing a police officer and sentenced to death, argued that Latin Americans were underrepresented in his original jury (1979). The court found that he did not sufficiently define this term or prove that that this group was discriminated against.

[53] "In order to establish a *prima facie* violation of the fair-cross-section requirement, the defendant must show (1) that the group alleged to be excluded is a 'distinctive' group in the community; (2) that the representation of this group in *venires* from which juries are selected is not fair and reasonable in relation to the number of such persons in the community; and (3) that this underrepresentation is due to systematic exclusion of the group in the jury-selection process" (*Duren* 1979 at 364).

This case recognized women as a cognizable class. *U.S.* v. *Alvarado* (1989) clearly declared Hispanics a cognizable class, citing the federal government's use of the term for the purposes of the Equal Employment Opportunity Commission and for set-aside programs for minority businessmen:

Though issues may arise as to whether a particular individual is properly included within the category of "Hispanics", the classification has sufficient cohesiveness to be "cognizable" for jury discrimination claims. Indeed, it is somewhat surprising that the Executive Branch, which uses the term "Hispanic" and similar categories in implementing anti-discrimination standards . . . should disclaim the pertinence of the category "Hispanic" in the context of jury selection. (*U.S.* v. *Alvarado* 1989, at 444)

Is "language other than English" a cognizable class? Even without a common linguistic background, those whose native language is other than English can constitute a significant percentage of the population – almost 30 percent statewide in New Jersey, reaching almost 60 percent in Hudson County (Jersey City and surrounding communities).[54] As we shall see in the following, one court was willing to consider English speakers as a cognizable class that should not be the object of discrimination.

In the transition from the jury pool to the empanelled jury, using the challenge process, race was again the initial focus of protection against discriminatory peremptory challenges. This principle was established in the landmark case *Batson* v. *Kentucky* (1986), in which the prosecution struck all African-Americans in the jury pool. Batson was accused of burglary and receipt of stolen goods. The US Supreme Court ruled that while there was no right to a jury with members of one's racial minority, the exclusion of potential jurors on the basis of race was impermissible under the Equal Protection Clause.

It established a three-prong test to determine if the challenge is legal: (1) a prima facie case of discrimination raised by the defense; (2) a race-neutral explanation of the challenge raised by the prosecution; (3) the trial court determines if purposeful discrimination has taken place. This emphasizes the intent of the prosecutor. Almost any non-discriminatory explanation has been accepted. The dissenting opinion written by Justice Stevens sought a more restrictive test that required plausibility and persuasiveness in the explanation of race-neutrality. California had set a higher standard for the first prong of the Batson test, in the case of *People* v. *Wheeler* (1978), then challenged in *Johnson* v. *California* (2005), which went to the US Supreme Court. The prima facie case required likelihood that discrimination had taken place, rather than "reasonable inference."

---

[54] Census Bureau figures from the 2010 Census.

At the US Supreme Court this requirement was deemed too onerous. A prima facie case could be based on historical patterns of discrimination or on comparative juror analysis (comparison of how jurors responded to similar questions or on statistical comparisons of the general population and the jury pool (Ali, 264–265)). In *Rivera* v. *Nibco, Inc.* (2010),[55] a case we will return to in Chapter 6, lawyers for the company used three of their four peremptory challenges to strike potential Latino jurors. Five reasons were given for striking juror TG, a Latina: (1) TG's sister was concerned about discrimination; (2) TG liked working with multi-linguals (she worked at Frito-Lay); (3) TG had filed a workers' compensation claim; (4) TG's sister had been fired; and (5) TG had previously served on a jury that failed to reach a verdict. The first two turned out to be false – her sister had never filed a discrimination claim and TG merely said "she loved working in a diverse workplace" – and the third was dismissed by comparative juror analysis: four non-Hispanic jurors who had filed unemployment claims were not stricken. The fifth was considered weak by comparative juror analysis, as one of the non-Hispanic jurors had said she had trouble judging others. As a result, the Ninth Circuit reversed and remanded the District Court ruling, concluding that "Nibco's stated reasons for striking juror TG were implausible, unsupported by the record, and/ or undermined by a comparative juror analysis," thus rendering them "pretext for intentional discrimination" (2010 at 761).

Application of these principles concerning discrimination in jury selection has had limited impact in the case of potential jurors whose English is questionable. Low representation or outright exclusion of jurors from linguistic minorities has not generally been recognized by the courts as a problem for impartiality. At the federal level, the linguistic requirement for inclusion in a jury is that potential jurors are competent enough in English to fill out the juror qualification form or can speak English.[56] State requirements vary, with some specifying that jurors must be able "to read, write, speak and understand English" (e.g., Pennsylvania).[57] Most other states include some form of this skill set in English, with only a few omitting any mention of linguistic competence (Montana, Florida, Tennessee, Texas, and Virginia; see Gonzales Rose (2014, 820)). This requirement has been used even to exclude native speakers of English if the judge has found them difficult to understand. In *Corona* v. *Almager* (2009 at 6), the judge accepted the prosecution's challenge to an

---

[55] This case started in 1998 and was finally settled in 2011.

[56] Jury Selection and Service Act of 1968, 28 U.S.C., §1865 (b) 2–3. The court deems any person qualified to serve unless he [*sic*]

(2) is unable to read, write, and understand the English language with a degree of proficiency sufficient to fill out satisfactorily the juror qualification form;

(3) is unable to speak the English language.

[57] Pennsylvania Statutes 42, § 4502 (a) (1).

African-American potential juror because "I had a substantial difficulty understanding him. I think that probably translated into a difficulty, or at least not a sophistication, in understanding English to the extent we are going to need it in this case."

At the other end of the spectrum, New Mexico has a constitutional guarantee for the inclusion of Spanish speakers who are not competent in English: "the right of any citizen of the state ... to sit upon juries shall never be restricted, abridged or impaired on account of ... inability to speak, read or write the English or Spanish languages" (Constitution of 1911, Article VII, Section 3, cited in Chávez (2008, 306)). This policy goes back to territorial days, as in *New Mexico v. Romine* (1881; see Chávez (2008, 305–306)), and has been upheld in recent years.[58] In 2014, Illinois proposed a pilot program in five counties that would offer interpretation services for any LEP jurors, regardless of native language. Such programs increase minority representation and thus contribute to the cross-section principle of jury composition.

Given the English-language requirement, the disparity between the raw census number of people from a linguistic minority and the number of those who are jury eligible can be considerable. In *State of Washington v. Gladstone*, the lawyers showed that the representation of Latino jurors was approximately 1/8th the presence of Latinos in the general population. The mathematical methods used to determine if minorities are underrepresented implicitly approve discrimination against certain sectors of the population. For example, the courts have accepted that when comparing minority representation of the *venire* to the general population, one must consider only the "jury-eligible" members of the minority, that is, excluding those whose English is limited or non-existent: "a district court need not and may not take into account Hispanics who are ineligible for jury service to determine whether Hispanics are underrepresented on grand jury *venires*" (*U.S. v. Torres-Hernandez* 2006, at 704). Using this metric, courts have frequently found the disparity "constitutionally insignificant."[59]

The decision in *Taylor v. Louisiana* (1975) requires that the *venire* represents a cross-section of the community, but the empaneled jury does not have to reflect the diversity of the *venire*. Even were the *venire* diverse, the actual

---

[58] *State ex. rel. Martinez v. Third Judicial District Court* (2000); *State v. Rico* (2002). In the first of these, the Supreme Court of New Mexico upheld a District Court ruling prohibiting the excusal of a non-English-speaking juror simply because his inclusion would require the use of an interpreter. In the second, a Navajo potential juror was excused because the Navajo interpreter was absent, and the next nearest one way 2½ hours distant. Even though the New Mexico constitution does not protect Navajo, the same expectation of accommodation was accepted. However, in *State v. Samora* (2013), failure to admit a juror with limited English proficiency was recognized as an error, but not an error requiring reversal.

[59] *Torres-Hernandez* (2006, at 705); for further discussion of the mathematical models used in determining discriminatory disparity in jury selection, see Re (2011).

composition of the *voir dire* often excludes minorities, based on racial and ethnic stereotypes. While most of the appeals involving peremptory strikes have been by the defense, occasionally the defense itself has been found guilty of discrimination against a class, in attempting to exclude all members of the victim's racial/ethnic group (*Norona* v. *State* 2014). On the belief that African-American jurors will be more sympathetic to the accused, prosecutors tend to use peremptory challenges to strike people of color, while the defense has the opposite tactic: in a study of thirteen jury trials in North Carolina, Rose (1999) found that 71 percent of the challenges of African-American jurors were made by the prosecution, and 81 percent of the challenges of white jurors came from the defense. Studies of the relationship between race/ethnicity and willingness to convict have had conflicting results, leading Ali to conclude that "striking potential jurors based on stereotypes produces a homogenous jury that denies a defendant a right to an impartial jury" (Ali 2013, 257–258). A number of legal scholars have argued that peremptory challenges should simply be abolished.

Dismissal of potential jurors because they are native speakers of the non-English language of testimony is another barrier to minority representation on juries, but one that has been accepted by the courts. Court instructions require jurors to listen only to the interpreter, not to the original language. Furthermore, English alone is the language of record, the official record of the verbal evidence. Testimony in other languages has until recently rarely been recorded, and thus cannot be challenged. Rubert (2014), himself a court interpreter, sees the requirement to listen only to the interpreter as a matter of fairness: "fairness requires that all jurors consider the same evidence." Ali, however, argues that with proper intervention on the part of bilingual jurors the ability to understand the witnesses' original testimony "can positively contribute to the truth-seeking function of a jury trial" (2013, 260).

The principle of attending only to the words of the interpreter was affirmed by the decision in *Hernandez* v. *New York* (1991), even as the Supreme Court recognized the problems with excluding bilingual jurors. Dionisio Hernandez was accused and convicted of attempted murder and criminal possession of a weapon. The prosecutor used two of his peremptory challenges to exclude Latino potential jurors on the basis that "there was a great deal of uncertainty as to whether they could accept the interpreter as the final arbiter of what was said by each of the witnesses" (1991, at 365). The defense objected, and the case went ultimately to the Supreme Court, which affirmed the conviction by accepting the prosecution's claim that the challenges were neutral and non-discriminatory.

Though it affirmed the decision in this particular case, the Supreme Court observed that "our decision today does not imply that the exclusion of bilinguals from jury service is wise, or even that it is constitutional in all cases. It is a harsh paradox that one may become proficient enough in English to participate in trial, only to encounter disqualification because he knows a second language as well" (1991 at 371). The court continued:

We would face a quite different case if the prosecutor had justified his peremptory challenges with the explanation that he did not want Spanish-speaking jurors. It may well be, for certain ethnic groups and in some communities, that proficiency in a particular language, like skin color, should be treated as a surrogate for race under an equal protection analysis. (*ibid.*)

Once again language is considered important only to the extent that it can be equated with a protected class, race, or national origin.

It is, however, not easy to win a *Batson* appeal. *People* v. *Cardenas* (2007) exemplifies the difficulty of a *Batson* appeal based on language. The prosecution struck two potential Latino jurors claiming that the jurors would not disregard testimony in Spanish, even though the judge had told them they would have to do so. On appeal, the California Court of Appeal recognized the problems with the prosecutor's tactic but refused to overturn the trial court's conclusion that the prosecutor's reasons were "race-neutral."

People v. *Gonzales* (2008) is a rare example of a successful *Batson* appeal. The prosecution claimed that its peremptory challenges were based not on "stereotypical assumptions about Latinos or bilinguals" (2008 at 629) but rather on the belief that the prospective jurors would not listen to the interpreter rather than the witness. However, the Spanish-speaking jurors were asked if they could listen only to the interpreter, and all but one responded that they could. In particular, the prosecution's peremptory challenge of juror "J.C.," a bilingual (Spanish-English) was justified on perceptions of "maturity." This explanation was considered "unsupported by the record and implausible" (2008 at 632) and therefore suspect.[60]

When bilingual jurors are seated, they should never challenge directly the interpretation, but only by passing a note to the judge. If a juror recognizes that an error has been made, a message should be delivered to the bailiff, so that the disputed interpretation can be resolved. What should not happen, and was labeled juror misconduct in *People* v. *Cabrera* (1991), is that a juror who has understood the original language testimony offers a different translation for the other jurors. The goal is to resolve any disputed translation before the jury begins deliberations.

Most of the focus in American jurisprudence has been on the right of a defendant to a fair and impartial jury, but a growing concern is the civil right of citizens to be eligible for jury duty. The inclusion of LEP jurors has been

---

[60] See discussion of this case in Ali (2013, 254–255), who speculates that had the prosecution simply asked juror J.C. about his ability to listen to the interpreter – whatever the answer – the prosecution's peremptory strike would probably have been accepted.

mandated by the constitution of the state of New Mexico and has been proposed by State Senator Iris Martinez of Illinois. These jurisdictions permit persons who are not fluent in English to serve as jurors and to have the trial proceedings translated for them. This guarantee is enshrined in the New Mexico Constitution, Article VII, Section 3, though it limits the protection to Spanish speakers:

The right of any citizen of the state to vote, hold office or sit upon juries, shall never be restricted, abridged or impaired on account of religion, race, language or color, or inability to speak, read or write the English or Spanish languages except as may be otherwise provided in this constitution.

The proposed Illinois law (Senate Bill 977) would extend this right to all LEP persons, otherwise qualified, without restriction as to language. In a pilot program in five counties with a high proportion of LEP prospective jurors, this bill

Provides that in the counties of Cook, Lake, DuPage, Kane, and Will, the court shall implement a pilot program to appoint a qualified interpreter to interpret or translate proceedings for a juror whose predominant language is not English. Provides that the interpreter shall be available throughout the trial and may accompany and communicate with the juror throughout any period during which the jury is sequestered or engaged in its deliberations. Provides that the court shall determine and allow a reasonable fee for all interpreter services provided which shall be paid out of general county funds. Provides that the Administrative Office of the Illinois Courts shall record specified information regarding the pilot program. Provides that an interpreter shall make an oath or affirmation that the interpreter will make a true interpretation, will not interject the interpreter's own thoughts, beliefs, or conclusions regarding the proceedings, and will not express any opinion as to what the verdict should be.

Ironically, the protection of a juror's right to serve has been invoked to protect English monolinguals.

This was the claim of defendant Garcia in *U.S.* v. *Lopez et al.* (1987). The vast majority of the testimony in this case consisted of recordings in Spanish. The appellant argued that only Spanish-speakers could truly evaluate the recordings, even though translated transcripts would be provided, including translations by the defendant herself. In English-language recorded testimony, transcripts are used to assist the jury, but do not substitute for them. Garcia sought to apply the same rule to Spanish-language recorded testimony. However the US District Court held that to require a pre-screening for bilingual jurors would be a national origin discrimination against English monolinguals:

[18 U.S.C.] § 1862 prohibits the exclusion of jurors based on their national origin, and while it is true that many people are bilingual who are not Hispanic, there can be no question that the majority of Spanish-speaking jurors in the Chicago area are Hispanic . . . since the exclusion of jurors who speak only English would, in the circumstances of this case, be statutorily prohibited, Garcia's motion for a bilingual jury must be denied. (*Lopez* at 3–4)

Given what we have considered earlier, two aspects of this decision are curious: (1) claiming a national-origin class of English speakers, while other courts have denied a national-origin class of Hispanics/Latinos; (2) claiming that the class of English speakers would be the object of discrimination.

Fairness and impartiality are the cornerstones of the American legal ideology. The edifice itself, however, is built on the other foundations of the American character, practicality and "common sense." These sometimes prove to be contradictory tendencies in the shifting linguistic layers that make up the American populace. With the doors opened for immigration from Asia and Africa and the rapid growth of the Spanish-speaking population, the percentage of Americans who are less comfortable in English is increasing. In California, 19.8 percent of the population is described as speaking English less than "very well" (US Census 2010). The increased numbers of LEP residents constantly increases the need for linguistic negotiation in the legal system. A consistent extension of protections for LEP persons also strains the ability of the courts to provide the services necessary for fairness. The draft Language Access Plan for California (2014) recommends that the right to an interpreter be extended first to domestic violence and other family court matters and then to civil suits. The combination of increased LEP population, increased services, and increased scrutiny of the quality of those services, along with decreases in the budget available to provide the services, is a challenge to the principles of fairness demanded by society.

Fairness is usually associated with the ability to understand the legal action being taken, requiring interpretation that is accurate and unbiased. The federal district courts reported a 13.8 percent increase in interpreter use between 2009 and 2010. State courts are experiencing similar demands, while administrative budgets are pared. California similarly noted a 14 percent increase between 2004 and 2008, and expenditures on interpretation services of over $93 million for the fiscal year 2009 (more than $1 million over the state budget allotment).[61] The logistical problem of supplying an adequate number of certified or qualified interpreters to meet this demand encourages courts to minimize the need for interpretation in marginal cases. The discretion of the trial court in assessing the need for interpretation is rarely challenged successfully.

Similarly, appeals based on errors in translation are very hard to win. The very nature of interpretation and translation makes the standard of plain error

---

[61] See the interpreter need document available at www.courts.ca.gov/documents/language-inter preterneed-10.pdf, pp. xv and 1–2.

hard to reach. As recording technologies become more prevalent, the potential for closer scrutiny is possible, and with it the end of the conduit metaphor of court interpreting.

These disparities between ideology and practicality lead to sometimes confusing and conflicting judicial precedents. By the nature of American common law some time lapse is required for the practice of the courts to catch up to the evolving standards of fairness.

Impartiality has generally been guaranteed by limiting the government's power through citizen involvement in the jury system. Language questions limit the participation of a significant portion of the citizenry, who are first excluded for knowing too little (English) and then for knowing too much (the non-English language of testimony). The redefinition of cognizable groups protected from discrimination has lowered de jure and de facto barriers to jury participation by those whose native language is other than English, but practical issues remain. The ideology of inclusion continues to press against the "common sense" acceptance of English dominance.

In the common-law system, philosophy and practicality are both constantly adjusting to each other. Fairness and impartiality are not absolutes but rather continuously negotiated goals of the American legal system. These negotiations are carried out in court cases and hearings as the facets of each individual situation are generalized into the law.

4 Language and Education

From the earliest days of the Republic, government at all levels has recognized its vital interest in education. An educated citizenry is crucial to participation in government and to economic productivity. To achieve these goals competence in languages other than English has sometimes been perceived as a threat, sometimes as a boon. Equality and liberty are at play, invoking the competing powers of the levels of government in a federal system and the competing powers of the divisions of government in our checks-and-balances system.

What is the goal of language education? For some education seeks reproduction of the dominant culture, presenting its history as the common heritage of the nation. This approach is justified as providing students with the practical knowledge necessary to function economically and socially in our society. The curriculum in the schools and the books chosen to support it teach children what it is to be American (Ramsey 2010, 9), defined, often, as white, Protestant, and of English origin. A contemporary example is E. D. Hirsch, Jr. (1988), who describes a "civil religion" and a "national vocabulary" as "national givens": "Our civil religion defines our broadly shared values as a society, and our national vocabulary functions, or should function, as our broadly shared instrument of communication (1988, 103)."[1] These are not, he argues, reflections of the "coherent culture of a dominant class" (*ibid.*).[2] Constant through this approach, from the Know-Nothings of the 1850s to the English-only movement of the early twenty-first century, is

---

[1] Hirsch protests that he is not prescriptive but merely being descriptive of what "literate Americans" know (1988, xiv), but when he insists that what his literate Americans know should be the standard curriculum for all young Americans, he crosses the line into prescriptivism. Hirsch worries that "well-meaning bilingualism could erect serious barriers to cultural literacy among our young people and therefore create serious barriers to universal literacy at a mature level" (1988, 93). He raises the specter of ethnolinguistic division, as in Belgium or Canada.

[2] He further claims that "Neither in origin nor in subsequent history have national languages been inherently class languages" (1988, 106). Most sociolinguists would argue the exact opposite. Standard French is certainly the product of the centralization of power in the royal court in the seventeenth century (see my introduction to a new edition of Scipion Dupleix's *Liberté de la langue françoise dans sa pureté* (1651), forthcoming).

a fear that new immigrants are different from previous immigrant groups,[3] that they are refusing to assimilate,[4] and that their knowledge of a second language and culture will diminish allegiance to the dominant national culture. Early in the twentieth century the Commission on Naturalization found that "the proposition is incontrovertible that no man is a desirable citizen of the United States who does not know the English language" (1905, 11).[5] The learning of English does not mean that the mastery of the immigrants' native language is not a valuable goal for American society. Often, however, it has been perceived as an either/or rather than a both/and proposition, and the dominant group has sabotaged English acquisition while stoutly demanding it.

For others, the common heritage is a set of principles defining equality and the constitutional protections of all, including minorities. In part this is what

[3] In 1845, the Native American Party declared in its convention platform that earlier immigrants were "recruited chiefly from the victims of political oppression, or the active and intelligent mercantile adventurers of other lands" while the new immigrants (at that point the Irish victims of the potato famine) were "the feeble, the imbecile, the idle, and intractable" which Europe foisted upon the New World (cited in Sarason & Doris 1979, 185–186). The claims were not without some basis, as European governments sometimes assisted the poor and convicted criminals to emigrate, England alone sending at least 30,000 felons to the United States. In colonial times several colonies passed laws against or demanding duty payments for the transportation of criminals, but the king ignored them, one of the many grievances listed in the Declaration of Independence (see Abbott 1931, 23–30). The Immigration Act of 1882 formally denied entry to criminals, paupers, and other undesirables, and created the federal bureaucracy for immigration control. The Immigration Act of 1917 continued these activities, inspired by spurious eugenics research by Henry Laughlin and others.

[4] The most recent example is Huntington (2004). He feared that the size and demographic distribution of the Spanish-speaking community led Latinos to reject assimilation. His conclusions are directly contradicted by an extensive longitudinal study in Rumbaut, Massey, and Bean (2006), which shows that third-generation Latinos prefer speaking English at home at virtually the same rate as other immigrants, though they are more likely to still be able to speak their heritage language.

[5] The Commission report was the basis for the Naturalization Act of 1906 which gave the federal government control of the naturalization process, previously subject to state-to-state variation. The Commission was unable to agree on a single bill, and sent two proposals to President Roosevelt. One required that the candidate for naturalization be able "to read and speak the English language and to write in his own language" (1905, 109). The other that "no such alien shall hereafter be admitted as a citizen of the United States who can not write in his own language or in the English language and who can not read, speak and understand the English language" (1905, 97). The final text excluded the written requirement: "No alien shall hereafter be naturalized or admitted as a citizen of the United States who can not speak the English language." Current law 8 U.S.C. §1423 (a) stipulates that

no person except as otherwise provided in this subchapter shall hereafter be naturalized as a citizen of the United States upon his own application who cannot demonstrate – (1) an understanding of the English language, including an ability to read, write and speak words in ordinary usage in the English language: *Provided*, That the requirements of this paragraph relating to ability to read and write shall be met if the applicant can read or write simple words and phrases to the end that a reasonable test of his literacy shall be made and that no extraordinary or unreasonable condition shall be imposed upon the applicant.

Hirsch meant by the American "civil religion," but he did not pursue the inherent conflicts between the principles. The American tradition of freedom allows parents and students to choose other educational goals, in addition to or in place of what has been deemed common. Local control of the schools is perhaps a good example of the "laboratory" of creative solutions to diverse problems, as envisioned by Justice Brandeis in 1932.[6] Local control and private and parochial schooling increased the diversity of education, sometimes allowing indigenous and immigrant communities to pursue cultural survival through the schools. Local control could also permit repressive measures by the majority population, the suppression of identity and even maintenance of segregated schools. Similarly, according to the way the political winds were blowing, federal and state funding, accreditation and assessment through testing has sometimes promoted a uniform curriculum and a uniform language, using a principle of equality to limit educational options, or it sometimes has promoted dual-language programs and language-maintenance efforts. Equality of opportunity, providing all children with the knowledge and skills to succeed, requires an understanding of the system of government and the ability to understand and to express oneself in the English language. The society as a whole benefits from the contributions of all cultures, and linguistic competence beyond English is a major advantage in global competitiveness.

Education thus presents important questions for American society as a whole. How much uniformity is required for unity? How much room is left for freedom? What is the role of the student's native language and culture in learning the dominant language and culture? Is monolingualism a national asset or a national weakness? These are not new questions: they were already hot topics in colonial America. The local/state/federal funding formulas for schooling have, on the positive side, encouraged experimentation to determine best practices. On the negative side, they have allowed bigotry to deny educational opportunity. Each new wave of immigrants has been pronounced

---

[6] In his dissent to *New State Ice Co.* v. *Liebmann* (1932), Justice Brandeis argued that the state of Oklahoma should be able to limit competition in the ice business, if it so chose, as an experiment in how to balance production and consumption in a time of high unemployment. He concluded:

To stay experimentation in things social and economic is a grave responsibility. Denial of a right to experiment may be fraught with serious consequences to the Nation. It is one of the happy incidents of the federal system that a single courageous State may, if its citizens choose, serve as a laboratory; and try novel social and economic experiments without risk to the rest of the country. (at 311)

Although he acknowledged that the Supreme Court had the power to prevent an experiment, he cautioned that "we must ever be on our guard, lest we erect our prejudices into legal principles" (*ibid.*) and urged that we "let our minds be bold." The constraints on such experimentation were recently expressed in denying the states' ability to prohibit same-sex marriages, overturning Wisconsin's statutes (*Wolf* v. *Walker* 2014): "States may not 'experiment' with different social policies by violating constitutional rights" (at 994); affirmed by the Seventh Circuit in *Baskin* v. *Bogan* (2014).

"unassimilable" and "uneducable," with such evaluations consigning students to special education or even segregated schools; each has then been assimilated and educated and has contributed its own genius to American society.

Indigenous communities have suffered a similar fate. As noted in Chapter 1, indigenous communities today are protected, in theory, by special rights of cultural preservation incumbent in that status. The history of their education, however, is one of linguistic extermination. For many it was a reverse Trail of Tears, as children were forcibly removed from their families and sent east to boarding schools, where their native language would be lost.

In 2009, almost 10 percent of the students in the public schools required English-language assistance, a figure that is rapidly increasing (12 percent increase between 2002 and 2011).[7] The highest growth rate has been in the South, with South Carolina registering a 400 percent increase. How English-language learners have been and are being educated has been controversial from the founding of the Republic, and even earlier. The ways of addressing the issue have changed with the advent of statistical social sciences in educational research, but the pedagogical and public debate has followed the same basic lines since those earliest days. The divisions concern the purpose of education, the meaning of "American," the nature and role of identity, and economic competitiveness.

Though formal schooling was spotty at the time of the Revolution, the founding fathers were already thinking about the role of education in a republic. Benjamin Rush (1806 [1798]) found education necessary for unifying the diversity of his native Pennsylvania:

I conceive the education of our youth in this country to be peculiarly necessary in Pennsylvania while our citizens are composed of the natives of so many different kingdoms in Europe. Our schools of learning, by producing one general and uniform system of education, will render the mass of the people more homogeneous and thereby fit them more easily for uniform and peaceable government.[8]

Thereby, he would "convert men into republican machines." For him religious training was the primary focus of education, but he valued learning languages,

---

[7] Table 47. Number and Percentage of Public School Students Participating in Programs for English Language Learners, by State: Selected Years, 2002–2003 through 2010–2011, National Center for Education Statistics, https://nces.ed.gov/programs/digest/d12/tables/d t12_047.asp).

[8] Benjamin Rush, "On the Mode of Education Proper in a Republic" (first published in 1798; we have used the 1806 second edition, where this essay is found on pp. 6–20). His dream of common schooling was based on Protestant Christianity and the teaching of social and personal responsibility. While these elements remained strong components of nineteenth-century pedagogy, the goal of homogeneity through uniform instruction would be thwarted by local control.

both ancient and modern, and mastering English rhetoric as necessary skills for all professions.

Accordingly, the federal government required new states to put aside 1/16th of the land in every township to help fund public schooling, including higher education. Illinois, in order to become a state in 1818, incorporated this requirement into its earliest code,

> believing that the advancement of literature always has been, and ever will be, the means of developing more fully the rights of man, that the mind of every citizen in a republic is the common property of society and constitutes the basis of its strength and happiness, it is therefore considered the peculiar duty of a free government like ours to encourage and extend the improvement and cultivation of the intellectual energies of the whole. (cited in *Powell* v. *Board of Education* 1881, at 381)

This conception of education stresses the benefits to society rather than to the individual: the pursuit of happiness is a collective endeavor dependent on the contributions of all to a common good.

The desire to use public schools to develop citizenship through Protestant moral teaching and English-language instruction sharpened with industrialization in the first half of the nineteenth century, and with the first waves of mass immigration, German and Irish. Catholicism and linguistic difference felt like a threat to the Protestant English-speaking communities, a threat that could be countered by assimilation through the public school system. The common school movement advanced rapidly in the period 1830–1860. New York's Free School Society, essentially a charity school system, was transformed into the Public School Society, funded through taxation. State schools attempted to establish uniform curricula based on Protestant moral teachings,[9] but at the same time a fierce attachment to local control prevailed. Local control and competition from parochial schools challenged the nativist tendencies from the middle of the nineteenth century through the strong Americanization[10] campaigns of the early twentieth century.

---

[9] Private religious schools thrived in large part because of the liberal Protestant orientation of public school education. The use of the King James Bible was particularly abhorrent to both Catholic and Lutheran communities. In 1890, the Wisconsin Supreme Court banned the Bible from public school classrooms, noting that the choice of translation and the choice of passages constituted doctrinal religious instruction, banned by the Wisconsin Constitution (*State ex. rel. Weiss* v. *District Board of School District No. 8 of the City of Edgerton* 1890).

[10] In some instances, Americanization was accompanied by the desire to open the eyes of the English-speaking community as well, as when the editor of the *Wisconsin Journal of Education* suggested, in 1862, that "Wherever there is a somewhat equal intermingling of Americans and Germans, we conceive it would be an advantageous plan, if practicable, to provide for instruction in both languages. Under a judicious arrangement, many American children might learn to read and speak German; and this interchange would help and hasten the assimilation of the races" (cited in Kuyper 1980, 118). However, this was not the dominant view: Wisconsin law in 1866 decreed that "no branch of study shall be taught in any other than the English language"

Legal intervention started at the state level, particularly in the newly founded states on the frontier. In the first half of the nineteenth century the rich agricultural lands of Ohio, Indiana, and Illinois beckoned American-born and immigrant families, their almost simultaneous arrival leading quickly to language conflicts. The control of language in the classroom could be effected in several ways: by direct order to instruct in English or to permit other languages, by teacher certification, and by the selection of acceptable textbooks. The earliest state law noted in this respect is Indiana's law of 1824, establishing a funding system and an administrative structure for schools in the Hoosier State. The law required that a prospective teacher be examined "touching his qualifications, and particularly as respects his knowledge of the English language, writing, and arithmetic."[11] In Pennsylvania, school law provided more flexibility to local control, thus promoting bilingual education in the public schools from the 1830s (Ramsey 2010, 43–45).[12] The Pennsylvania School Law of 1837 approved of schools in German, explicitly rejecting monolingualism: "In other states having one language, one people, one origin and one soil, a system suited to one district, satisfies the whole. Not so here."[13]

The conflicting opinions on bilingual education in the antebellum era are illustrated in Ohio. German schools were established by 1831, with more students than the English schools. In 1836, the governor sent Calvin Stowe[14] to Europe to study Prussian education; his glowing report further promoted German education. Nonetheless, the Ohio legislature passed a law in 1838 banning the use of languages other than English as the medium of instruction. Confronted by an angry and unified German population, Ohio repealed its English-only education law in 1839 to allow any community with seventy-five freeholders of a particular language in a given township to demand a school

---

(Kuyper 1980, 121). In spite of that statute, many school districts continued using German, particularly in the lower grades.

[11] Kloss (1998, 105) interpreted this (and many have repeated his findings) as establishing English as the dominant language of instruction. Though English as the language of instruction was probably a fact in the few existing schools, we have found no evidence of any restriction on the language of instruction. A French school was being operated by a certain M. Jean at the time, and instruction in French was specifically included in the curriculum of the school in Vincennes, though as a subject rather than as the medium of instruction. At that time there was a residual French population along the Ohio River, but new immigration of Europeans was not yet significant.

[12] In Harrisburg a "German convention" with representatives from six states was held in 1837, demanding that German be recognized as an official state language and collecting funds to start a German teacher training school. The school opened in Philipsburg, but closed two years later (Bureau of Education (1902, 557); Chapter 14 of this report is devoted to "German Instruction in American Schools").

[13] *Journal of the House of Representatives of the Commonwealth of Pennsylvania, 1836–1837*, vol. 2 cited online in a paper by Sarah K. Myers, http://comenius.susqu.edu/journals/spectacles/2012/myers.pdf.

[14] Stowe was the future husband of Harriet Beecher, the author of *Uncle Tom's Cabin*.

in their language; if German were not offered, students could attend school in another district at their home district's expense. In Cincinnati, the German schools first were aimed at transition to English over a three-year period, but in 1847 they switched to a format calling for a half day of instruction in each language, so that students would learn both cultures. The German schools flourished from the beginning, with 327 students enrolled in the first year (1840–1841) and 17,000 by the end of the century (Toth 1990, 61).[15]

Laws specifically permitting instruction in other languages were common in the middle of the nineteenth century. Colorado allowed instruction in Spanish or German. New Mexico had almost equal numbers of Spanish and English schools (Kloss 1998, 170). In the south, Louisiana towns had the option of French schools throughout the nineteenth century, except briefly during Reconstruction (Handschin 1913, 28–29). Chicago instituted its first experiment in German-language instruction in 1865. By 1893, 44,000 students were studying German in the Chicago public schools, more than half of those children not of German origin (Kloss 1998, 114).

Private schools offering fully bilingual education flourished in the first half of the nineteenth century. In Buffalo, at least four German private schools were established before the first public school opened in the German Twelfth District, and the role of German in that public school was a political issue throughout the 1850s, with real bilingual education instituted only after the Civil War (Gerber 1984, 37). Private schools, both religious and secular, were often established to ensure language instruction in the home language along with other cultural values of the home country. In order to compete, the public schools began to offer German classes, but the real push for full bilingual education came after the Civil War. A combination of political opportunism[16] and demographic pressure changed German from a subject to be studied to the medium of instruction.

The way this transformation worked out depended on local conditions, as the power of state superintendents and that of local boards varied enormously from place to place and from one era to the next. Indeed, the history of bilingual education in the United States has thousands of variants depending on local

---

[15] The German schools were so successful that many students of other national origins enrolled. Separate German schools for African-Americans were established after the Civil War, aided by a donation from King Ludwig of Bavaria (Toth 1990, 62). African-American parents later demanded German instruction in the segregated schools of Indianapolis (Ellis 1954b, 252). In more modern times, both the Cincinnati and Milwaukee dual-immersion German bilingual programs were attracting minority students – 37–50 percent of the total enrollment – in the late 1980s (Toth 1990, 117).

[16] The Republican Party had absorbed the nativist Know-Nothing element, and continued to oppose bilingual education, fearing the "Germanizing of America." In Buffalo, in the 1870s, this opposition unified Germans for the Democratic Party and resulted in the replacement of five Republican city councilmen by Democrats. The bilingual education programs were subsequently not just re-established but reinforced (Gerber 1984, 48–49).

conditions.[17] Local control of the schools in the urban ethnic enclaves provided a rallying point for the rise of ethnic political power. In the urban setting, the politics of ethnic identity were crucial to local control. In San Francisco, which in the 1860s had a large German population, the ethnic politics of the Democratic Party and the vision of School Superintendent John Pelton led to the opening of "Cosmopolitan Schools," in which the primary languages of instruction were German and French, with English taught as a second language (Shradar 1974, 29–32). However, the Chinese, more numerous in San Francisco than either of these ethnicities but lacking the right to vote, remained excluded from all public schools until 1885 (Dolson 1964, 120–121).

In the central states of the plains, local control permitted rural ethnic communities to maintain their distinctive identities, including language.[18] An 1821 law in Michigan (then a territory) allowed schools to be in French or English. In the era of the Know-Nothings in the 1840s and 1850s, some of this openness disappeared: the Illinois statute on education in 1847 required all schools receiving state funding to certify that "the school was an English one, in which the medium of instruction was the English language" (cited in *Powell* 1881, at 383). With the demise of the Know-Nothings and the rise of immigrant voting power, the pendulum swung the other direction; the 1857 Illinois law provided for "an English education" but specified that "nothing herein contained shall prevent the teaching of a foreign language in a common school" (*Powell* 1881, at 384). The Illinois law of 1869 provided for any modern language to be used as a medium of instruction. In *Powell*, a taxpayer objected to instruction being given in German. The state Supreme Court ruled against Powell, noting that "directors [of the schools] are invested by law with large discretion in all matters pertaining to the management of schools," though a dissent by Justice Walker found that without specific wording to the contrary, "the directors are powerless to authorize the teaching of any foreign language"

[17] Texas permitted bilingual education from the earliest days of the Republic of Texas, as Stephen Austin was a strong supporter, as was Jacob De Gress, the German-born first superintendent of public instruction. Toward the end of the nineteenth century, support for some form of bilingual education varied greatly from county to county, and included Poles, Germans, Czechs as well as the Spanish-speaking population. For an extensive study of the topic, see Blanton (2004). Other place-based studies include Toth on Cincinnati, Sommerfeld on Cleveland, Kuyper on Wisconsin, and Gerber on Buffalo (all specifically about German instruction). Zeydel (1964) studied German instruction across the country. Gehrke (1935) described the demise of German schooling in North Carolina early in the nineteenth century.

[18] A Department of the Interior report studied rural schools in Nebraska, where more than half of the teachers were foreign born or the children of foreign-born parents. In Washington County, 37 percent of the teachers were born in Denmark or of Danish parents (1919, 26–27), while in Cuming County only a quarter of the population was "native white of native parentage" (information drawn from the 1910 Census, reported in 1919, 26). This is the context for *Meyer* v. *Nebraska* (1923), see below p. 97.

(at 389).[19] Matters came to a head shortly after *Powell* with the passage of the "Edwards Bill" (1889).

In Texas, the politics of Reconstruction and post-Reconstruction led to the elimination of the post of state school superintendent. Democrats resented this administrative vestige of Reconstruction, but also rejected bilingual education. The new policies left control in the hands of county judges, which, contrary to the Democrats position, favored bilingual education in areas with large numbers of immigrants (Blanton 2004, 21–22). The Czech community in Fayette County elected a Czech county judge who blithely sidestepped laws concerning the certification of non-English-speaking teachers (*ibid.*, 40). In Missouri, the State Supervisor of Public Instruction complained that the immigrant populations were controlling the school boards and superintendent positions, guaranteeing a place not just for their heritage languages but for teachers who didn't know English:

In a large number of districts of the State the German element of the population greatly preponderates and as a consequence the schools are mainly taught in the German language and sometimes entirely so. Hence if an American family lives in such a district the children must either be deprived of school privileges or else be taught in the German language ... Some of the teachers are scarcely able to speak the English language. (1888; cited in Kloss 1998, 89–90)

Concern over the quality of rural education led the National Education Association to establish a "Committee of Twelve on Rural Schools" to promote school consolidation and expert governance (Tyack 1974, 23), with the result that the number of rural schools was cut from 200,000 to 20,000 between 1910 and 1960 (*ibid.*, 25). More and more states required that English be the language of instruction and that teachers prove their competence in English. In 1874, for example, Kansas reversed an earlier law permitting instruction in other languages.

By the turn of the twentieth century, the dominance of immigrants from eastern and southern Europe, their concentration in urban environments, and the transformation from an agrarian to an industrial society profoundly changed the circumstances, the focus, and the methods of education.[20] The schools were given the charge of preparing the children of these immigrants not only to be citizens but in the skills to be productive workers. First and foremost for both of

[19] A similar case in Michigan noted that the territorial laws of 1827 required every township with 200 or more students to employ a teacher "well instructed in the Latin, French and English languages" (*Stuart* v. *School District No. 1 of Kalamazoo* 1874, at 78). When the state constitutional convention convened in 1850, an attempt was made to insist on English-only instruction ("the English language and no other shall be taught in such schools" [free public schools], *Stuart* 1874, at 83). This provision was explicitly rejected.

[20] Tyack (1974) outlined the perception of a "Rural School Problem" and the quest for professionalization of public schools and even private schools (through accreditation practices).

those goals was the mastery of the English language. In urban schools and in consolidated rural schools, educational reform meant the establishment of a system, with grade levels, standardized testing,[21] a focus on order and obedience, and a hierarchy of administrative oversight.

Changes in both attendance policy and in the length of the school year reflect the gradual shift from an agrarian to an industrial society, as demonstrated by the geography of these measures. Compulsory attendance for ever-longer school years was attached to child labor laws, swelling the enrollments in the schools, particularly the public schools. One of the most dramatic changes in American education was the expansion of education in the late nineteenth and early twentieth centuries. Between 1890 and 1940, the percentage of children aged 5–17 attending school grew from 44 percent to 77 percent (Fass 1989, 38). Massachusetts passed the first compulsory education law in 1852, with the great impetus in most states occurring between 1890 and 1910, and the southern states the last to adopt such laws (Richardson 1984, 476). Compulsory education combined with state oversight of curriculum to pursue goals of Americanization, in its nativist sense of American – that is, a white, Anglo-Saxon Protestant.

This modernization was presented as neutral and progressive, an attempt to get politics out of the schools, but politics played an important role. In the last quarter of the nineteenth century, and even more so in the first quarter of the twentieth century, school reform meant the exclusion of languages other than English as the medium of instruction, and sometimes even as a subject of instruction. In the north, the Democratic Party sought to attract the ethnic vote by promising bilingual education in the public schools, while Republicans pursued a policy of English-only education. In Texas, after the Civil War, the divisions were more complicated. Local control pitted Democrats for antebellum liberties against Reconstruction Republicans seeking uniformity through English-only education and English-language certification for teachers. Those Reconstruction measures were overturned in the Democratic backlash at the end of Reconstruction (1876–1884), but gradually they were reintroduced through the pressures of the State Superintendent's office and of the Texas State Teachers Association.[22] Progressive politics and xenophobia joined forces to attack bilingual education.

---

[21] Already in the nineteenth century, teachers and administrators were adept at manipulating test results, teaching to the test and encouraging students who would do poorly to drop out of school (Tyack 1974, 48). And if immigrants outshone the natives, they were immediately suspect: when Poles at St. Adalbert School in Buffalo, during the height of anti-immigrant feelings during World War I, outperformed the public students in State Regents Exams, the Buffalo Chamber of Commerce demanded an investigation, sure that the Poles were cheating (Seller 1979, 51).

[22] The political battles over this change delayed the imposition of the district system until 1910. For full details on this process, see Blanton (2004), Chapter 3 "The Gradual Demise of the Bilingual Tradition, 1884–1905" (pp. 42–55).

Toward the end of the nineteenth century anti-foreign-language sentiment grew with the arrival of new immigrants and economic depression. One by one states began requiring that English be the medium of instruction. In 1903, fourteen states had such a requirement; by the end of World War I the number had grown to thirty-four. These laws had the effect of pushing immigrant children into parochial schools. Soon enough state school superintendents sought to enforce the same provisions in private schools. In Illinois, the Edwards law was proposed in 1889 by Richard Edwards, the State Superintendent of Public Instruction. Officially titled "An Act Concerning the Education of Children," the bill sought to enforce compulsory schooling from the ages of 7–14. The controversy arose over the right the law gave to public school authorities to determine the minimum standards that a private school had to meet to be considered a school. The law required that instruction of the primary subjects of elementary education be conducted in English, which was already the case in public schools. The threat to bilingual education, as well as to the autonomy of private schools, spelled doom for the politicians who supported the bill. Republican dominance was overthrown as the immigrant vote went overwhelmingly to the Democrats.

The Bennett law (1889, Wisconsin)[23] copied Illinois' Edwards law, applying to parochial schools the same strictures against instruction in languages other than English. The controversial part of the text read:

No school shall be regarded as a school under this act unless there shall be taught therein, as part of the elementary education of children, reading, writing arithmetic and United States history in the English language. (cited in Jensen 1971, 124)

At the time there were roughly 75,000 students in denominational schools, the majority of which received some or all of their education in German or Norwegian. The Bennett law was supported by one German group, the liberal Turnerbund composed primarily of Forty-Eighters, and by a majority of the Scandinavians, though their displeasure might be sensed in a low voter turnout.[24] However, the Catholic Bishops united with the Lutheran Synods to urge defeat of those who had supported the law. Germans and Scandinavians

---

[23] For a detailed analysis, see Ulrich (1980).

[24] Though the immigrants wanted to preserve their language and religion, these cultural components were hardly unified in the old country. Germany only became a single state in 1871, and German dialects differed widely reflecting the political fragmentation of the German-speaking peoples in Europe. The Kingdom of Italy re-established in 1861, though some areas only joined the Kingdom after World War I. Poland had no political existence through the nineteenth century, as it was partitioned between Russia, Prussia, and the Austro-Hungarian Empire. Regional settlement patterns also influenced the politics of bilingual education. In urban areas, linguistic homogeneity among speakers of a single language was rare, rendering bilingual education all the more problematic. In the rural settlements, homogeneity was more likely. In the rural German communities in Wisconsin, the majority of the population came from Prussia (Kuyper 1980, 84), but in urban centers like Milwaukee, differences in dialect along

constituted more than half of the eligible voters in 1890; foreign-born and second-generation children constituted 73.7 percent of the total population, according to the 1890 Census (cited in Wyman 1968, 269). The law was repealed in 1891, after it cost Republicans control of the state government.

One justification for targeting language in school reforms was supported by intelligence testing, a new science of psychology at the turn of the twentieth century. The "neutral" tests of intelligence developed in the early twentieth century were language based, resulting in "scientific" proof of the intellectual inferiority of the new immigrants. The advent of broad studies of intelligence seemed to give support to those who would limit immigration and contributed to the passage of immigration laws in 1920 and 1924 that essentially limited immigration to those coming from northwestern Europe.[25] Using language-based tests immigrant children and African-Americans scored significantly lower than white children whose families spoke only English. 69.9 percent of Polish-Americans and 63.4 percent of Italian Americans tested by the Army were classified as being of a "mental age of less than eleven years" (Sweeney 1922, 602). This fed the eugenicists' worries about "mixed blood" children lowering the national intelligence.

Social scientists were deeply divided over the scientific value of intelligence testing. Rudolf Pintner (1923) had compared verbal intelligence testing with non-verbal intelligence testing, rather timidly urging "caution in drawing conclusions as to the intelligence of foreign children when tested solely by means of tests which presuppose the understanding or reading of the English language" (1923, 295).[26] Margaret Mead's MA thesis at Columbia (1924) analyzed the results of intelligence testing among the children of Italian immigrants, her findings published in 1926 and 1927. She found that language played the most important role in determining how the Italian children would score: the intelligence test was really testing English proficiency. Similarly, Hisakichi Misaki's (1927) study of Japanese-American students concluded that "it is most probable that the innate mental capacity of Japanese children is

---

with religion, class, political viewpoints, and general attitudes toward education divided the German community.

[25] Psychology journals of the 1910s and 1920s are full of such studies: Garth (1923) on Mexican-Americans and Native Americans, Ferguson (1916) on African-Americans, Fukuda (1923) on Japanese-Americans, etc. H. H. Goddard interpreted the Binet tests in ways Binet himself never intended, fueling nativist prejudices. Carl Brigham (1923), a Princeton professor who would later develop the SAT college entrance examination, gave an elaborate account of the threat to the national intelligence of the mixture of "Nordic" with "Mediterranean" blood (e.g., 1923, figure 46, 198–199). For an overview of this type of scholarship, see Gould (1996), and for its application to Italian immigration, Messina (2010). Such arguments show surprising persistence, for example in *The Bell Curve* (Herrnstein & Murray 1994).

[26] The non-verbal test was Pintner's own. His findings were disputed by V. T. Graham (1925), who also used a combination of verbal and non-verbal tests and still rated Italian children as lower than "American" and Jewish students.

greater than the Binet IQ would indicate when the tests are given only in English" (cited in Strong & Bell 1933, 32). The practice of English-only intelligence tests was not legally put to rest until *Diana v. California State Board of Education* (1970), a case involving nine students from Monterey. Citing the Fourteenth Amendment, the Civil Rights Act of 1964, and the ESEA of 1965, a consent decree ordered that both entering students must be tested in their primary language and those already placed must be retested.

In the first decades of the twentieth century, progressive education fueled by the new psychology and old prejudice turned against additive Americanization in favor of subtractive Americanization, a move exacerbated by the extreme anti-German propaganda of World War I. During the first years of World War I, before the United States joined the war, America was bombarded by stories of German atrocities coming from England and France. Organizations like the Council of National Defense stoked anti-German feelings here. Once the United States entered the war, in 1917, the anti-German hysteria reached a fever pitch. In 1918, the governor of Iowa declared that English would be the sole medium of instruction in public and private schools and that English would be the sole means of communication in public places, on trains and on the telephone. This even extended to religious services. Governor William Harding claimed that "God is listening only to the English tongue."[27] People who could not understand English were to conduct their religious services only in private homes. He relented slightly, allowing a Lutheran pastor in Davenport, Iowa, to give a sermon in German, after the English service was over, and only if those attending the German had sat through the English. In Montana, a mob stormed the high school in Lewiston, seized German textbooks and burned them while they sang patriotic hymns. A young German immigrant was lynched in Collinsville, Illinois, in April 1918 (Ross 1994, 45–47). In 1918, a number of states banned the teaching of German, either outright or before students reached the age of 14. The California State Board of Education stated that German was "a language that disseminates the ideals of autocracy, brutality and hatred." Louisiana prohibited the teaching of German at any level, both private and public schools, even in the universities.

In January 1919, nineteen states restricted the teaching of foreign languages. By the end of the year thirty-seven of the forty-eight states had such restrictions, though the restrictions vary considerably from state to state.[28] Some

---

[27] Ironically, Harding was able to win his election by attracting the German vote, championing the sale of alcohol and attacking President Wilson's pro-British stance. Then, when the United States declared war on Germany, he became the most rabid anti-German.

[28] A useful chart outlining these differences is in Edwards (1923, 272). The survey was described by the Catholic hierarchy as "secret" and "bigoted," a "dastardly act of espionage on our private schools" (Nepper 1919, 269).

applied to all schools, others only to public schools. Some applied only to elementary grades, 1–6 or 1–8. Some specified that foreign languages could be taught as a subject for up to one hour per day. Some limited the subjects that could be taught in a foreign language. The absence of a federal mandate allowed such diversity.

It was in this context that two of the US Supreme Court's landmark cases were decided in the 1920s, *Meyer* v. *Nebraska* and *Farrington* v. *Tokushige*. As we have seen, Nebraska had a large number of schools operating in foreign languages, primarily but not exclusively in German, and many teachers with little or no knowledge of English. The German–American Alliance in Nebraska led the state to enact, in 1913, the Mockett law allowing public school instruction in a foreign language from the fifth grade on, if fifty-five parents demanded it. The tide turned as the war dragged on. The Mockett law was repealed in 1918, after the governor described it as "vicious, undemocratic and un-American" (cited in Ross 1994, 80).

The State Council of Defense, formed to coordinate civil defense and civilian support for the war, surveyed foreign-language schools, identifying 262 schools in which a foreign language was the primary language of instruction, usually taught by teachers with no certification.[29] In some counties, the public schools were unable to be sustained because of the immigrants' allegiance to their parochial schools (*Report of the Nebraska Council of Defense*, January 14, 1917, cited in Thompson 1920, 147). The Council subsequently passed a resolution (December 18, 1917) recommending that "no foreign language shall be taught in any of the private or denominational schools in Nebraska, and that all instruction, whether secular or religious, shall be given in the English language" (*ibid.*, 148).

These recommendations were put into effect through the Burney law (subjecting all schools, including private and parochial, to state supervision) and the Siman law ("An Act Relating to the Teaching of Foreign Languages in the state of Nebraska"), prohibiting instruction in a foreign language in grades 1–8, both enacted in 1919.[30] The Burney law was a compromise after another bill that

---

[29] The survey was led by Šárka Hrbková, herself a Czech immigrant, who was chair of the Slavonic Languages Department at the University of Nebraska. Her work as chair of the Women's Committee for the Council gave her a role in the University's loyalty trials and may have contributed to her non-reappointment and the dissolution of the Czech language program at the university after the war. See http://unlhistory.unl.edu/exhibits/show/czechprogram1903-1919/DepartmentChairmen/Šárka-b–hrbkova. She was a strong advocate for what immigrants contribute to America, often drawing sharp comparisons with less upright Anglo-Americans (Hrbková 1919).

[30] Section 1 of this law states that "No person, individually or as a teacher, shall, in any private, denominational, or parochial or public school, teach any subject to any person in any language other than the English language" (cited in *Nebraska District* v. *McKelvie* 1919, at 95). It further stipulated (Section 2) that languages other than English could be taught as subjects of study to students who had passed the eighth grade.

would have closed all private and parochial schools was narrowly defeated (Ross 1994, 93–94). The congregations that sponsored these schools challenged the laws immediately, though many had complied with the thrust of the Siman bill, limiting foreign-language instruction to recess or after-school programs. The strategy was based on defense of their property rights, the right to pursue one's professional vocation, and religious liberty.

The initial claim was brought by the Nebraska District of the Evangelical Lutheran Synod of Missouri against Nebraska Governor Samuel McKelvie (*Nebraska District* v. *McKelvie* 1919). The Supreme Court of Nebraska found no conflict between the Siman act and religious freedom (at 98), and interpreted the law to mean that teachers and parents had complete freedom to teach whatever they wanted provided that the foreign-language instruction did not interfere with the regular school hours.

The intent evidently is that none of the time necessarily employed in teaching the elementary branches forming the public school curriculum shall be consumed in teaching the child a foreign language, since whatever time is devoted to such teaching in school hours, must necessarily be taken away from the time which the state requires to be devoted to education carried on in the English language. Furthermore, there is nothing in the act to prevent parents, teachers or pastors from conveying religious or moral instruction in the language of the parents, or in any other language, or in teaching any other branch of learning or accomplishment, provided that such instruction is given at such time that it will not interfere with the required studies. (Nebraska District 1919, at 100)

This interpretation directly contradicts the explicit language of the statute. In terms of pedagogy, the court rejected the claim that children who arrived at school knowing no English needed to receive their first instruction in their native language (at 101).[31] Instruction in the native language was, according to the court, not only unnecessary but an "evil" that needed to be corrected (at 97).

The Zion Lutheran Church in Hampton, Nebraska, decided to adapt to the law by offering its German instruction during an extended lunch recess period. The school day remained 9–4, but instead of a one-hour lunch period, students had one and a half hours, with the last half hour devoted to German-language instruction. As such, the half-hour of German was taking away from English instruction. It was in this context that on May 25, 1920, schoolmaster Robert Meyer was arrested for teaching a biblical lesson in German to 10-year-old Raymond Parpart during the extended recess.

While the case was under appeal, Nebraska passed a more severe school language law, the Norval Act (1921), which denied any opportunity to teach

---

[31] "We are not bound to draw the conclusion that because children, when they first attend school, cannot understand or speak English, they must be taught the language of their parents, whether Polish or Bohemian, in order that they may learn English" (*Nebraska District* 1919, at 101).

any foreign language in a school before the ninth grade. No longer could the interpretation of "regular school hours" permit foreign-language instruction to sneak into the recess or after-school periods of the elementary schools (*Meyer* v. *Nebraska* 1922, at 665–666). The Nebraska synod as well as other church groups[32] immediately challenged this law, winning at the District Court in Platte County but losing at the Nebraska Supreme Court (*Nebraska District* v. *McKelvie* 1922). Citing its own decision two months earlier in *Meyer*, again the court argued that the state had a compelling interest in regulating foreign-language education. Justice Morrissey dissented, arguing that the language education legislation "violate the provisions of both the state and federal Constitutions" (*Nebraska District* 1922, at 455).

Meyer then pursued his case to the federal courts, where it was bundled with similar cases from Iowa and Ohio. August Bartels in Iowa, where the law was virtually identical to Nebraska's, was accused of teaching a secular subject, reading, in German so that students could participate in religious training in that language. All of the instruction he offered in this school was in English, save this one subject. The Iowa Supreme Court narrowly ruled against Bartels (4–3), with the dissenters claiming that teaching the reading of religious texts is religious not secular instruction and therefore protected (*State* v. *Bartels* 1921).

The Ohio Supreme Court ruled unanimously that Emil Pohl had broken a law that was reasonable for ensuring the common welfare of the state. The common welfare was expressed by Governor James Cox in his message of support to the legislature: "If any person in Ohio wants his child indoctrinated in the Prussian creed, let our safeguards be such that he must go elsewhere for it" (cited in *The Guardian* October 21, 1922, p. 8). Pohl argued that the right to teach and to learn a foreign language was a privilege protected by the privileges and immunities clause in the federal constitution, and that the legislation was arbitrary because it banned only German instruction prior to the eighth grade. The Ohio Supreme Court deferred to the legislature, assuming that the enactors of the statute must have had good reason to pass such a bill: "if the legislature found such facts to exist as to warrant it in the enactment of the sections in question it is not within the province of a court to redetermine the existence or nonexistence of such facts" (*Pohl* 1921, at 477).

The three cases attracted nationwide attention, even before the appeal to the US Supreme Court.[33] Justice McReynolds wrote the opinion for the court based on the Fourteenth Amendment's provision that no state can deprive an

---

[32] Representing the Catholic parochial schools was John Siedlik of Omaha, who argued for Polish instruction at St. Francis School. His attorney argued that any school whose students can enter without a problem the local high schools (with curriculum entirely in English) after eight years of instruction in Polish and English has proven itself a success.

[33] *New York Times*, October 11, 1922; *The Guardian* (official newspaper of the Diocese of Little Rock, Arkansas); *America* (Jesuit publication), January 10, 1920, p. 262.

individual of liberty without due process. Meyer's right to teach and parents' right to hire him, McReynolds concluded, "are within the liberty of the Amendment" (*Meyer* 1923, at 400). Coercion to impose a single language, however desirable a single language might be, constitutes excessive police power: "a desirable end cannot be promoted by prohibited means" (*Meyer* 1923, at 401). The court approved the right of the state to insist on the teaching of English but denied the right of the state to bar the teaching of other languages alongside English, at least in private and parochial schools. The control of the curriculum in state-funded schools was not questioned. The plaintiff in all three cases was the teacher, whose right to teach could not be denied, as language learning per se could not be considered harmful to the individual or to society: "proficiency in a foreign language seldom comes to one not instructed at an early age, and experience shows that this is not injurious to the health, morals or understanding of the ordinary child" (at 403). This finding of fact is the crux of the Meyer bundle as well as of the cases concerning Japanese schools in Hawaii.

The Japanese-language school case in Hawaii stressed the parents' freedom to determine the education of their children. The Japanese population of Hawaii increased from 153 in 1869 to 61,111 in 1900 (Matsubayashi 1984, 44); another 71,281 arrived between 1900 and the institution of the "Gentlemen's Agreement" (1907).[34] The first Japanese-language school in Hawaii was founded on Maui in 1892, and in California in 1903. Most were associated with Christian or Buddhist missionary groups. By 1908, there were 88 Japanese schools in Hawaii (*ibid.*, 53), and 163 in 1920.[35] Japanese schools operated in the Hawaiian Islands primarily as supplemental education after the public school day had ended. Initially, Japanese parents nurtured the idea of returning to Japan, and wanted their children to be able to be reinserted into the Japanese educational system;[36] in this goal the schools were aided by the Japanese Ministry of Education, which provided textbooks. After the Gentlemen's Agreement, the focus shifted to English education with a Japanese language and culture component.

[34] The Gentlemen's Agreement, never ratified by Congress, ended Japanese immigration by barring Japan from issuing passports to those who wanted to emigrate to the United States. In return, President Theodore Roosevelt used his bully pulpit to shame the San Francisco School Board into abandoning a move to isolate Asian-Americans, including the Japanese, in an Asian School. Given the increased military power of Japan, after the Japanese victory in the Russo-Japanese War, Roosevelt was inclined to seek a middle ground. Cullinane (2014) outlines Roosevelt's compromise, which promised to bring a halt to the immigration of the "coolie class" of Japanese, both directly from Japan and indirectly from Hawaii.

[35] In addition to the Japanese schools, there were ten Korean schools and twelve Chinese schools at the time of the federal survey (Bureau of Education 1920, 112).

[36] Japan had a strong public school system already, and Japanese immigrants to the United States had a higher level of schooling than most Americans at the turn of the twentieth century (Wollenberg 1978, 52, citing Kitano).

The fate of the Japanese schools in Hawaii was intimately tied to the desire for statehood, already being discussed in 1920, and to resentment of Japanese sugar-cane workers who went on strike that year. White mainland politicians worried that the majority of voters of Hawaii would be of Japanese descent, as projected by federal survey (Bureau of Education 1920, 19–20). The Americanizers feared that Japanese emphasis on filial piety would reinforce their allegiance to the Emperor, much as Nativists feared that American Catholics would have first allegiance to the Pope.

The Americanization of Japanese, Chinese, and Korean children thus became a focus for civic organizations like the Chamber of Commerce, the American Legion, the Daughters of the American Revolution, and the Ad Club, a Hawaiian businessmen's organization founded in 1912. In preparation for statehood, Governor Lucius Pinkham requested an evaluation of the schools in Hawaii.[37] The federal Bureau of Education sent a team to the islands in 1919, resulting in the 1920 *Survey of Education in Hawaii*. The commission recommended closing all language schools, acknowledging that there was a fine line between constitutionally closing the schools and unconstitutionally attacking the religions that supported them.

Although the commission recognizes the inherent right of every person in the United States to adopt any form of religious worship which he desires, nevertheless it holds that the principle of religious freedom to which our country is unswervingly committed does not demand that practices and activities must be tolerated in the name of religion which make the task of training for the duties and responsibilities of American citizenship a well-nigh hopeless one. (Bureau of Education 1920, 134)

Closing the schools was not an attack on the languages: the second recommendation of the commission was

to organize in every school, where there is sufficient demand, a class or classes, in any foreign language desired, the same to be held for one hour per day at the close of the regular public school session, in the public school building, by teachers regularly employed for the purpose by the Territorial department of education. Work of this character to begin with the first grade if it be desired. (Bureau of Education 1920, 140)

With the commission's report in hand, legislators passed a teacher certification requirement that would bar monolingual Japanese teachers (cited in Matsubayashi 1984, 140–143) and place all schools under state control, including school hours and textbook selection. The Department of Public Instruction subsequently restricted attendance at foreign-language schools to students who had already finished first grade.

---

[37] For details about the origins of the request and its implementation, see Asato (2003).

The Japanese-language schools met with the Japanese consul and devised a plan to launch a test case that they could take to the courts. By August of 1923 more than eighty Japanese-language schools had joined forces to lead the court challenge. In 1925, Justice De Bolt granted an injunction preventing enforcement of the contested school laws. In 1926, the Ninth Circuit ruled in favor of the schools (*Farrington* 1926). The state appealed to the US Supreme Court, protesting that "it would be a sad commentary on our system of government to hold that the Territory must stand by, impotent, and watch its foreign-born guests conduct a vast system of schools of American pupils, teaching them loyalty to a foreign country and disloyalty to their own country, and hampering them during their tender years in the learning of the home language in the public schools" (*Farrington* 1927). The parents responded that the Hawaii statute "takes from the parent of a child attending a foreign language school all control and direction of the education of his child." The court again ruled in favor of the schools: "The Japanese parent has the right to direct the education of his own child without unreasonable restrictions; the Constitution protects him as well as those who speak another tongue" (at 298).

While the territorial government was rebuffed in its attempt to control the curriculum in the Japanese schools, it successfully pursued its program of delaying entry, so that only students who had passed the fourth grade could attend Japanese schools. Even then they had to have attained a score "not lower than normal for his grade" in English reading and composition.[38] Below-average students in English had to wait until eighth grade or the age of 15 to attend a foreign-language school. These restrictions were then challenged by Chinese schools in *Mo Hock Ke Lok Po v. Stainback* (1947), and rejected by the District Court.

The state and territorial governments in the German and the Japanese cases claimed that allowing children to learn a foreign language was injurious both to the child and to the society. The harm to society was disloyalty. After the conclusion of World War I the focus of disloyalty was shifting from Germans to Bolshevism,[39] but fear of a foreign threat made any language other than English suspect. This finding justified state intervention to control what was taught and to whom, to prevent the poisoning of the mind just as it prevented poisoning of food.[40] However, countered Arthur Mullen, Meyer's lawyer, excessive state control of the content of education was precisely one of the threats of Bolshevism (Ross 1994, 123). The liberty of the instructor to teach

---

[38] Atkinson (1947) supported the challenges against these laws.

[39] Pohl attempted to distinguish German instruction from instruction of Eastern European languages, as the German threat was supposedly over and Bolshevism came from Russia (Ross 1994, 116).

[40] Thus argued the state of Iowa in defending the *Bartels* case (Ross 1994, 121).

a language, of the child to learn it, and of the parents to choose this option is based on the rejection of the factual claim of harm.[41] Without harm there is no reason to take the chance that religious freedom or freedom of speech is threatened.

The widespread statutes concerning foreign-language education had a long and pernicious effect. By banning such instruction before the ninth grade, legislators assured that few students would ever become proficient in the language they were studying, as the "critical period" for language acquisition ends around age 12.[42] The problem became almost immediately apparent in the 1920s, leading some states to reverse course. In 1933, Texas revised its school code to permit the teaching of modern languages starting in the second grade, noting that "the present law greatly hinders the teaching of foreign language by restricting it to high school grades" (cited in Blanton 2004, 78). Nonetheless, the vast majority of school districts in the United States offer foreign-language education only in high schools, and even then often for two years only. In Cincinnati, for example, no foreign languages were taught in the elementary schools from 1919 to 1959 (Toth 1990, 90–91). Monolingualism in America is a self-inflicted wound.

A different type of harm was being inflicted by various schemes to segregate "white"[43] students from others. The segregation of African-American students was legally enforced in the southern states that had seceded from the union, and in many border states, while schools elsewhere were often segregated in fact if not by law. In the south all non-white groups were classified as "colored" and therefore placed in separate and decidedly unequal schools. This restriction

---

[41] Justice Oliver Wendell Holmes, in his dissent (*Bartels* v. *Iowa* 1923, at 412), deferred to the legislature in its finding of fact, as in the *Lochner* case (1905) concerning the regulation of bakeries. See Chapter 1, footnote 57. In case of uncertainty, he would not contravene the statute:

Youth is the time when familiarity with a language is established and if there are sections in the State where a child would hear only Polish or French or German spoken at home I am not prepared to say that it is unreasonable to provide that in his early years he shall hear and speak only English at school. But if it is reasonable it is not an undue restriction of the liberty either of teacher or scholar. No one would doubt that a teacher might be forbidden to teach many things, and the only criterion of his liberty under the Constitution that I can think of is "whether, considering the end in view, the statute passes the bounds of reason and assumes the character of a merely arbitrary fiat." I think I appreciate the objection to the law but it appears to me to present a question upon which men reasonably might differ and therefore I am unable to say that the Constitution of the United States prevents the experiment being tried.

[42] The Critical Period Hypothesis was first posited for first-language acquisition (Penfield & Roberts 1959) and then for second-language acquisition (Lenneberg 1967). In second-language acquisition, it generally refers to the inability to gain full bilingualism, especially a completely native accent, after the onset of puberty, and ascribes this result to biological factors. It is not a 100 percent predictor, and the theory has been challenged by those who believe that the difficulties encountered by older learners can be attributed to social and educational factors (e.g., Birdsong (1999) and Hakuta et al. (2003)).

[43] We must always keep in mind the various definitions of "white" in the peculiar American fascination with race.

could include Chinese students, such as Martha Lum a 9-year-old Chinese-American placed in a "colored school" in Mississippi (*Gong Lum* v. *Rice* 1927).

California law first prohibited "Negroes, Mongolians, and Indians" from attending the regular public school though it did permit but not require schools for the banned children (1863, reported in Wollenberg 1978, 13). A year later anti-Confederate forces in the legislature required opening schools for children of color, but also permitted these pupils to attend the regular public schools with the permission of the white parents. By 1880 all de jure segregation for African-Americans was forbidden, though residential restrictions often created African-American schools, but separate schools for Asians and Native Americans were allowed.

San Francisco opened its first Chinese public school in 1859, but the obligation to educate Chinese students was not recognized, even though the Burlingame Treaty with China (1868) required school districts to admit them.[44] Private Chinese-language schools flourished in San Francisco, but Chinese students were generally barred from public school education (Dolson 1964, 120–121). Although one of the board members recognized that education was desirable for those who were US citizens and likely to become voters (Wollenberg 1978, 40), it took a decision by the California Supreme Court in 1885 to open the doors of the public schools to Chinese-American students.[45]

In 1885, a separate Chinese school was hastily established to prevent 8-year-old Mamie Tape from enrolling in the local white school, even though by newspaper accounts she spoke English well. The segregation of Chinese students was challenged in 1902 (*Wong Him* v. *Callahan* 1902), but the District Court found no violation of state or federal law as long as there is "no discrimination in the educational facilities" and the "course of study is the same in one school as in the other" (at 382). By the 1920s Chinese students were segregated only by residential patterns (Wollenberg 1978, 44).

The segregation of Japanese students followed fear of Japanese power engendered by the Japanese victory in the Russo-Japanese War (1905). In October 1906, Japanese and Korean students were ordered to join the Chinese students at the Oriental Public School. Almost all the Japanese students boycotted the school, encouraged by the Japanese consul, leading to the intervention of President Theodore Roosevelt. Among the boycotters was 10-year-old Keikichi Aoki, who had attended an integrated school the year before (Washington), but was forced to move after the earthquake, where he

---

[44] "Chinese subjects shall enjoy all the privileges of the public educational institutions under the control of the government of the United States" (Article VII).

[45] *Tape* v. *Hurley* (1885). Until 1880 California state law required admission for "all white children between five and twenty-one years of age, residing in the district" (cited in *Tape* v. *Hurley,* at 474). The 1880 revision struck the word "white," thus permitting admission to all children, regardless of race.

attended Reading Primary School until the October order requiring Japanese students to attend the Oriental school. He challenged the order in *Aoki v. Deane* (Mary Deane was the principal of the Reading School). The case was dropped after the San Francisco school board withdrew its segregation resolution, in exchange for the limitations on Japanese immigration of the Gentlemen's Agreement.

While the Japanese were integrated into the public schools of California, they also established more than 200 Japanese schools, conducted after regular school hours or on the weekends (Wollenberg 1978, 69). Unlike the Hawaiian case discussed above, the California Japanese schools were not connected to the Japanese consulate and did not attempt to emulate Japanese instruction in Japan. While they taught Japanese language and culture, they focused on Americanization of second-generation Japanese-American children, the *Nisei*. In spite of this focus, they were targeted by Valentine S. McClatchy, the publisher of the Sacramento and Fresno *Bee*, the most widely read newspapers of central California, in his pamphlet *California's Japanese Language Schools. Dangerous and Un-American* (December 13, 1922).[46] His efforts led to legislative attempts to follow Hawaii's model, first regulating the certification of teachers for these schools and then seeking to close the schools (vetoed by the governor). The Nisei turned out to be model students regularly outperforming their white counterparts and even earning the grudging respect of Mr. McClatchy, who lamented in 1929 that whites and Japanese did not intermarry, because he valued the "national homogeneity" that would result.[47]

Mexican-Americans and Asian-Americans were supposedly segregated for their own good because of their lack of English, but the absence of segregation of other students with no knowledge of English and the material inferiority of the schools[48] made it clear that race and ethnicity were the deciding factors, not linguistic ability. One of the early triggers for protest in Crystal City, TX (see following), was the treatment of Arnold López's children when they arrived from Houston in 1960: his son was refused entry to the "Anglo" school first

---

[46] The full text is available in the digital collection of the California State University Dominguez Hills, http://cdm16855.contentdm.oclc.org/cdm/compoundobject/collection/p16855coll4/id/1 38/rec/7.

[47] The full text of *The Japanese Problem in California. Racial Relations and the Second Generation. The Aftermath of Japanese Immigration*, originally published in the *Japanese-American News* on January 1, 1929, is available at https://archive.org/stream/japaneseproble mi00mccl/japaneseproblemi00mccl_djvu.txt.

[48] *Wong Him* (1902) established the "separate but equal" principle in California, but the equality requirement was not enforced. University of Southern California researchers hired by the Santa Ana School District in 1928 found appalling conditions at the Mexican-American schools, but their report did not change the district's practices (Strum 2010, 16). Similarly, in Texas, Carlos Calderón's MA thesis (University of Texas, Austin, 1950) catalogued the differences between Mexican-American and Anglo schools in the Rio Grande valley (for details and photographs, see Valencia 2008, 42–49).

grade, even though his score on an entrance test – not required of Anglo children – clearly demonstrated his proficiency.

For Mexican-Americans the denial of any schooling gradually gave way to segregated schooling around the turn of the twentieth century. Nueces County, Texas, offered no schooling to Mexican-Americans until 1891, twenty years after the founding of public schools in the county (Taylor 1934, 192). Corpus Christi, Texas, established a segregated Mexican-American school in 1892. Other Texas districts followed quickly; by the 1942–1943 school year, 122 districts in fifty-nine counties had separate schools for Mexican-Americans (Rangel & Alcala 1972, 315).

Many school districts in the southwest followed suit, creating segregated schools for Mexican-origin children. Santa Ana and Pasadena (CA) created "Mexican Schools" in 1913.[49] By the mid-1920s there were fifteen schools for Mexican-Americans in Orange County, California, which offered a different curriculum from that offered to the Anglo population, a curriculum preparing the Mexican-American children for menial labor[50] (Strum 2010, 15). Here too no language test was given to determine English proficiency before assigning children to the segregated schools. In 1919, parents in the Santa Ana, California, school district protested that those children who spoke English should be sent to the "white" school. The school district admitted that they could not discriminate on the basis of race, but could do so based on the aptitude of the Mexican-American children "to advance in the grades to which they shall be assigned," a reference to the eugenics arguments we discussed earlier (p. 94). This theme, that Mexican-Americans were more prone to repeating grade levels, was advanced by Merton Earle Hill,[51] who studied the San Bernardino, California, schools and concluded Mexican-American children did not have "as much native ability as normal American children" (cited in Strum 2010, 17).

An Arizona rancher, Adolpho Romo, mounted the first legal challenge to the equality of "separate but equal" schools for Mexican-American students (*Romo*

---

[49] Smaller school districts were often integrated because they could not afford the maintenance of separate schools, however dilapidated the minority students' schools might have been. Similarly, high schools were typically integrated, but by then most Mexican-American children had dropped out, having passed the age of compulsory attendance because they were forced to repeat early grades.

[50] The difference in the curriculum also violated the decision in *Wong Him* (1902): "When the schools are conducted under the same general rules, and the course of study is the same in one school as in the other, it cannot be said that pupils in either are deprived of the equal protection of the law in the matter of receiving an education" (at 382).

[51] Hill (1882–1970) wrote his doctoral dissertation on the development of an Americanization program (1928, University of California, Berkeley), a degree he pursued while working full time in a number of schools. He remained a professor at Berkeley and UCLA until his retirement.

v. *Laird* 1925).[52] His four children, Antonio (15 years old), Henry (14), Alice (11) and Charles (7), were assigned to the Eighth Street School in Tempe, along with all other Mexican-American students. Instruction was given by student teachers rather than certified teachers. The judge ordered that the children be admitted to the Tenth Street School and that the school district use certified teachers in the Eighth Street School. While the Romo children henceforth went to the "Anglo" school, the school system remained segregated into the 1950s.

In Texas, Jesus Salvatierra and other Mexican-Americans through the League of United Latin American Citizens (LULAC) challenged the segregated school system in a suit filed against the Del Rio, Texas, school system (*Del Rio Independent School District* v. *Salvatierra* 1930).[53] The Mexican-American community across Texas had fund-raising events to support the legal battle.[54] Del Rio had three elementary schools, one of which was used exclusively for Mexican-American children, through the third grade. Mexican-American children above the third grade attended the same schools as other white children. But by the third grade most of the damage had been done: a high percentage of Mexican-American children repeated first and second grades, sometimes by explicit school policy: in Laredo, in the 1920s, 81 percent of the Mexican-American children were "overage," that is, had been held back because they had not made sufficient progress in English[55] (Blanton 2004, 87). Even into the 1950s, standard school practice in southern Texas districts was to require Mexican-American students to spend four years in grades one and two, regardless of their abilities.[56]

The superintendent of the Del Rio, Texas, schools insisted that he had only the well-being of the students in mind in segregating the Mexican-American pupils. They were primarily the children of migrant laborers who came to school only after the harvest was done, and usually spoke no English. These children, he claimed, would suffer from low morale and self-esteem if thrown in with the Anglo children. Segregation benefited all students by meeting each

[52] The text of Judge Joseph Jenckes's decision is included in Muñoz (2001, 31–32).

[53] A 1928 case in Texas never reached the courts as the school superintendent admitted Amada Vela to the Charlotte (TX) "white" school. See San Miguel (1987, 76–78) for further details.

[54] The Texas State Historical Society website devotes a page to the organization of the Mexican-American community in support of Salvatierra and the other families in the class-action suit: https://tshaonline.org/handbook/online/articles/jrd02. According to this site, in the 1920s, 122 districts in fifty-nine counties of Texas operated segregated schools for Hispanic children.

[55] Blanton (2004, 74–91) describes in detail the English-only curriculum that led to this failure rate.

[56] "The Driscoll school authorities have drawn the line, not only for beginners but through the first and second grades, not on a basis of individual aptitudes or attainments but against all children of Latin-American extraction *as a class*" (*Hernandez* v. *Driscoll Consolidated Independent School District* 1957, at 8; italics in the original). The court went on to conclude: "This is not a line drawn in good faith, based upon individual ability to speak and understand the English language. It is the very opposite. It is unreasonable race discrimination against all Mexican children as a group throughout the first two grades" (at 14).

group's "peculiar needs." However, children of non-Mexican migrant workers were not separated from other children. In the name of local control of the schools, the appeals court ruled against the segregation of the school district, but not against the board's discretion in the use of funding that instigated the suit: "in none of them [school districts] should this liberty of discretion or administration be exercised in derogation of the letter or spirit of the constitutional or statutory rights, privileges, or immunities of the citizen or his children, of whatever race; or, in short, to effectuate an arbitrary segregation of the races, or unjust discrimination against any race or the individual members thereof" (*Del Rio* 1930, at 794).

LULAC continued to contest segregation, winning admission of Mexican-American students to Goliad (TX) High School in 1934, and to the Beeville (TX) schools in 1939 (Garcia 1991, 55). In California, the Comité de Vecinos de Lemon Grove, supported by the Mexican Consul, brought together parents who boycotted the schools to protest the erection of a second-class segregated school (1931). The children, led by 12-year-old Roberto Alvarez,[57] took the stand to prove that they could speak English and were being unfairly treated. Segregated schooling for Mexican-Americans was not explicitly rejected until the landmark case of *Mendez* v. *Westminster*.[58]

The *Mendez* case developed in the atmosphere of the "Zoot Suit Riots"[59] and the frustration of Mexican-Americans who sent their children to fight overseas in World War II but could not get equal treatment at home. Westminster had two schools, the Main School for the Anglo students and Hoover for the Mexican-Americans. Gonzalo and Felicitas Mendez, Lorenzo Ramirez, William Guzman, Frank Palomino and Thomas Estrada combined to challenge segregation in Westminster, Garden Grove, Santa Ana, and El Modena school districts. Ramirez had just moved from the fully integrated Whittier school district to El Modena and was shocked when School Superintendent Harold Hammersten would not let his children attend the Roosevelt School (for Anglo children) and required them to go to the Lincoln School (for Mexican-Americans). As a child Gonzalo Mendez had moved from the Hoover (Mexican) school of Westminster to the Main School after demonstrating his proficiency in

---

[57] Alvarez would go on to serve in the Navy during World War II and start a successful fruit importing business. He died in 2003 (*Los Angeles Times* obituary, http://articles.latimes.com /2003/feb/26/local/me-alvarez).

[58] The petitions, briefs, conclusions, and trial transcripts as well as the decisions are available through the online services of the National Archives:
    https://research.archives.gov/search?q=*:*&rows=20&offset=0&tabType=all&facet=true& facet.fields=oldScope,level,materialsType,fileFormat,locationIds,dateRangeFacet&highlight=t rue&f.parentNaId=294939&f.level=item&sort=naIdSort%20asc. For a thorough description of the evolution of the Méndez case, see Strum (2010). Much of the detail presented here is drawn from that book.

[59] The Zoot Suit Riots is how journalists described ten days of wanton violence against Mexican-Americans by whites, many of them members of the armed services, in June of 1943.

English. By the time his children entered the schools he was a relatively prosperous tenant farmer and café owner. He and Felicitas, a native of Puerto Rico, spoke more English than Spanish in their home, and their children were fluent English speakers. Nonetheless, they were relegated to the Hoover School, despite repeated trips by Gonzalo Mendez to the superintendent and to the school board during the 1944–1945 school year. His lawyer, David Marcus,[60] filed suit on March 2, 1945, in the Federal District Court for the Southern District of California.

Segregation of Mexican-Americans was based on national origin rather than race, a category of discrimination that at the time did not have legal sanction in California, or more broadly in the United States, though racial segregation of Asian and African-Americans did. Interestingly, Asian and African-American students were admitted to the "white" schools in Orange County, but not Mexican-Americans (testimony of Manuela Ochoa, cited in Strum 2010, 80–81). Could a state-funded institution use language as a pretext to justify segregation, without testing for language ability? Even if the segregation were authorized, we have seen that separate was never equal.

The attorney for the school districts argued that in some cases the segregation was residential rather than educational, local schools serving homogenous populations, and in other cases that the segregation was based on language ability, not ethnicity. However, none of the schools tested for language ability, and one of the school superintendents, James Kent of Garden Grove, had written his master's thesis at the University of Oregon on segregation of Mexican-Americans in Southern California, arguing that Mexicans were "an alien race that should be segregated socially" (cited in Strum 2010, 82). Expert witnesses called by the Mexican-Americans claimed just the opposite: only by combining English-speaking and Spanish-speaking students could the Mexican-Americans attain the level of English to succeed. Ultimately, Judge McCormick sided with those experts: "The evidence clearly shows ... that commingling of the entire student body instills and develops a common cultural attitude among school children which is imperative for the perpetuation of

---

[60] Marcus, the son of Jewish immigrants, had a Mexican-American wife and pursued a number of cases involving Mexican-Americans, including overturning the widespread practice of segregated use of swimming facilities in Southern California (*Lopez* v. *Seccombe* 1944). In that case Judge Yankwich cited the Fifth and Fourteenth Amendments to conclude that

petitioners are entitled to such equal accommodations, advantages, and privileges and to equal rights and treatment with other persons as citizens of the United States, in the use and enjoyment of the facilities of said park and playground and to equal treatment with other persons and to equal protection of the laws in their use and enjoyment of said privileges as provided, and afforded, to other persons at all times when the same is open and used by them. (at 772)

In 1939, swimming facilities for Mexican-Americans were also discussed in Tempe (AZ), but only to consider building a separate pool for the Latino population. Integration was not contemplated (Powers & Patton 2008, 136).

American institutions and ideals."[61] The educational goal of English-language mastery and the social benefits of that education could only be achieved through integration. The segregation of students "of Latin and Mexican descent in separate schools" was ruled "arbitrary and discriminatory and in violation of plaintiffs' constitutional rights" (Judge McCormick's "Judgment and Injunction," filed March 21, 1946).

The schools appealed together but reacted differently to the injunction. Westminster integrated its elementary schools and the Mendez children were able to attend school with students of all races and nationalities together. El Modena agreed to test the English-language skills of incoming students but persisted in segregating children at higher levels, until a court found the school system in contempt. Santa Ana school officials indicated a willingness to let a few students transfer from the Mexican-American school, if the students proved to be "socially acceptable." A year later the Ninth Circuit upheld the District Court's ruling, though Judge Stephens was far more restrained than Judge McCormick. He found only that the practice of segregating Mexican-Americans was contrary to California law, refusing to judge the case on the basis of the educational goals.[62] Soon thereafter the California legislature passed an antisegregation law, signed on June 14, 1947, by Governor Earl Warren, who, as Chief Justice of the US Supreme Court, would hear *Brown v. Board of Education* seven years later. The school districts did not appeal the Circuit Court ruling and started implementing, very reluctantly, some form of integration of Mexican-American students. In 1948, a survey of schools in southern and central California found that 78 percent of them had segregated schools in the past, but only 18 percent continued the practice (Strum 2010, 149).

The *Mendez* case was decided in a District Court, on the basis of California law. Therefore, it did not set a nationwide precedent against segregation of Mexican-Americans. But it did inspire similar suits in Texas (*Delgado v. Bastrop* 1948) and in Arizona (*Gonzales v. Sheely* 1951). The *Delgado* ruling followed the *Mendez* decision closely, permitting separate classes only in the first grade and only upon English-language testing of all students.[63] *Delgado* made it clear that not only de jure segregation but also that segregation based on "customs, usages and practices" was illegal. The Texas Superintendent of Public Instruction L. A. Woods ordered all schools to stop "segregation of

---

[61] P. 11 of Judge McCormick's "Conclusions of the Court," filed February 18, 1946, available in the National Archives website (see above footnote 58).

[62] Justice Denman's concurring opinion went much further, citing the San Bernardino swimming pool case and condemning segregation as a "vicious principle" that would infect the "adolescent minds of American children" (*Mendez v. Westminster* 1947, at 783).

[63] Superintendent Woods authorized the use of a test devised by Dr. Herschel Manuel of the University of Texas Austin, allowing a year's experimentation to determine the proper level for English proficiency in the first-grade classes (Blanton 2004, 115).

Mexican or other Latin American descent in the public schools," but the following year the legislature created a new post, the Commissioner of Education, and the governor appointed J. W. Edgar, who was much less sympathetic to the desegregation cause. Where Superintendent Woods had decertified the Del Rio schools for non-compliance, Commissioner Edgar recertified them. He remained in office for twenty-four years, during which time desegregation complaints were frequently buried in bureaucracy.[64] Only with the *Driscoll* case in 1957 (see above, Footnote 56) did the separate but equal argument begin to die. Mexican-American student boycotts in the late 1960s had mixed results: in Crystal City (1969–1970) they led to a number of policy changes and to the election of Mexican-American members of the school board, while in Kingsville (1969) there were no concessions and 110 marchers were arrested (Rangel & Alcala 1972, 369).[65]

In Arizona segregation was challenged in 1951 by Porfirio Gonzáles and Faustino Curiel (*Gonzales* v. *Sheely* 1951).[66] The Tolleson school district had two elementary schools. All but ten of the 370 Mexican-American children in grades 1–7 were forced to attend Unit 2. Assessment of language ability was performed by first-grade teachers, and students assigned to Unit 2 at that point (95 percent in the year described in the suit) remained in Unit 2 through the seventh grade, regardless of language ability. When appeals to the school board were rebuffed, the parents took legal action. Their case was buttressed by the Supreme Court's decisions in *McLaurin* v. *Oklahoma State Regents for Higher Education* (1950) and *Sweatt* v. *Painter* (1950).[67] These decisions reprised the terminology of *Mendez*, arguing that state restrictions on "commingling" of students were unconstitutional. The educational goals of integration are all the

---

[64] In 1953, Commissioner Edgar rejected the contention of parents in the Pecos Independent School District that the site of a new junior high school would perpetuate segregation, finding no "intent to segregate." Fifteen years later, the East Pecos Junior High remained 100 percent Mexican-American (Valencia 2008, 55). When *Brown* v. *Board of Education* was decided in May of 1954, Edgar sent a letter to all the districts in the state telling them to do nothing different in the 1954–1955 school year, because "The Texas public school system is administered under the Texas constitution and the statutes passed by the Texas legislature, and no change should be contemplated until further action has been taken by the United States Supreme Court and until the Texas Legislature points the way for such changes" (cited in Russell 2011, 325).

[65] Shockley (1974, 111–149) provides a full description of the Crystal City boycott and the changes instituted as a result.

[66] For a full discussion of the case, see Powers and Patton (2008). Many of the details provided here are drawn from that article.

[67] In *McLaurin*, an African-American admitted to a graduate program in education was forced to sit in a designated seat in the classroom, in the library, and in the cafeteria. In *Sweatt*, an African-American was denied admission to the University of Texas law school, on the basis that there was a state law school reserved for African-Americans at Texas State, an unaccredited school with no library and no full-time faculty. In *Sweatt*, however, the Supreme Court explicitly refrained from challenging the *Plessy* v. *Ferguson* "separate but equal" doctrine, contenting itself to rule that the conditions were definitely not equal.

more evident in language acquisition; it is clearly harder to master a second language when contact with speakers of that language is limited.

Unfortunately, as recognized by Chief Justice Vinson in his opinion in *McLaurin* (1950, at 641), "the removal of state restrictions will not necessarily abate individual and group predilections, prejudices and choices." The states proved inventive in creating segregated schools without de jure segregation. Judge Seals listed these tactics in his opinion in *Cisneros* v. *Corpus Christi Independent School District* (1970):

administrative decisions by the school board in drawing boundaries, locating new schools, building new schools and renovating old schools in the predominantly Negro and Mexican parts of town, in providing an elastic and flexible subjective, transfer system that resulted in some Anglo children being allowed to avoid the ghetto, or "corridor" schools, by bussing some students, by providing one or more optional transfer zones which resulted in Anglos being able to avoid Negro and Mexican-American schools, not allowing Mexican-Americans or Negroes the option of going to Anglo schools, by spending extraordinarily large sums of money which resulted in intensifying and perpetuating a segregated, dual school system, by assigning Negro and Mexican-American teachers in disparate ratios to these segregated schools, and further failing to employ a sufficient number of Negro and Mexican-American school teachers, and failing to provide a majority-to-minority transfer rule, were, regardless of all explanations and regardless of all expressions of good intentions, calculated to, and did maintain and promote a dual school system. (at 617–620)

As we have seen in *Hernandez* (1954, relating to jury selection, Chapter 3, p. 73), authorities argued that desegregation required by *Brown* could not be applied to Mexican-Americans because they were officially "white."[68] The arguments used by the Mexican-American litigants for the previous twenty-five years were turned against them, leading them to join forces with African-Americans, as in *Cisneros*. This decision extended protection of the Fourteenth Amendment to groups beyond race:

This court reads *Brown* to mean that when a state undertakes to provide public school education, this education must be made available to all students on equal terms, and that segregation of any group of children in such public schools on the basis of their being of a particular race, color, national origin, or of some readily identifiable ethnic minority group, or class deprives these children of the guarantees of the Fourteenth Amendment. (*Cisneros* 1970, at 605)

The group's history of discrimination sufficed to establish eligibility for protection under *Brown*; minority status was not even necessary. A numerically larger group could still be an oppressed group (Footnote 27 of the court's

---

[68] The jury selection case is discussed in Sheridan (2003). For a full discussion of the use of "whiteness" both by Mexican-American litigants and by state actors in education cases, see Gross (2007) and Wilson (2003).

opinion), prevented from being "full participants in the dominant society" (Footnote 30). Such discrimination was not limited to the South, as demonstrated by the Supreme Court's decision in *Keyes* (*Keyes* v. *School District Number One* 1973), confirming the protection of identifiable minority groups under the *Brown* ruling. Subsequent cases, such as *Diaz* v. *San Jose United School District* (1985), have focused on the means to achieve integration and the results of such efforts.

The Supreme Court in *Parents Involved in Community Schools* v. *Seattle School District No. 1* (2007) rejected all racial classifications in order to protect white students' prerogatives, a perspective that undercuts all previous desegregation efforts, claimed Justice Breyer in his dissent.[69] Judged by the percentage of minority students in overwhelmingly minority schools, segregation has increased. In 1969, 55 percent of Latino students in the United States attended schools that were majority-minority. Integration reached its highest point in the late 1980s, but by 2009, following the Supreme Court's retreat in numerous cases, 80 percent of Latino students attended such schools (Dorsey 2013, 534).

The goal of desegregation for English Language Learners (ELLs) was to promote acquisition of English. Actual implementation of better language pedagogy for ELLs required another level of legislative and judicial intervention. In the Mexican schools of Texas, a monolingual English-only approach, accompanied by pantomiming and other teaching techniques, was favored until the 1960s (see Blanton 2004, 74–91). The method was ineffective, as generally 70–80 percent of the elementary school students failed each year (Blanton 2004, 87), a result that was attributed to lower intelligence in the Mexican student population, as measured by English-language intelligence tests.

---

[69] Chief Justice Roberts argued that because Seattle had never had *de jure* segregation and Louisville had been declared compliant with previous desegregation plans, there were no past wrongs to be righted through judicial intervention. All racial classifications were automatically suspect, regardless of the relative power of different groups. In a case involving a Michigan state constitutional amendment barring racial considerations in university admissions, *Schuette* v. *Coalition to Defend Affirmative Action, Integration and Immigrant Rights* (2014), the Supreme Court reaffirmed this opinion, much to the consternation of dissenting Justices Sotomayor and Ginsburg. Article 1, Section 26, in the revised constitution provides that public universities in the state "shall not discriminate against, or grant preferential treatment to, any individual or group on the basis of race, sex, color, ethnicity, or national origin in the operation of public employment, public education, or public contracting." They contended that by majority vote Michigan voters "changed the basic rules of the political process in that State in a manner that uniquely disadvantaged racial minorities" (at 1652). After the amendment, minority enrollment in the University of Michigan's undergraduate and graduate programs dropped precipitously, as in California after *Bakke*, even though the African-American and Hispanic percentage of the general population grew. When the state contravenes constitutional protections "our role as judges includes policing the process of self-government and stepping in when necessary to secure the constitutional guarantee of equal protection" (at 1654). The dissenting judges reasoned that "there are some things the Constitution forbids even a majority of citizens to do" (at 1667).

Other approaches always existed, but had no formal, legal support. By the beginning of the 1960s, frustration with the failure of English-only pedagogy combined with new pride in ethnic heritage to inspire different educational models. The political will to pursue those models led to the passage of the first Bilingual Education Act (BEA) in 1968. The ideological, scientific, and pedagogical winds have shifted frequently in the intervening years, with the pressures increasing at each re-authorization of the bill, required every five years. The competing models with competing experts have led most judges to accept any approach that had some basis in educational theory and research. State intervention – through statute, constitutional amendment, and referendum – has tried to limit the range of options available to school districts, with more of an eye to expense than to effectiveness.

For the past fifty years federal statutes and jurisprudence have required schools to acknowledge the special needs of ELLs and the need to hire teachers appropriately trained to meet those needs. However, the methodology has not been specified as long as it is supported by educational research, opening a range from fully bilingual-bicultural programs to transitional bilingual education to English immersion. Educational experts can be found to justify any of these approaches, leading judges to abstain from requiring any particular method and states and local school districts to embrace the least expensive options, making funding an important point of contention. The schools are constrained, to a certain degree, by requirements to prove success through assessment, but statistics are easily manipulated, explained away, or simply ignored.

Through the first half of the twentieth century, bilingualism was most often assumed to have negative consequences for children's cognitive development.[70] Attitudes began to shift in the 1950s, furthered by the research of Elizabeth Peal and Wallace Lambert on French–English bilingualism in Québec in the 1960s.[71] They concluded that "intellectually his [the youngster's] experience with two language systems seems to have left him with a mental flexibility, a superiority in concept formation, and a more diversified

---

[70] For example, Smith and Saer's studies of Welsh bilinguals and monolinguals (1923). Saer found "mental confusion" in bilinguals that he judged as permanent because he detected it in university students as well as elementary school students (1923, 38). These findings came at a time when Welsh nationalism was growing, including the demand to make Welsh the sole official language in Wales. Toward this aim, Plaid Cymru was founded in 1925.

[71] In the context of the "Révolution Tranquille," furthering the political and economic aspirations of the French majority in Québec, Peal and Lambert (1962) found that bilingual children, all from francophone families, performed a variety of tests better than their monolingual counterparts. The sociolinguistic context is referenced by their attention to attitudes toward English and French, noting that "parents of higher intelligence might be more inclined to encourage their children to learn English" (1962, 13, also discussed 17–18), while monolinguals were possibly constrained by a "conservative nationalistic sentiment for the retaining of the French language" (1962, 21).

set of mental abilities, in the sense that the patterns of abilities developed by bilinguals were more heterogeneous" (1962, 20). Success at true bilingualism and the benefits derived from it were dependent, in their study, on parental attitudes toward the dominant (English) language.

The change in the scientific position on bilingualism combined with the rise of the Civil Rights Movement to promote bilingual education and positive attitudes toward students' first language along with the desire to master English. After the Cuban Revolution in 1959, the arrival of many Cubans in South Florida encouraged experimentation in this regard, which the Ford Foundation funded. The Coral Way Elementary School in Dade County opened a true bilingual/bicultural program for grades 1–3 in 1963, with an even mix of native Spanish speakers and native English speakers. Schools in Texas, New Mexico, and Arizona soon followed this model. The National Education Association sponsored a survey of successful programs and published the findings in 1966. At the same time, two federal programs of President Lyndon Johnson's War on Poverty included recognition of the issues for LEP students that needed to be addressed, Title VI of the Civil Rights Act of 1964 and Title I of the Elementary and Secondary Education Act of 1965 (ESEA).

The ESEA attempted to address the academic achievement of school districts with large numbers of low-income families. In particular, Title I of the Act favored the development of pre-school and early elementary education. Grants would be provided to state and local education authorities, which would be overseen by a National Advisory Council on the Education of Disadvantaged Children (Sec. 212 (a)). The ESEA constituted the first major federal intervention in education, but included protection of the principle of local control:

Nothing contained in this Act shall be construed to authorize any department, agency, officer, or employee of the United States to exercise any direction, supervision, or control over the curriculum, program of instruction, administration or personnel of any educational institution or school system or over the selection of library resources, textbooks, or other printed or published instructional materials by any educational institution or school system. (Section 604)

The ESEA did not directly target those whose native language was not English, but some of the funds supported such programs. A Title III grant designed to "accelerate creativity" supported an ESL program in the San Diego area (Petrzela 2010, 417).

Using Title I funds the Tucson, Arizona, school district adapted the Coral Way program in 1965, but still perceived the use of Spanish as a handicap rather than an advantage (de la Trinidad 2008, 165). Starting in 1959, María Urquides, Henry Oyama, and Adalberto Guerrero developed a Spanish-for-Spanish-speakers program, and they later would be part of the National Education

Association (NEA) survey team. Senator Ralph Yarborough, Texas, attended the NEA conference in October of 1966 and was inspired to propose the first federal bilingual education legislation, which amended the Elementary and Secondary Education Act, adding Title VII, now known as the Bilingual Education Act. It was, as he put it, "a magnificent opportunity to do a very sensible thing – to enable naturally bilingual children to grow up speaking both good Spanish and good English" (cited in Valencia 2008, 164). His original proposal was to support language programs only for Spanish speakers, but to gain broader support in the Senate the bill extended coverage to all "children of limited English-speaking ability" (Bilingual Education Act of 1968, Declaration of Policy). In the 1968 vote support came from both Democrats and Republicans; a simultaneous bilingual education bill in the California senate had the support of then Governor Ronald Reagan. As president he would take a much different stand.

The original BEA allocated $85 million to support experimental programs, particularly those aimed at low-income school districts.[72] It did not specify the type of curriculum that could be funded, nor did it require all school districts to address the particular needs of non-English-speaking students. The vast majority of school districts offered no bilingual education (less than 10 percent across the Southwest), and fewer than 3 percent of Mexican American students were enrolled in such programs (Valencia 2008, 167, citing a 1972 report by the US Commission on Civil Rights). The initial grants were for a maximum of three years. One of the larger ones was for $442,216, granted to Project Frontier, which combined several districts along the California–Mexico border in a program that grew out of cooperation between the Mexican government and the school districts (Petrzela 2010, 418). While the minimal funding for a national program inhibited widespread implementation, the emphasis on bilingual-bicultural education did shift attitudes, encouraging more positive attitudes toward minority languages and toward bilingualism in general.

It may seem surprising to us today that the Nixon administration was interested in supporting language minority groups against discriminatory practices, at the same time as it was professing a policy of "benign neglect" toward African-Americans. The "Southern Strategy" to gain a Republican majority in the former states of the Confederacy was accompanied by a Southwestern Strategy to attract Latino voters. Under the leadership of Nixon-appointee Leon Panetta, and then J. Stanley Pottinger, the Office of Civil Rights (OCR) in the Department of Health, Education and Welfare actively pursued discrimination cases, issuing guidelines for school districts with more than 5 percent

---

[72] Moran (1988, 1265) points out that authorization and expenditure are two very different things. In the first four years of the BEA, only $35 million of $135 million authorized was actually spent.

language minority students (May 25, 1970). These guidelines required any such district to "take affirmative steps to rectify the language deficiency in order to open its instructional program to these students" and prohibited the use of intelligence assessment based on "criteria which essentially measure or evaluate English language skills." Furthermore, it required outreach to parents, in a language other than English if necessary.[73] Nixon himself would, in 1972, propose an "Equal Educational Opportunities Act" to give students "who start their education under language handicaps" an "educational bill of rights."[74]

In March of 1970 Kinney Kinmon Lau and twelve other non-English-speaking students started a class action law suit against the San Francisco Unified School District, arguing that English-only instruction with no assistance was a violation of Title VI of the Civil Rights Act of 1964. By the time the District Court heard the case, the Office of Civil Rights (OCR) guidelines had been issued. Lau was a first-grader who recently arrived from Hong Kong. His mother Kam Wai Lau was concerned that he could not understand any of the instruction provided, a problem she mentioned to Neighborhood Legal Services while seeking help in a landlord–tenant dispute. She was connected to Ed Steinman, an attorney, and Ling-chi Wang, a community organizer in Chinatown.

With the opening of immigration to Asians through the Hart-Celler Act (Immigration and Nationality Act of 1965), Chinese immigration was increasing rapidly. Lau was one of almost 2,856 Chinese-speaking students in the school system who had limited or no English proficiency.[75] At the District Court and the Ninth Circuit the decisions sided with the school district: the students were receiving the same education as the English-speaking students. However, the Supreme Court, drawing on Judge Shirley Hufstedler's vigorous dissent at the Ninth Circuit, ruled unanimously in favor of the children. Just as Negrón was found absent at his own trial (see Chapter 3), the children were essentially absent at their own education, rendered "functionally deaf and mute" by the curriculum offered by the district (at 805). Because the state mandates compulsory attendance, and the use of English as the language of

---

[73] The full text of the guidelines is available at www2.ed.gov/about/offices/list/ocr/docs/lau1970.html.

[74] Address to the Nation, March 16, 1972. The primary focus of the address was to reject busing as a means to arrive at desegregation. The bill he proposed was never passed though another version was approved in 1974. The full text is available at www.presidency.ucsb.edu/ws/?pid=3775.

[75] The initial case in the federal courts was heard in District Court in 1970; the appeal was decided in 1973 and then at the US Supreme Court (1974). For a longer description of the background, see Salomone (2010, 119–138). Initially, all Chinese-language students were included in the class action, but 1,066 students were receiving some kind of language assistance, so they were removed from the case, leaving 1,790. Roughly 16 percent of the total school population was of Chinese origin in 1969.

instruction, the state creates the "language problem" and does nothing to remedy it (at 806).

Before the *Lau* case reached the highest court, the Supreme Court had ruled on discrimination and school funding in *San Antonio* v. *Rodriguez* (1973).[76] Inequities in school funding were a constant issue across the country, as the most common source for school funds is property tax, a local tax that depends on the property values of the community. It is not a new issue.[77] In Illinois, the wealthiest districts spend almost three times as much per pupil as the poorest districts.[78]

In *Rodriguez*, the parents of students in the Edgewood School District outside of San Antonio observed that though they had the highest property tax rate in the area, the school district was still among the poorest, with the result that from the facilities to the percentage of fully certified teachers, the Edgewood district had less to offer the mostly Mexican-American students. The nexus of wealth and ethnicity offered an opportunity to challenge school funding based on the Equal Protection Clause of the Fourteenth Amendment. A suit was filed in 1968. The state argued that equalized expenditures constituted socialism, but the District Court's three-judge panel disagreed (*Rodriguez* v. *San Antonio ISD* 1971): "The *type* of socialized education, not the question of its existence, is the only matter currently in dispute" (at 284; italics in the original). However, the decision made no mention of ethnicity or language; the disparity in wealth was the crux of the matter. The Supreme Court (1973) rejected relative wealth as a suspect class meriting the "strict scrutiny" standard, finding no absolute equivalency of the wealth of the school district and the wealth of the inhabitants of that district. It also rejected the requirement of "equal education" as long as "adequate education," a minimum standard, was maintained. As a result, it

---

[76] The inequities of school funding in the San Antonio region are discussed more fully in Sracic (2006).

[77] Already in 1907 John R. Commons commented on the idea of using education as a basis for suffrage: "The educational test is a rational test, but it is rational only when the state makes an honest and diligent effort to equip every man to pass the test. The former slave states spend $2.21 per child for educating the negroes, and $4.92 per child for educating the whites" (1907, 45, citing a government report from 1900–1901). This was probably an optimistic comparison of spending.

[78] The "Illinois Report Card" from the Illinois State Board of Education (ISBE) showed that New Berlin, near Springfield, spent $4,656 per pupil while New Trier in the Chicago suburbs spent $13,187 (instructional costs as opposed to operating costs, based on 2013–2014 data; http://illinoisreportcard.com issued by the ISBE,). Average per pupil expenditure in Illinois (operating and instructional) was $12,040 in FY 2012–2013. Again the richest districts spent about three times as much per pupil as the poorest districts. (www.iasb.com/pdf/playingfair.pdf, a report by the Illinois Association of School Boards). Illinois funding formulas for education were challenged in *McInnis* v. *Shapiro* (1969), but the court found in the school funding question "no discoverable and manageable standards by which a court can determine when the Constitution is satisfied and when it is violated" (at 335). Unequal expenditures did not equal "invidious discrimination" (at 336).

reversed this decision, primarily based on the fear that the principle of local control would be abandoned, brushing aside Justice Marshall's concern that the majority's ruling "can only be seen as a retreat from our historic commitment to equality of educational opportunity and as unsupportable acquiescence in a system which deprives children in their earliest years of the chance to reach their full potential as citizens" (at 71). Neither the majority and concurring opinions nor the dissents addressed the linguistic inequality of the pedagogical situations, and the differences in funding that the linguistic factor might entail.

The distinction between "adequate" and "any" education was crucial then to the success of the *Lau* appeal. Because the Chinese students could not participate at all in their education without special assistance, the Supreme Court found that students like Kinney Kinmon Lau were "effectively foreclosed from any meaningful education."[79] No specific means to facilitate their participation were identified; bilingual education was just one choice among several. After some hesitation, the school board in San Francisco ultimately acquiesced to the plan jointly crafted by their task force, the Justice Department, and the Center for Applied Linguistics (Salomone 2010, 130). This plan called for bilingual-bicultural education, more than the Chinese parents had originally demanded. It remains a popular option as the San Francisco schools have been precluded by the *Lau* court order from following the general California rule to offer only English immersion (per Proposition 227, see following).[80]

Nationally, the *Lau* decision led to the creation of the "*Lau* remedies," guidelines for school districts that described what would and would not satisfy the educational obligations to ELLs. As a first step, the school district has to identify the students' language skills, the language of their home, and the language they use most frequently in different contexts (such as on the playground). Next the schools must diagnose the students' needs and devise a program to address those needs. Initially, three types of programs were described: transitional bilingual education, bilingual-bicultural education, and multilingual multicultural education. Within those programs, districts need to offer courses and/or modules that value minorities, and minorities cannot be funneled into programs because of their ethnicity (as when Mexican-Americans were assigned to vocational tracks devoted to unskilled manual labor). Schools must also commit to hiring appropriate instructional personnel, though the commission recognized that some temporary certification might be necessary. Temporary or lower-level certification has remained a major issue.

---

[79] The consent decree was filed in 1976. The full text is available at www.justice.gov/crt/about/edu/documents/lauor1.pdf. Lau himself never benefited from the changes. Though he achieved perfect fluency in English, he lost his Chinese and later regretted that he could not use that skill for international work (from a 2002 *Boston Globe* interview cited in Salomone 2010, 130).

[80] Reardon *et al.* (2014) analyzes the success of the various programs. We will return to this study later.

Schools are expected to contact parents in whatever language is necessary to assure communication.[81] Finally, programs must be evaluated regularly with progress reports delivered to the OCR. These remedies were sent to all school districts; over the next five years they would be used as the basis for over 500 consent decrees between the OCR and the schools. But they had never gone through the standard approval process for federal regulations. When Shirley Hufstedler, the Secretary of the newly formed Department of Education, finally attempted to pursue formal approval, opposition came from all sides and they were ultimately withdrawn from consideration by the man who had originally written them, Reagan's Secretary of Education Terrel Bell (appointed in 1981).

The same year as the *Lau* decision, 1974, the Congress passed the Equal Educational Opportunities Act, first proposed by President Nixon in 1972 (see above, p. 116). This statute required states to take "appropriate action" to overcome language barriers. "Language barriers" were a less demanding threshold than the "inability to speak and understand the English language" specified in the 1970 guidelines (Salomone 2010, 137). Exactly what constituted appropriate action was outlined in a 1975 report by the US Commission on Civil Rights. The recommendations went well beyond the requirements of the 1970 memo, stating that "the constitutional principle is not invalidated because there may be but a single or just a few non-English-speaking students attending a particular school," but it acknowledged that numbers might be critical in determining the most appropriate program and the length of the program[82] (1975, 169; the choices are outlined in the same report, pp. 78–83).

The three-prong approach to evaluating the appropriateness of a school district's program was established in the case *Castañeda* v. *Pickard* (1981), concerning the practices of the Raymondville TX Independent School District.[83] Raymondville had historically operated a segregated school system,

---

[81] For example, an agreement with the Dekalb County (GA) schools in 2014 required that "A brief statement regarding the availability of translated materials and instructions for requesting translation and interpreter services will be provided on school and District websites, in the Code of Conduct, and at school and District offices"; the statement was to be made available in the ten languages most spoken by students in the district (www.justice.gov/crt/about/edu/docu ments/dekalbagree2.pdf).

[82] The length of programs has been a matter of considerable controversy over the years. The 1975 report anticipated these questions, noting that the proper length depended largely upon the sociolinguistic context. "Navajo children who live on the Navajo Reservation and are isolated from English speakers may need 12 years of bilingual bicultural education. In some areas of the Southwest, particularly those that receive continual immigration from Mexico, Mexican American children might need at least six years of bilingual bicultural education" (1975, 83).

[83] Raymondville is a town of about 10,000 inhabitants, the onion-growing capital of Texas, about fifty miles north of Brownsville in far southern Texas. Willacy County is one of the poorest in Texas. Raymondville was the object of a documentary *Valley of Tears* (2003). After the *Castañeda* case was filed, a week-long strike in April of 1979 further galvanized the Mexican-American community.

and over 80 percent of the students in the district were Mexican-American. The complaints focused on the ability grouping of students, the hiring of professional personnel, and the nature of the educational programs for ELLs. The Fifth Circuit found the *Lau* guidelines irrelevant, as they simply required the district to do something (which the district was), and Title VII required proof of discriminatory intent, which was not clear. However, the court was willing to consider the application of the Equal Education Opportunities Act §1703(f) in order to assess the appropriateness of a language remediation program.

The first prong concerns research support for the type of program being used: the underlying theory must be "recognized as sound by some experts in the field, or, at least, deemed a legitimate experimental strategy" (at 1009). The second assesses the application of that theory, the "practices, resources and personnel necessary to transform the theory into reality" (at 1010). Finally, the court requires results: the application of the theory must overcome the language barriers encountered by the students. Not only that, the district must help students to recoup the academic deficits that might result from the extra time spent on English instruction. The goal is "parity of participation in the standard instructional program within a reasonable length of time" (at 1011). The court found the program reasonable, but the teacher training component questionable, as some of the teachers had only a crash course in Spanish designed to provide them with a basic 700-word vocabulary. The court too was unconvinced by the evaluation of progress toward the desired goal of parity of participation.

Individual states' weak enforcement of bilingual education policies has regularly been challenged. In the 1980s, the Onarga, IL, school district regularly responded to the state-mandated audit of LEP students by claiming that it had fewer than twenty such students. The local Mexican-American community knew that there were many more than twenty, but hesitated to protest because many had undocumented status. Finally, one woman, Margarita Gómez, risked deportation to demand the legally required services for her children. In *Gomez* v. *Illinois State Board of Education* (1985 and 1987), the State Board of Education issued rules but failed to monitor or enforce them, claiming such authority was held only by the individual school district superintendents. The Seventh Circuit rejected such delegation of authority, and a settlement was reached in 1988. The *Gomez* decision subsequently was cited to require the Texas Education Agency to enforce minimum LEP guidelines.[84]

Cost and the availability of appropriately prepared teachers were issues that dogged the BEA throughout its history. School districts perceived the Lau guidelines and the provisions of EEOA as unfunded mandates: the federal

---

[84] For background on the *Gomez* case and the subsequent influence, see Badillo (2011).

government funded experimental programs of limited duration, but the EEOA required permanent solutions with verifiable results. The Office of Bilingual Education (OBE), established by the EEOA in 1974, and the Office of Civil Rights within the Justice Department approached the questions from different perspectives: the OBE was interested in developing and evaluating pedagogical approaches, while the OCR, related historically to desegregation efforts, was concerned about bilingual-bicultural education as a new segregation. Each renewal of the BEA circumscribed the types of programs that would be considered acceptable, but only a small fraction of the school districts would receive federal funding to help implement them.

The amendments to the BEA's reauthorization in 1978 were influenced by the Supreme Court's decision in *U. of California* v. *Bakke* (1978)[85] and by a report issued by the American Institutes for Research (AIR). The *Bakke* decision indicated that intent to discriminate had to be proven as well as discriminatory effect, and thus made it more difficult to challenge whether or not a school district's program kept students from the "meaningful participation in the curriculum" required by Title VI. In the same year, the AIR report suggested that the form of assistance given to ELLs did not significantly alter the results: students in bilingual programs (both dual language immersion and transitional bilingual education) performed slightly better in math tests, and slightly worse in English, than did children in English immersion programs. Furthermore, it found that children in bilingual programs were frequently kept in bilingual classrooms even after they had achieved sufficient mastery of English to pursue an English-only education. This conclusion raised fears of a new type of segregation and introduced the economic argument that scarce resources should be devoted to those most in need.[86] While these findings were criticized and applauded, along political/ideological lines, the general results were amendments to the reauthorization bill of 1978 limiting the discretion of local school districts: the goal of bilingual education was to be the speedy acquisition of English and the insertion of ELLs in regular (English-only) classrooms. The goal of promoting bilingualism and biliteracy was effectively abandoned.

---

[85] *Bakke* concerned admission to medical school at the UC Davis campus. The Superior Court of California issued an injunction against the University of California in considering race in any admissions decisions. The Supreme Court found the admission process at the University unconstitutional, but did not ban all consideration of race.

[86] This was also the conclusion of journalist Noel Epstein's book (1977), which remains a primary source for English-only advocates (see Barry 2001, 298–299, and below in Chapter 7, p. 190–191). For an evaluation of the scientific credibility of studies concerning different approaches to bilingual education, see August, Goldenberg, and Rueda (2010). They are particularly critical of the Baker and de Kanter study (1981) that so heavily influenced the Reagan administration and subsequent opponents of bilingual education. The Baker and de Kanter study is available online as an ERIC document: http://files.eric.ed.gov/fulltext/ED215010.pdf.

Soon after Ronald Reagan's inauguration, in March of 1981, another government study was launched within the Office of Planning, Budget and Evaluation, under the direction of Beatrice Birman and Alan Ginsburg. Their study stated that the ultimate goal of bilingual education was monolingualism in English: "Although bilingualism is a laudable and a worthwhile outcome, we judge benefit in terms of English language acquisition and subject-matter learning" (1983, xx). In the 1984 reauthorization of the BEA, native language instruction was limited to supporting transition to a completely English curriculum. Promoting bilingualism was cast as divisive, risking separatism.[87] Seventy-five percent of the funds were allocated to transitional bilingual education rather than bilingual maintenance programs.

Four percent of the grant funds were devoted to "Special Alternative Instructional Programs" that did not require any use of the native language instruction at all, on the grounds that any type of bilingual instruction might be "administratively impractical" in some school districts (Wiese & Garcia 1998, 8). The practicality justification was related to numbers of students in each language[88] and the availability of bilingual qualified teachers. Introducing practicality was an escape valve for school districts: funding for the alternative programs was increased to 25 percent of the funding in the 1988 bill, and the possibility of exceeding that cap in the 1994 reauthorization. Far from the heady days of the early 1970s when bilingual education was described (though never by law) as a right, by the early 1990s bilingual education was considered an expensive frill.

The winds shifted a bit under the Clinton administration. The 1994 reauthorization restored the preference for bilingual education and described such programs as developing "our Nation's national language resources, thus promoting our Nation's competitiveness in the global economy." It also reinforced interest in bilingual programs for the indigenous populations, Native Americans, Native Alaskans, Native Hawaiians, and Native American Pacific Islanders. (We will consider language programs for indigenous populations later in this chapter.)

---

[87] Québec was often cited as an example, though the sociolinguistic context is entirely different. In Québec, the French-speaking majority, which was descended from an immigration that preceded the arrival of the English, was seeking to assert its right to equality with the English minority.

[88] In 2010, the Illinois State Board of Education identified 144 native languages of its students (other than English), eighty-seven of them with fewer than fifty speakers statewide. Spanish speakers constituted 81 percent of the ELLs. Justice Blackmun stressed in the *Lau* decision that "numbers are at the heart of this case": "When, in another case, we are concerned with a very few youngsters, or with just a single child who speaks ... any language other than English, I would not regard today's decision ... as conclusive upon the issue whether the statute and the guidelines required the funded school district to provide special instruction" (1974, at 572).

Among skeptics of bilingual education emphasis on accountability and efficiency grew through the 1980s and 1990s, usually defined by standardized testing and the rapidity of students' transition to an English-only classroom. The assumption was that three years should be enough time to make that transition. One part of the Birman and Ginsburg study challenged the pedagogical efficacy of bilingual-bicultural programs, another focused on the added expense of such programs, another on the lack of properly certified personnel, and finally on the frequency of mistaken placement of ELLs. The use of federal funds of Title VII projects was investigated by the Office of the Inspector General (1982). At the same time Senator S. I. Hayakawa (R, CA) began organizing opposition to a wide variety of accommodations to LEP Americans, in the form of the organization U.S. English (founded 1983) and an English-language amendment to declare English the official language of the United States (see Chapter 5).

Through the 1980s total federal funding through the BEA stagnated in the range of $130 million to $150 million, and the number of students affected dropped from 300,000 to 182,000 (San Miguel 2004, 65). Under Secretary of Education William Bennett, the requirements for native language instruction were decreased and the enforcement arm for compliance with the BEA was greatly reduced.

In 1983, the Department of Education commissioned a long-term study of the effectiveness of the various approaches to providing equal educational opportunity to children who arrived at school not speaking English, or not speaking it well. The study covered the period 1983–1989, considering data relating to the language skills of the children, to their home background, to the context of the school district, to the preparation of teachers, and to the classroom itself. One of the conclusions was that the three approaches studied had similar results, which encouraged the US Congress and state legislatures to encourage or even require the cheapest solution, commonly believed to be English immersion, with the minimum amount of bilingual assistance possible. The low-cost solution was to hire or retrain monolingual English teachers, providing them with a short intensive second-language course to make them "bilingual." This approach tended to work acceptably in the short term but to fail in the long term, as teachers of bilingual classes who were not really bilingual could not provide the assistance necessary for success in subject matters other than English itself.

The deficiencies in the pedagogical studies are largely the product of local control and local conditions.[89] The outcomes depend on the programs selected:

---

[89] For a summary of the longitudinal study's failings, see Dolson and Mayer (1992), at www.ncela .us/files/rcd/BE018850/Longitudinal_Study_of_Three_Program_Models.pdf. They focus on the selection of which programs nationwide would represent the three approaches to bilingual education being studied.

for example, the definition of "early-exit bilingual education" required only one hour per day of instruction in the students' native language, and the second language qualifications of the teachers were minimal (averaging 2.7 on a 5.0 scale, compared to 4.7 in English; Dolson & Mayer 1992, 112). This in turn transmits to the students a negative attitude toward their native language and culture, which further inhibits their overall progress. Similar problems are evident in the evaluation of the other programs. The conclusions of the longitudinal study, that all three programs were equally effective, depended on how one defines effective: in the short term, English-immersion programs made it possible to remove support for the ELLs after grade three; in the long run (considered through grade seven), the immersion students failed to progress while students in "late-exit bilingual programs" continued to advance and surpassed the students in the other programs.

Another longitudinal survey, conducted in the San Francisco public schools from 2002 to 2012 by Stanford University researchers, compared four programs within two language groups (Spanish and Chinese): English immersion, early exit bilingual, maintenance bilingual, and dual immersion.[90] Again the general conclusion was that the short-term gains of English immersion in grades one to three were surpassed in the later grades by bilingual programs.

Predictably, advocates of bilingual education stress the long term while opponents stress the short term, which is less costly and makes fewer demands in teacher preparation. The question remains as to what constituted success. For the opponents of bilingual education, the rapidity of integration into the full English curriculum was enough. For the advocates, long-term success in the full curriculum was a higher standard.

In the period 1998–2002, statewide referendums took center stage in the bilingual education debates. In 1998, California overwhelmingly passed Proposition 227, which prescribed English immersion methods and a limit of three years for students to be integrated into the regular curriculum. Arizona followed suit in 2000 with Proposition 203. The transition period was reduced to one year. Massachusetts voters passed a similar law in 2002, Question 2. Ballot initiatives can be seen as the ultimate in democratic decision-making, or as the ultimate in political demagoguery. These initiatives replaced local control by state control, educational policy by political policy.

The results of these propositions have been interpreted along familiar lines: short-term gains touted by supporters, long-term failures lamented by detractors (e.g., Wentworth *et al.* (2010), Uriarte *et al.* (2010)). Political support for the constraints imposed by these referendums seems to be wavering. In 2014

---

[90] A set of graphs illustrating the results is available at Reardon *et al.* (2014); a more detailed analysis of one aspect in one group – reclassification of Latino students as fluent in English – can be found in Umansky and Reardon (2014).

a bill to repeal Question 2 in Massachusetts died in committee. The same year the California assembly voted to include a ballot initiative to repeal Proposition 227 in the November 2016 election.

Accountability has been a dominant theme in bilingual education, as it has been in educational policy more broadly. Here too ideological divisions with competing experts complicate rational decision-making. In 2001, the "No Child Left Behind Act" (NCLB), the reauthorization of the Elementary and Secondary Education Act first passed in 1965, repealed the Bilingual Education Act and replaced the Office of Bilingual Education with the Office of English Language Acquisition. Additionally, it instituted a rigorous program of annual testing and made progress in the tested areas the basis for continued federal funding. ELLs are tested for their proficiency in English as well as tested in English for academic content (along with native speakers of English). Even for native speakers the testing program has been controversial, with opponents urging a broader-based assessment program. Because so much rides on the outcome of the tests, "teaching to the test" is a constant temptation, and sometimes temptation crosses the line into cheating, as in the Atlanta Public Schools.[91]

The federal statute requires that ELLs be "assessed in a valid and reliable manner and provided reasonable accommodations on assessments" and provided guidelines for what would constitute acceptable accommodations.[92] For ELLs a few states have provided translations of the subject area tests into the most common languages found in their schools. In 2014–2015, New York City, for instance, offered the tests in Arabic, Bengali, Chinese, French, Haitian Creole, Korean, Russian, Spanish, and Urdu.[93] Such accommodations have been deemed by two state courts as acceptable but not mandatory.[94]

NCLB requires states to identify the languages other than English in each district and "to indicate the languages for which yearly student academic assessments are not available and are needed" (*Reading* 2004, at 172).

---

[91] An investigation by the Georgia Bureau of Investigation (2011) found that 178 teachers in the district had altered answers by students. In 2015, eleven teachers were convicted of racketeering, with nine receiving prison sentences of five years or longer. Cheating can take many forms, including encouraging parents to label their children "learning disabled" in order to give their children extra time to take the tests. A list of fifty ways to cheat, certainly not exhaustive, was compiled by the National Center for Fair and Open Testing and published in the *Washington Post*, March 31, 2013: www.washingtonpost.com/blogs/answer-sheet/wp/2013/03/31/50-ways-adults-in-schools-cheat-on-standardized-tests/.

[92] The statute is at 20 U.S.C. § 6311(b)(3)(C)(ix)(III); the guidelines were issued in March 2003 by the Department of Education. Both are cited in *Coachella Valley Unified School District* v. *State of California* 2009, at 103.

[93] http://schools.nyc.gov/Accountability/resources/testing/default.htm.

[94] *Reading School District* v. *Department of Education* (2004) and *Coachella* (2009). In *Reading*, the school district challenged the commonwealth's Department of Education's designation of thirteen schools as failing to achieve adequate yearly progress. One of the three bases for this challenge was that the failure of the state to provide native language testing was discriminatory.

The court concluded that "it is not practicable at this time to provide native language testing" (*ibid.*). Practicality was the key word: both the Pennsylvania and the California courts raised the specter of having to provide tests in over 100 languages, though tests in two or three languages would cover over 90 percent of the needs. The *Coachella* court cited Proposition 227 in determining that the state required testing to be in English, and accepted the Educational Testing Service's procedures "to reduce any avoidable disadvantages to English language learners," primarily through attention to the linguistic level in English of test questions (*Coachella* 2009, at 106). The court took note of a state report that many of the ELLs did not have academic skills in their native language and reasoned that translated tests for those students would not be any more accurate than English-language tests (at 108). English-only provisions in Proposition 227 ensured that students would not have academic skills in their native language.

Most importantly, the courts did not want to get embroiled in sorting out the conflicting claims of educational professionals. The *Coachella* court had no interest in becoming "the official second-guesser on the issue of how to assess LEP students under the NCLBA" (at 117). The judiciary had no desire to constrain the discretionary power of the state Department of Education and found no abuse of discretion in the testing program.

As one of the most prominent expenses of government, spending on education is constantly under surveillance. In this context legislators and taxpayers look for efficiency, which can conflict with the goal of equality. When in 1992 the Arizona legislature failed to fund ELL programs in a rational manner, parents in Nogales, along the Mexican border, brought suit in the name of Miriam Flores, an 8-year-old third grader who was not getting the help she needed to succeed in school. By the time the Supreme Court finally ruled on the case in 2009, she was a student at the University of Arizona. Subsequently, further litigation led to decisions by the District Court (2013) and the Ninth Circuit (2015). Thus ends, perhaps, twenty-three years of litigation. The case started as a funding debate and ended as a segregation case, testing at each stage the issues of federalism and separation of powers in the pursuit of equality.

At the first stage, the US District Court ruling in 2000, sixty-four "findings of fact" documented the problems: in Nogales in 1992, 80 percent of the elementary school students, 70 percent of the middle school students, and 65–70 percent of the high school students were classified as limited English proficient. Both in the elementary school and in the middle school, students were "mainstreamed" (i.e., put in all-English classrooms) as soon as they were judged to have a command of oral English, without regard to their ability to read or write English; middle school students were found to be up to five years behind their peers in academic English skills. More than half the teachers in the system lacked the required bilingual or ESL certification. Budgetary constraints prevented the district from hiring and retaining qualified teachers. State and Office of Civil Rights oversight of a consent decree signed in 1992 was extremely limited in the period between the filing of the suit and the District Court ruling in 2000. In the ruling the court found the state's minimum support level "arbitrary and capricious" (*Flores* 2000, at 1239), as it bore no relation to actual need. Therefore, the state was determined to have violated the Equal Education Opportunity Act. With little progress toward rectifying the problems, the state was found in contempt of court in December 2005.

In 2006, the Arizona legislature passed House Bill 2064, an education reform package, in an attempt to meet the court order. The new funding for English learner programs was increased from $355 to $432 per student, but still fell $18 per student short of the goal set eighteen years before. Furthermore, the Bill required districts "to misuse previously allocated federal funds" by applying federal money supplied for desegregation efforts to the English-learner programs (*Flores* 2006, at 11). This judgment was set aside by the Ninth Circuit, and reheard by the District Court in 2007. While acknowledging some progress, the court reaffirmed the inadequacy of the state's funding formulas, the continued failure to meet standards for progress, particularly at the high school level, and condemned the state's policy that ELLs can receive only two years of special assistance in English before being mainstreamed. The court found that "on average, it takes ELL students in the NUSD [Nogales Unified School District] four to five years to be reclassified as English proficient" (*Flores* 2007, at 1163). In short, seven years after the initial ruling, the state still did not comply with the court's decree, and the District Court gave the state until the end of the current legislative session to comply.

The state's appeal to the Ninth Circuit Court of Appeals had a similar result. The state asked for relief from the District Court order, on the basis of *Federal Rules of Civil Procedure* 60(b)(5), which allows the court to "relieve a party from a final judgment when the judgment has been satisfied, released or discharged" (cited in 2008, at 1162). The court order could also be modified if the terms turned out to be unworkable or counterproductive, or if the lower court were deemed to have abused its discretion. The Ninth Circuit noted that the success rate of ELLs on standardized tests (now mandated by NCLB) continued to lag far behind other students. In 2006, only 20 percent of tenth-grade ELLs passed the math test, and just 10 percent passed the reading test. Furthermore, the state's direct funding of ELL programs still failed to meet the most basic needs of the students, requiring districts, when they were so inclined, to take funds from other sources to support these programs. The state claimed that the passage of NCLB rendered the EEOA-based ruling of the District Court obsolete. The Ninth Circuit disagreed: "The first [EEOA] is an equality-based civil rights statute, while the second [NCLB] is a program for overall, gradual school improvement. Compliance with the latter may well not satisfy the former" (*Flores* 2008, at 1172). The EEOA provides for "the current rights of individual students, while NCLB seeks gradually to improve their schools" (*Flores* 2008, at 1173).

The following year the Supreme Court, in a 5–4 ruling, reversed this decision, finding that in this case "a federal court decree has the effect of dictating state or local budget priorities" (*Horne* 2009, at 448). Citing the rule 60(b)(5), the majority declared that a "flexible approach" must be taken "to ensure that responsibility for discharging the State's obligations is returned promptly to the State and its officials" (*Horne* 2009, at 450). The majority claimed that the lower courts had focused too much on funding and not enough on the basic claim of equality, a reading that is hard to justify based on the texts of the previous decisions. Furthermore, the majority inserted itself into educational policy-making by claiming that "Research on ELL instruction indicates there is documented, academic support for the view that SEI is significantly more effective than bilingual education" (*Horne* 2009, at 460–461), a highly selective reading of the professional literature. Most fundamentally, the Supreme Court, focused on states' rights, failed to consider the outcome for the students: whatever Arizona was doing was not working by any standard available. Similar results seem to be coming from the other states that restricted approaches to educating ELLs through ballot initiatives.[95] By its deference to the discretion of the states, the Supreme Court severely restricted the ability of the federal government to enforce constitutional principles of equality and the statutes that derive from them. The burden of proof is on the students to show that they are being failed, rather than on the states to show that they are taking appropriate action.[96]

The dissent, written by Justice Breyer, observed that "[t]hree decades ago, Congress put this statutory provision in place [EEOA] to ensure that our Nation's school systems will help non-English-speaking schoolchildren overcome the language barriers that might hinder their participation in our country's schools, workplaces, and the institutions of everyday politics and government" (*Horne* 2009, at 515). He concluded that "I fear that the Court's decision will increase the difficulty of overcoming barriers that threaten to divide us" (*Horne* 2009, at 516).

---

[95] O'Sullivan (2015, 702) cites a 2014 California Superior Court decision finding that "there existed credible evidence 'that districts are denying required instructional services' to ELLs altogether." Guo and Koretz (2013) noted that Massachusetts had not pursued any comprehensive evaluation of the effectiveness of its policy; while their own work attempts to fill in some of the gaps, they acknowledge that it is just a first step towards that goal. We must always keep in mind, as in King's (2014) thesis, that policy and what teachers choose to do in the classroom are potentially quite different.

[96] For further discussion of this point, see Asturias (2012).

The Supreme Court's decision ordered the District Court to revisit its previous order in light of the state's changes in educational policy and the federal government's changes through NCLB. One change in educational policy was the implementation of the "Four-Hour Model," which requires four hours daily of "English Language Development" (ELD) instruction for all ELLs, at every level, until they can pass the state's English language proficiency test.[97] The state claims that students can typically pass the exam after a year of ELD instruction, though the majority of ELLs continue to fail the state's exam (2013, at 28–29). For students in the more advanced grades, ELD instruction takes the place of subject matter instruction (e.g., in math, science, history, etc.). No effort is made to remediate the lost instruction in those subject areas. The drop-out rate of ELLs remains much higher than for the general school population.

This program was then challenged as a new form of segregation, a claim that was denied by the District Court on the basis that the Four-Hour Model was not "driven by a deliberate attempt to discriminate on the basis of race, color, or national origin" (*Flores* 2013, at 33). Intent, as we have seen, is extremely difficult to prove, and constitutes a much higher bar than impact. In the end, the District Court came back to the original consideration, school funding, noting that statewide there was a "lack of funding at all levels." It concluded that the state's choice in funding the education of ELLs "may turn out to be penny wise and pound foolish, as at the end of the day, speaking English, and not having other educational gains in science, math, etc. will still leave some children behind" (*Flores* 2013, at 38). The Ninth Circuit, in affirming the District Court ruling, rejected the arguments that the Four-Hour Model constitutes segregation when continued past the first year, and that this approach denied students the necessary education in subject areas. The court cited the diversity of programs instituted by different districts to address that issue (*Flores* 2015, at 30–31). If some districts integrated ELLs into academic content, the state as a whole could not be held in violation of the EEOA. Local control obviated the state's responsibility for inequities that continued.

A similar case concerning the state of Texas wended its way through the various levels of the federal judiciary, starting in 1970 as a desegregation case.[98] In 1970, the District Court issued an injunctive order against the Texas Education Agency (TEA) to ensure that "no child will be effectively denied equal opportunity to educational opportunities on account of race, color or national origin" (cited in 2007, at 5). The League of United Latin American

---

[97] An outline of the program is included in the Findings of Fact, items 39–46 (*Flores* 2013, at 11–14).

[98] We will analyze only the 2007 and 2008 rulings.

Citizens and the GI Forum joined the suit in 1975, to add the English learner component to the equal education suit. A 1981 decision found that the TEA had failed "to take appropriate action to address the language barriers of LEP students" as well as "to remove the disabling vestiges of past *de jure* discrimination against Mexican-Americans" (*U.S.* v. *Texas* 1981, at 434), using an impact rather than an intent standard, as in the third prong of the *Castañeda* test (see above p. 118–119): "Good intentions are not enough. The measure of a remedy is its effectiveness, not its purpose" (*ibid.*). The court determined that "bilingual education is uniquely suited to meet the needs of the state's Spanish-speaking students" (*U.S.* v. *Texas* 1981, at 433). The court ordered immediate relief, regardless of the funding issues: "Remedying past injustices suffered by an ethnic minority may be politically inexpedient and economically burdensome; but citizens cannot be compelled to forego their constitutional rights because public officials fear public hostility or desire to save money" (*U.S.* v. *Texas* 1981, at 434).

In 2007, the District Court found that Texas' programs for ELLs were having the desired effects, and that the state was making good-faith efforts to meet the needs of those students (*U.S.* v. *Texas* 2007). The next year (*U.S.* v. *Texas* 2008) the District Court reversed itself, citing the Ninth Circuit's ruling on *Flores* (itself subsequently reversed by the Supreme Court). Using a results test, the court found that the "Performance Based Monitoring Analysis System" (PBMAS) used by the state had serious gaps, amounting to a lack of appropriate oversight of local districts. Finally, in 2010, the Fifth Circuit (*U.S.* v. *Texas* 2010) cited the Supreme Court's ruling in *Horne* v. *Flores* to determine that removing "language barriers" should not be judged by "the equalization of results between native and nonnative speakers on tests administered in English" (*U.S.* v. *Texas* 2010, at 367). The complexity of the factors that might contribute to unequal results could not support a "causal connection" between the results and the actions taken (or not taken) by the Texas Education Agency (*U.S.* v. *Texas* 2010, at 372). The burden of proof of such a causal connection is virtually impossible to meet.

The debates about language in education are largely surrogates for other issues: What does it mean to be American? What does equality mean? Throughout the history of the United States, and even before the United States were formed, to the extent that languages other than English represent foreignness, maintenance of another language has been perceived as allegiance to another country. But this narrow-minded nativism, which certainly has existed and continues to exist, is not the only reason education partially or wholly in another language has been the object of scrutiny.

Education, as one of the most important functions of government, has been the nexus for debates about local, state, and federal powers. Local control can be an opportunity for exciting innovation, and an opportunity for the expression of the worst forms of prejudice (*de facto* segregated schools). State intervention can be a way of imposing standards, or a way of imposing rigid constraints that limit adaptation to local conditions or desires (the Bennett and Edwards bills in the nineteenth century, or the referendums at the turn of the twenty-first century). Federal intervention can be an opportunity for experimentation (the programs funded by the Bilingual Education Act) or a means to impose through accountability measures a single vision of what education must be (a perhaps unintended consequence of the NCLB).

Education is also the nexus for debates about legislative, executive, and judicial powers. Both legislative and executive branches have tried to shape education of ELLs, sometimes pushed, sometimes pulled back by a judiciary that has had to grapple with the meaning of equality and freedom in education. Congress, through the Elementary and Secondary Education Act of 1965, and the Bilingual Education Act of 1968 recognized a fundamental inequality in American society but left the resolution to state and local authorities, with oversight from educational experts (the Office of Bilingual Education) and from legal experts (the Office of Civil Rights). The judiciary's *Lau* decision pushed the executive to be more specific, but then constrained the executive from acting without following proper procedure.

Education of ELLs is also the nexus for debates within the educational establishment. Every approach has its proponents and its detractors within the realm of academic research, in universities, the US Department of Education, state boards of education and the think tanks they contribute to and utilize to justify their perspectives. The variables in this educational research are quite diverse, and that diversity facilitates the justification of opposing viewpoints. Rarely are researchers comparing apples to apples, which provides fodder for opposing legislative and executive solutions and frustration for all judges called on to evaluate whether any given program meets the standards of equality.

The masses of conflicting data encourage government at every level to opt for the least expensive approaches to educating ELLs and to constrain the freedom of individual school districts to offer different choices to their students. The conflicting data also prevent the judiciary from establishing the measures of success in that endeavor, to determine if the constitutional and statutory requirements of equality have been met. In the sequence of cases involving Miriam Flores, the Supreme Court's majority urged that we not lose "sight of the forest for the trees" (*Horne* 2009, at 474), but itself chose a rather small grove rather than a vast wood for its own focus. The broader issue is how freedom can and must create equal opportunity for participation in the broader society. Incremental improvements that fail more than half of the ELLs have not met that goal.

Indigenous Languages and Educational Policy in the United States

In international human rights laws indigenous peoples have rights claims to their language and culture that are not accorded to immigrants. The assumption is that immigrants have chosen to move to a given country, and must adapt to that country's language. Indigenous peoples have been absorbed into a given country, through some means of territorial expansion.[99] The rights include the right to use one's native language in most official capacities, the right to maintain one's native language and to learn the official language of the country, and the right to a public education whatever one's native language might be. For almost two centuries after the founding of the Republic, the United States failed to distinguish the educational goals for immigrants and those for indigenous peoples. American Indian nations have, in theory, sovereignty over their own affairs, but are subject to congressional and judicial control, limiting their ability to control education offered to their children.[100] Only in 1972 did the Congress pass the Indian Education Act, followed subsequently by various measures to preserve and promote Native languages. However, federal policies requiring standardization of curricula and assessment continue to challenge Native peoples' authority over education.

Indigenous, in US history, is usually applied only to non-Western languages and cultures, excluding others whose lands were absorbed into the national territory – Spanish speakers in the Southwest, French speakers in Louisiana, Russian speakers in Alaska, etc. By statute the recognized categories of indigenous languages are Native American, Native Alaskan, Native Hawaiian, and Native Pacific Islander. At the arrival of Columbus in the New World it is estimated that 300 Native languages were spoken in the territory now included in the United States. In 2006, an estimated 175 were still in existence, 70 percent of those spoken only by the elderly, some of them by fewer than ten speakers (Dussias 2008, 7–8). Given the fragile existence of most Native languages, language revitalization has been, since 1990, a primary focus of federal legislation.

---

[99] In the United States, this distinction was explicitly recognized in *Morton* v. *Mancari* (1974), which supported an Indian-preference hiring practice within the Bureau of Indian Affairs, rejecting an anti-discrimination claim by non-Indians, in favor of Indian self-government, citing a 1943 case that required the United States "to prepare the Indians to take their place as independent, qualified members of the modern body politic" (at 552). The Supreme Court declined to judge whether the indigenous status extended to Native Hawaiians in *Rice* v. *Cayetano* (2000), though Justices Stevens and Ginsburg dissented, recalling the Congress' joint resolution apologizing to Native Hawaiians for the seizure of 1.8 million acres without their consent (at 531).

[100] The Indian Self-Determination and Education Assistance Act of 1975 "recognizes the obligation of the United States to assure maximum Indian participation in the direction of education" (cited in Winstead *et al.* 2008, 48).

The field of Native education is littered, throughout the nation's history, with scathing reports of failure followed by congressional action, an oft-repeated cycle. The results have not been impressive. Performance gaps by all standards are still significant, as the Obama administration recognized "that [American Indian/Alaska Native] students are dropping out of school at an alarming rate, that our Nation has made little or no progress in closing the achievement gap between AI/AN students and their non-AI/AN student counterparts, and that many Native languages are on the verge of extinction" (Executive Order 13592, 2011, Section 1). Language issues are at the heart of many of these failures.

From the earliest period of European colonization in North America missionaries established schools for Native Americans, translating the Bible into their languages and teaching them English. The English Society for the Propagation of the Gospel in New England funded the creation of an Indian College (1650), and the erection of a building in Harvard Yard (1655). Caleb Cheeshahteaumuck graduated from Harvard College in 1665. John Eliot, translator of the Bible into Wampanoag (1663), established fourteen towns of "Praying Indians" and funded through his will a school open both to Native Americans and to African-Americans, as well as to English colonists.[101] In the eighteenth century, Eleazar Wheelock founded the Moor's Charity School in Lebanon, Connecticut, which provided to Native children a classical education in Latin and Greek as well as in English and theology.

The connection between Christian missionaries and Indian education continued through the nineteenth century, the government often quite oblivious to the notion of the separation of church and state. Even before the creation of the "Civilization Fund" (1819), the federal government assisted missionaries like Cyrus Kingsbury to establish mission schools.[102] The Civilization Fund regularized such efforts, offering $10,000 per year to establish schools for Native Americans. The Civilization Fund provided for the teaching of agricultural methods along with reading, writing and arithmetic, and further stipulated that "the means of instruction can be introduced with their own consent."

The teachers recognized quickly that teaching the students in their own language worked better than teaching them in English, a language they did not understand. Steven and Mary Riggs established a mission at Lac qui parle (now in Minnesota), translating the Bible into Dakota and establishing

---

[101] For full details of Eliot's work and legacy, see Cogley (1999).

[102] Beaver (1962a) traces the expansion of mission schools from the Revolution through the 1820s. Kingsbury received material support (farm implements and school buildings) from the Secretary of War, who had jurisdiction over Indian affairs, and established schools among the Cherokees, Creeks, and Choctaws (1962a, 22–23). By the mid-1820s thirty-eight schools were in operation, all from Protestant denominations. The Civilization Fund contributions to the schools constituted less than 10 percent of the total budget (Beaver 1962a, 27).

a phonetic alphabet for the language which greatly facilitated the students' acquisition of reading and writing skills, as noted in missionary reports later in the century (Reyhner 1993). Riggs' method of teaching was adopted later in the century at the Crow Creek, Yankton, and the Santee Agencies (Spack 2002, 49–52). Annual reports from the Board of Indian Affairs in the 1870s repeatedly reported that Native students could memorize English but not understand it, while they were perfectly literate in their mother tongues.

Nonetheless, President Grant's "Peace Policy,"[103] instituted in 1869, insisted on the importance of English in "civilizing" the Native peoples. The Peace Commission believed that if the Native children learned English "civilization would have followed at once" (cited in Prucha 2000, 106). The policy recommended that "Indian languages should be eradicated and replaced with English" (cited in Dussias 1999, 910). The Treaty of Fort Laramie, in 1868, instituted compulsory school attendance and provided for a teacher "competent to teach the elementary branches of an English education" (cited in Prucha 2000, 111). About half of these "contract schools" were assigned to religious groups. Both Bureau schools and missionary schools were to teach in English only, "except in so far as the native language of the pupils shall be a necessary medium for conveying the knowledge of English," a policy formalized in 1885 (Dussias 1999, 912).

The same arguments being used at this time to require English only in schools for immigrants were applied to the indigenous populations. English language instruction would instill "American values." To facilitate that process, Native languages were banned not only in the classroom but also in the schoolyard, or anywhere in the boarding schools. When Commissioner of Indian Affairs Hiram Price took office in 1881 he immediately ordered that "the Indian child . . . must be compelled to adopt the English language" (cited in Spack 2002, 24). Boarding schools had the advantage of mixing Native children from different linguistic backgrounds, thus obliging them to speak amongst themselves in the only common language, English.

There were occasional protests from the missionaries who found that English-only did not work and hindered their proselytizing efforts. A special exception was granted for religious instruction. Even the Superintendent of Indian Schools, William N. Hailmann,[104] in his 1896 report, harshly criticized this policy: "the unreasonable offensive warfare made in the Indian schools against the Indian vernacular is largely to blame for the apparent stubbornness

---

[103] See Beaver (1962b). The policy was instituted to combat corruption in the Bureau of Indian Affairs, through oversight by a Board of Indian Commissioners, mostly drawn from the ranks of Protestant philanthropists. The Grant Administration was hardly one to combat corruption, however, and in 1874 the commissioners resigned in protest.

[104] Hailmann himself was a German immigrant who had learned English as a second language, which might explain his empathy.

with which older Indians refuse to learn English" (cited in Dussias 1999, 918). He instituted a kindergarten program taught by speakers of Native languages. His sympathetic though paternalistic approach was soon abandoned.

The failure rate was overwhelming, a fact blamed on the intelligence of the children rather than on the pedagogical approach. Even the inability to learn English was blamed on "inherited characteristics" (Spack 2002, 30; see also Hoxie 1984, 199–204). The focus turned to vocational education of the most basic sort,[105] a diminished expectation that was excoriated by former commissioner Thomas J. Morgan in 1902: "The Indian child has a right that he shall not be hopelessly handicapped by such an inferior training as from the very beginning dooms him to failure in the struggle for existence" (cited in Hoxie 1984, 197). Morgan died soon afterward, as did hope for improved education. Francis Leupp became commissioner in 1905, institutionalizing the lowered expectations for an "inferior" race.

Following several years of revelations of Bureau of Indian Affairs scandals,[106] in 1926 the Secretary of the Interior, Hubert Work, asked the Institute for Government Research (the future Brookings Institution) to study the situation of American Indians. The director of the project was Lewis Meriam. He and his staff visited ninety-five reservations or other Native American communities. In their report they chose not to focus on the notion of progress, i.e., whether or not Indians were better off in 1927 than they were forty or fifty years earlier. Instead, they compared what the current level of services were with what might be considered ideal, looking at "best practices" being provided by a variety of service providers.[107]

The chapter on education opened with "The most fundamental need in Indian education is a change in point of view." Meriam's commission rejected the types of intelligence testing being conducted in the schools at that time, recognizing the effect of language and social status on the results. The report focused on the lack of qualified personnel, exacerbated by the poor pay offered for work on the reservations. While seeking best practices, the Meriam report continued the policy of providing the minimal education necessary for unskilled labor:

---

[105] Vocational education could, in certain instances, be subversive to the federal government's program of racial subjugation. Superintendent of Indian Schools Estelle Reel, who served from 1898 to 1910, firmly believed Indians were inferior, but she promoted traditional crafts, including hiring traditional Native teachers (Lomawaima & McCarty 2002, 285). Most vocational education, however, was aimed at providing agricultural and mechanical laborers for white farmers and factories, though the education was often so far behind the times it scarcely helped even for these purposes.

[106] For a history of the movements that uncovered the scandals, see Downes (1945).

[107] The full text of the chapter on education can be found at: www.alaskool.org/native_ed/resear ch_reports/IndianAdmin/Chapter9.html#chap9.

The real goals of education are not "reading, writing, and arithmetic" – not even teaching Indians to speak English, though that is important – but sound health, both mental and physical, good citizenship in the sense of an understanding participation in community life, ability to earn one's own living honestly and efficiently in a socially worthwhile vocation, comfortable and desirable home and family life, and good character.

Though some desire was expressed to improve the situation, notably by John Collier,[108] Franklin Roosevelt's Commissioner of Indian Affairs, the pathetic state of Native education would persist until the Civil Rights era encouraged higher expectations.

A 1969 Senate committee report described Indian education as a tragedy and a challenge; it led to the passage of the 1972 Indian Education Act. Among the challenges identified was a Bureau of Indian Affairs (BIA) estimate that one-half to two-thirds of Native children were limited English proficient – or knew no English at all – and few of their teachers were trained to meet their needs or had bilingual materials to assist their students (cited in Dussias 2001, 846). While the public schools were receiving federal funds to help address these needs, poor oversight led to the diversion of these funds to other purposes (Dussias 2001, 848).[109]

Two sometimes conflicting tracks were developed to address these issues: one track considered all aspects of Native education, another specifically the preservation and promotion of Native languages, including Hawaiian and the languages of the island territories of the Pacific (e.g., Guam, Samoa). The first began with the Indian Education Act, and has continued with the Improving America's Schools Act of 1994, Executive Order 13096 of 1998,[110] the No Child Left Behind Act of 2001 (Title VII Part A), and Executive Order 13592 (2011).[111] The second included the Native American Languages Acts

---

[108] Collier pushed through the Indian Reorganization Act (1934), which restored some tribal self-government and expressed his desire that Native cultures be respected, and that Native peoples be bilingual. For a detailed look at self-government and education for Native Americans, see Szasz (1999).

[109] As in the *Rodriguez* case in Texas (see above p. 117) funding for Indian education has been a problem. The Montana constitution (Article X, § 1) guarantees all citizens the right to a quality education, and the Indian Education for All Act supplements the general funds. The definition of quality and its relationship to funding came to a head in a 2005 case at the Montana Supreme Court (*Columbia Falls Elementary School District No. 6 v. State* 2005). That court found the funding inadequate to meet the constitutional promise. Three years later the 1st Judicial District Court of Montana found that subsequent legislative action had met the constitutional obligation (*Columbia Falls* 2008).

[110] The full text of President Clinton's Executive Order is available at www.presidency.ucsb.edu /ws/?pid=54747.

[111] The full text of President Obama's presidential order is available at: http://energy.gov/sites/ prod/files/EO%2013592%20Improving%20American%20Indian%20and%20Alaska%20Nati ve%20Educational%20Opportunities%20and%20Strenghtening%20Tribal%20Colleges%20 and%20Universities_0.pdf.

of 1990 and 1992 and the Esther Martinez Native American Languages and Preservation Act of 2006.[112]

The Indian Education Act (IEA) stressed the importance of tribal control and cooperation between federal, state, and local educational agencies and tribal government and communities. Inspired by the success of the Rough Rock Demonstration School in the Navajo Nation, the IEA promoted the maintenance of Native languages (22-23A-2-B)[113] within a bilingual-bicultural framework, and created a new division within the Department of Health, Education and Welfare, the Office of Indian Education, designed to take authority from the BIA (situated in the Department of the Interior).

Subsequent amendments added a teacher training component and fellow-ships for postgraduate education (1974), provisions to encourage school districts to work with parents and tribes, and specific standards for BIA schools. Special funds to improve "gifted and talented" programs in BIA schools were added in 1988, along with grants for demonstration projects. These efforts showed some promise, but a 1991 report, "Indian Nations at Risk: An Educational Strategy for Action," demonstrated that significant barriers to equal or even adequate education remained.

At the same time, the second track, the Native American Languages Act (NALA) and its progeny, sought to preserve and revive Native languages. Warhol (2012) sees the second track growing out of a 1988 conference in Tempe, AZ, a reaction to the increasing power of the English-only movement. Native-language educators feared that the English-only movement spreading through the states would endanger Native-language education efforts already underway. The conference issued a resolution, the Indigenous American Cultural Survival Act, which served as the model for the first Native American Languages Act. The NALA passed both houses of Congress only after inserting the phrase "Nothing in this title shall be construed as precluding the use of Federal funds to teach English to Native Americans," a maneuver to placate the English-only forces within the Congress (Warhol 2012, 246). The 1992 NALA added $2 million in funding for Native language maintenance and revival.[114]

These efforts had limited success. A subsequent report by the Department of Education's National Center for Education Statistics (1997), based on surveys of teachers and principals, confirmed the continuing gap between the

---

[112] The Esther Martinez Act expired in 2012, but the language revitalization funding it supported has continued. In May 2015, senators and representatives from the southwest introduced bills in both houses to reauthorize the bill through 2020 (press release from the office of Senator Tom Udall (NM), available at www.tomudall.senate.gov/?p=press_release&id=1954).

[113] The full text of the Act is available at www.ped.state.nm.us/indian.ed/dl08/ARTICLE.23A.pdf.

[114] Reduced from $5 million to induce Congressman Harris Fawell (R., IL) to let it out of committee (Warhol 2012, 248).

performance of Native students and others in standardized testing.[115] At that time more than 20 percent of Native students were classified as limited English proficient, and 40 percent of the LEP students received no specialized language services, whether they were in BIA or public schools (NCES report p. 18, from 1993 to 1994 data).

President Clinton's Executive Order 13096 (1998) established an interagency task force to promote cooperation between the Department of Education and the Department of the Interior in order to create a comprehensive federal Indian education policy. The Executive Order focused on the lack of reliable data, seeking to establish bases for future evaluations of progress, and on the need for experimentation to find effective solutions to the enduring problems.

Executive Order 13592 (2011) also focused primarily on interagency coop-eration between the Department of the Interior and the Department of Education, the repetition demonstrating just how difficult it is to ensure such cooperation. It specifically prescribes early childhood education including Native-language immersion.

Between the two executive orders President George W. Bush's signature education program, No Child Left Behind (NCLB), instituted a strict account-ability program based on standardized examinations given in English. Alongside the annual tests, a standardized evaluation program for Native Americans has been established, with roughly the same tests administered to fourth and eighth graders in 2005, 2007, 2009, and 2011. Within the NCLB guidelines, specific provisions for Native children permit instruction in Native languages, if the end result is increased English proficiency. Success is mea-sured by progress in English. Failure to meet the standards of "adequate yearly progress" in the NCLB regime leads to sanctions on the schools, with the possibility, after five years, to close down schools that fail to make progress.

The overall results are unchanged. Few of the Bureau of Indian Education (BIE) schools meet the yearly progress standards of the NCLB: only 7/63 BIE schools in the Navajo Reservation were successful in this assessment in 2003 and 2004 (Winstead et al. 2008, 58). The gap between Native students and non-Native students has grown slightly. For fourth graders, just over 50 percent continue to score "below basic" in reading, with only 18 percent considered proficient or advanced. At the eighth-grade level there has been some improve-ment, as the percent below basic has dropped from 41 percent to 37 percent and the percent proficient or advanced has risen from 17 percent to 22 percent. The highest improvement was in students attending urban and suburban public schools. Students in BIE schools scored significantly lower, a result that could be attributed to the far higher percentage of ELLs in the BIE schools (40 percent

---

[115] The full text is available at https://nces.ed.gov/pubs97/97451.pdf.

vs. 7 percent at the fourth-grade level, and 25 percent vs. 5 percent at the eighth grade level; NIES report 2012, at 58).

Even when bilingual programs were instituted, they were not necessarily successful in maintaining Native languages or achieving proficiency in English. A long-term Crow bilingual program instituted in the 1970s failed to alter the downward trend of Native-language competence: Eighty two percent of the Crow children spoke Crow in 1969, but only 24 percent in 2002 (Crawley 2008, 239).[116] The lack of progress on either goal, English proficiency or Native-language competence, may contribute to the sense of hopelessness reflected in an exceptionally high rate of suicide: at the Fort Peck (MT) reservation 25/153 students at the Poplar Middle School attempted suicide in 2009–2010, five of them succeeding (Healey 2014, 39).

Does the failure to make progress in standardized tests designed for non-Native students constitute failure of Native education? Lomawaima and McCarty (2002) argue that indigenous education as part of Native self-determination may have very different goals that are not captured by nation-wide standardized testing. Cultural and linguistic maintenance are not tested by NCLB. Local control does not resolve the issues, as the Native communities themselves are torn between the desire to preserve their culture, while providing children with the skills to thrive, not just survive, in the broader economy.

Some of the issues involved in Native American education are also illustrated by the schools offering instruction in Hawaiian.[117] Hawaiian immersion schools do not introduce English until the fifth grade, but must give their students an English language Hawai'i State Assessment that year. Even though a Hawaiian-language version of the NCLB examinations was prepared, the failure rate remained high; the test in Hawaiian was deemed more difficult than the English-language tests for the same age group. Hawaii switched to a portfolio program, all in Hawaiian, and students in the Hawaiian immersion program achieved much higher scores, 100 percent proficiency in reading and 71 percent proficiency in math (fourth graders in 2007). However, the federal Department of Education questioned the technical quality of the portfolio approach. Subsequent failures to construct acceptable translations from

---

[116] Most of Crawley's data is from the 1980s; later evidence from the era of high-stakes testing is not encouraging: a little more than 60 percent of Native students are determined proficient in reading over the period 2009–2013, with decreases across the board in the 2013 testing cycle. Only 14.8 percent of LEP students in the Native population tested as proficient on the English Language Proficiency test. These statistics are drawn from the Montana American Indian Student Achievement Data Report Fall 2014, at http://opi.mt.gov/pdf/IndianEd/Data/14INE DStudentDataReport.pdf.

[117] For a more detailed account of the evolution of education and assessment in Hawaii, see Ka'awalowa (2014). The history of the suppression of the Hawaiian language is traced in Nu'uhiwa (2015).

English or even adequate examinations written originally in Hawaiian are indicative of issues that arise when Native languages that have no history of standardization need to create a standard to meet high-stakes testing requirements.

Alaska has also received a waiver from the NCLB testing program (2013), developing its own Alaska School Performance Index (ASPI). The "adequate yearly progress" standard of NCLB would have labeled all Alaskan schools as failing, according to Learning Support Director Susan McCauley of the Department of Education and Early Development.[118] In the 2013–2014 state report card, 99 percent of fourth grade ELLs in Alaska, and 93 percent of Alaska Natives, were at the "basic" or "below basic" level in reading; in the eighth grade, 100 percent of the ELLs and 88 percent of the Alaska Natives were in those categories (compared to 59 percent of white fourth graders and 56 percent of white eighth graders).[119]

Indigenous language and English language proficiency remain elusive goals. The development of the former for the achievement of the latter has shown promise, but generalized progress has not been forthcoming. Self-determination can promote distinct goals of indigenous education but those goals vary according to the desires of each local community, and vary over time. As in public education generally, competing definitions of success complicate the work of local, state, and national authorities, and the work of legislative, executive, and judicial branches of government at each level. Quality education, or even adequate education, for Native children will always be a matter of negotiation between different theories and different powers. Education is just one piece of the puzzle when equality of Native children's opportunity is the goal. The long-term goal of equal participation in American society is often compromised by the short-term expediencies of funding and electoral cycles.

Education and Dialectal Variation in English

In 1918 the Chicago Women's Club instituted "The Better American Speech Week."[120] Children recited the pledge:

---

[118] Quoted in a newspaper article about a legislative hearing, "State Legislature No Friendly Place for Department of Education," February 15, 2015, available at www.alaskacommons.com/2015/02/15/state-legislature-no-friendly-place-department-education, last visited July 13, 2015. This is probably an exaggeration, as the percent failing to meet the NCLB's progress standard in 2012 was 53 percent.

[119] *Alaska's Public Schools: 2013–2014 Report Card to the Public*, p. 41, available at https://education.alaska.gov/ReportCard/2013-2014/reportcard2013-14.pdf.

[120] The pledge imitates the Pledge of Allegiance composed in 1892 by Francis Bellamy. The pledge and creed were described in Treadwell (1919, 604). The "Better American Speech Week" developed an idea tried earlier in Brooklyn in 1915 and at Manual High

I love the United States of America. I love my country's flag. I love my country's language.

I promise:

1) that I will not dishonor my country's speech by leaving off the last syllable of words.
2) That I will say good American "yes" and "no" in place of an Indian grunt "umhum" and "nup-um" or a foreign "ya" or "yeh" and "nope."
3) That I will do my best to improve American speech by enunciating distinctly and by speaking clearly, pleasantly and sincerely.
4) That I will try to make my country's language beautiful for the many boys and girls of foreign nations who come here to live.

In an alternate "English Creed" students would proclaim:

> I believe that my mother tongue is worthy my [*sic*] admiration, respect and love.
> I believe that it is possible for me to speak my native language correctly, fluently and elegantly.
> I believe that this takes time, patience and care.
> I believe that the use of slang kills one's power to speak fluently.

As the issues facing ELLs began to be addressed in a constructive manner, some parents and school districts applied the bilingual education framework to the education of African-American children. Standard ELLs are proficient in English, but not in the dialect commonly referred to as Academic English, required by standardized nationwide testing in the high-stakes testing programs that have defined progress and success since the passage of the No Child Left Behind Act in 2001. The primary focus of Standard English Learner legal issues has been African-American English (AAE), and in particular improving the ability of teachers to assist students who speak AAE to master Academic English.

African-American English was described by Gordon Green (1963) as the "last barrier to integration."[121] It remains so not because of the speakers, but because of the listeners: a negative value is attached to certain varieties of English, as illustrated in the work of Dennis Preston (e.g., 1996, 2009) and Purnell *et al.* (1999). The target itself is a moving one: "standard English" is

School in Indianapolis, and formally approved by the National Council of Teachers of English in 1919 (Otto 1919).

[121] Although framed in language that makes modern sensibilities wince (AAE as "illiterate speech," "the last chain that binds him [the African-American] to the past" (1963, 83)), Green's recognition of the inequalities experienced for speaking a different dialect of English seems accurate. In *Martin Luther King Junior Elementary School Children* v. *Ann Arbor School District Board* (1979, at 1378), the court evinced the same attitude in slightly softer terms: "'Black English' is not a language used by the mainstream of society black or white. It is not an acceptable method of communication in the educational world, in the commercial community, in the community of the arts and science, or among professionals." The court's assumptions were confirmed by a 1983 study of employment, reported in Gaulding (1998, 645–646); see Chapter 6, on accent discrimination.

hard, perhaps impossible, to define. Hitting this moving target is hard, perhaps impossible, to attain. Even if the speaker has mastered virtually all aspects of an imagined standard, the persistence of one or two stigmatized traits can lead a listener to categorize the speaker: an African-American who speaks with standard grammar and vocabulary but says "bof" instead of "both" or "axe" instead of "ask" will still be judged and potentially discriminated against on the basis of the one telltale feature.[122] AAE speakers are not the only victims, but the attachment of this dialect to race and the legal sanctions against racial discrimination give the approaches to AAE in education a legal standing absent for other stigmatized dialects.

The first legal challenge to the language education of African-American children was launched by parents of students at the Martin Luther King Junior Elementary School in Ann Arbor, Michigan. Citing the ESEA, the court determined that the school district failed to address the language barrier encountered by African-American students at the school, a failure that constituted a denial of equal educational opportunity on the basis of race. The first step was establishing the application of the term "language barrier" to a variety of English, not to an entirely different language[123] and the connection of the students' language to race. The next step was showing how the existence of a language barrier between the teachers and the students contributed to the difficulties students encountered in learning to read, and then how the difficulties in reading hindered equal participation in the educational opportunities offered by the school.

The court did not require a specific remedy, only that an effective one be implemented.[124] Subsequently, a plan was developed to provide twenty hours of in-service instruction to the teachers. Initially, teachers would learn to recognize the characteristic features of AAE and how they contrast with those of standard English. At the same time the teachers' appreciation for the history and background of AAE would keep them from making the value judgments common in the broader society, thus valorizing the native dialect of the students. Finally, teachers would develop instructional approaches to help students bridge the gap between their native variety of English and the variety taught within the schools. The assessment of success of the program would be based on "whether or not, and if so the extent to which, the children

---

[122] As Flores and Rosa (2015, 167) note, because the linguistic norm continues to be determined by the white listening subject, the ultimate resolution of this type of discrimination would be "to dismantle the hierarchies that produce the white listening subject"; the means to achieve this goal are vague and as hard to realize as the elimination of any prejudice.

[123] The distinction between language and dialect is not linguistic but political and social.

[124] "It is not the intention of this court to tell educators how to educate, but only to see that this defendant carries out an obligation imposed by law to help the teachers use existing knowledge as this may bear on appropriate action to overcome language barriers" (*Martin Luther King Junior Elementary School Children* v. *Ann Arbor School District Board* 1979, at 1383).

have been assisted in learning to read" (1979, at 1390). Nationwide, the achievement scores on standardized tests for reading indicate that the goal is not being met. The NAEP report card from 2011 shows that between 1992 and 2007 only three states narrowed the gap between white and black students' reading scores at the fourth-grade level, and no states narrowed the gap on reading scores in the eighth grade.[125]

The Ann Arbor case inspired the State of California to recognize the importance of other dialects in the teaching of standard English in a 1981 policy statement "Black Language: Proficiency in Standard English for Speakers of Black Language" (for a discussion of the politics behind this development, see Baugh (2000)). While the State Department of Education sought to encourage innovation in leading African-American students to proficiency in standard English, it specified that it was not interested in teaching AAE either to students or to teachers, or in the preparation of instructional materials in AAE. The new state policy did move the Oakland Unified School District to adopt that year a Standard English Proficiency program, which soon spread to other school districts around the state (Deák 2007, 107). A separate program was developed in the Los Angeles Unified School District, the Academic English Mastery Program, which includes the reading of literature written in AAE[126] and contrastive analysis exercises that put the students' native variety[127] and Standard English on an even plane. As in the bilingual classrooms, the degree to which the students' native variety of English is permitted, in reading and in pronunciation, is central, as well as the use of correction or contrastive analysis when students' use their form of English.

The familiar story of failure in a variety of educational and social goals led the Oakland Unified School District to adopt a bold resolution in December of 1996 – perhaps too bold. Following a report from the Task Force on the Education of African-American Students[128] that detailed achievement gaps for African-American students in the district, the board issued its Program to

---

[125] The black–white achievement gap report is found at https://nces.ed.gov/nationsreportcard/pdf/studies/2009495.pdf. Over the same period the nationwide Hispanic–white gap narrowed slightly at the fourth-grade level, but not at all at the eighth-grade level, https://nces.ed.gov/nationsreportcard/pdf/studies/2011485.pdf.

[126] The literature includes (but is not limited to) books written in AAE. A list of the literature organized by grade level and by student language is available at http://achieve.lausd.net/cms/lib08/CA01000043/Centricity/Domain/217/CLASSRM%20CULTURALLY%20REL%20LIT.PDF.

[127] The AEMP includes materials and instruction for African-Americans, Native Americans, Hawaiian-Americans, and Mexican-Americans. An example of the contrastive analysis handbook provided to teachers of African-Americans can be found at http://achieve.lausd.net/cms/lib08/CA01000043/Centricity/Domain/217/AFRICAN%20AMERICAN.PDF.

[128] The report noted, among other issues, that while 53 percent of the students in the district were African-American, 71 percent of the students in special education were African-American and the Grade Point Average for African-American students was the lowest of all identified ethnic groups.

Improve the English Language Acquisition and Application Skills of African American Students. The problem may just have been poor wording, but the resolution provided a questionable history for AAE and gave the impression that AAE would be taught to students and that federal resources for bilingual education would be applied to African-American students.

The historical analysis stated that "African-Americans (1) have retained a West and Niger-Congo African linguistic structure in the substratum of their speech and (2) by this criteria are not native speakers of black dialect or any other dialect of English." The first part of this is a matter of considerable scholarly discussion,[129] the second clearly false: AAE is English and its speakers are native speakers of English.

By the time of the resolution, the use of contrastive analysis and AAE reading materials was uncontroversial, already implemented in Los Angeles and many other school districts, but the Oakland Resolution gave the impression that students would be taught AAE: "a program featuring African Language Systems principles in instructing African American children both in their primary language and in English." The Superintendent was directed to "devise and implement the best possible academic program for imparting instruction to African American students in their primary language for the combined purposes of maintaining the legitimacy and richness of such language . . . and to facilitate their acquisition and mastery of English language skills." The ambiguity of the wording and a predisposition to misinterpretation on the part of critics led the general public to assume that AAE would be the medium and the matter of instruction.

The funding of the program would be from the general and specific funding account of the District, but the prospect of applying bilingual education was mentioned: "African American pupils are equally entitled to be tested, and where appropriate, shall be provided general funds and State and Federal (Title VII) bilingual education and ESL programs to specifically address their LEP-NEP needs."

The combination of these factors – scientific/historical, pedagogical, and financial – unleashed a ferocious backlash in the media[130] and among politicians. L. Preston Bryant, a Virginia delegate, proposed a bill "to prohibit any nonstandard or poorly spoken English from being taught in the public schools

---

[129] For a succinct summary with bibliography, see Baugh's page "What is Ebonics (African American English)?" on the website of the Linguistic Society of America: www .linguisticsociety.org/content/what-ebonics-african-american-english.

[130] For a summary of this firestorm, see Collins (1999) and Rickford (1999). The proceedings of a conference devoted to "Language and Academic Achievement among African American Students" add perspectives from a number of leading scholars: http://files.eric.ed.gov/fulltext/ ED430402.pdf. For a summary of the misconceptions of the backlash, see the contribution of Anna Vaughn-Cooke in that Eric Document, pp. 137–168.

as the equivalent of standard English."[131] Peter King (R., NY), a congressman who has repeatedly introduced "English as the Official Language of the United States" bills in the House of Representatives, sought to deny funding to "any program that is based upon the premise that Ebonics is a legitimate language" (House Resolution 28, January 9, 1997). These bills were never passed but reflect the spirit of the times. Jokes about Ebonics became so widespread that the Equal Employment Opportunity Commission filed a workplace harassment suit against the Federal Home Loan Mortgage Corporation (Freddie Mac) contending that sending these jokes to co-workers by e-mail constituted the creation of a hostile work environment.[132]

In January of 1997, the Oakland School Board issued a revised resolution that removed the claim that AAE was not a dialect of English, clarified that any use of AAE in the classroom was meant to assist transition to standard English, and eliminated the suggestion that state and federal funds dedicated to bilingual education could be used to assist African-American students. Eventually, the public clamor over Ebonics died down, but it is easily revived, as a San Bernardino episode in 2005 illustrated.[133]

Throughout all of the discussion above concerning education policy and law as it relates to language, it is clear that inequality resulting from linguistic difference has not been resolved. It is not just educational inequality but the way societal attitudes about language reinforce other inequalities, economic, political, and social. We have devoted the longest chapter of this book to education because it has been recognized as a primary responsibility of government at all levels, and because of the faith placed on education to meet the needs of the Republic, and to improve the lives of all citizens. The persistent gaps in achievement for ELLs and for Standard ELLs demonstrate that education can contribute to the resolution of these inequities, but unless other inequalities are addressed at the same time, education alone cannot solve them.

---

[131] "Virginia Bill Targets Nonstandard English," *Washington Post* January 3, 1997.

[132] The case is described in Volokh (2001). I have not been able to determine the ultimate disposition. Similarly, circulation in the workplace of an "Oakland Ebonics Quiz" provoked hostile environment claims against Pepsi, Morgan Stanley, and Citibank (Browne 2001, 591–592).

[133] A professor at California State University, San Bernardino, suggested that the school district might consider some use of AAE in instruction. The press jumped to the conclusion that this was a formal proposal by the San Bernardino Unified School District to introduce instruction of AAE and alarmist headlines spread quickly across the country.

5   Government, Public Services, and the English-Only Movement

The federal government and many states have a long history of offering information and services in languages other than English, including but not limited to the publication of official records in other languages. The Civil Rights movement of the 1960s and Executive Orders issued by Presidents Clinton (2000) and Obama (2011) have transformed voluntary accommodations into obligatory actions, while "Official English" movements have attempted to limit those requirements. Legally, the primary issues have been discriminatory intent and disparate impact.

Accommodation of LEP residents long antedates the invention of the LEP label. The Continental Congress published a German version of the Articles of Confederation, and a congressional bill to publish the laws of the country in German (as well as English) failed by a single vote in 1795 (Kloss 1998, 28–29).[1] In 1794, the territorial laws of Illinois were translated into French (Baron 1990, 113), but in 1810, Congress refused to let the Michigan territory publish a French version of its laws:

If Congress were to authorize the translation of the laws into the French language, they would thereby give to the translation a sanction which would entitle it to be received in the courts of that Territory as evidence of the laws of the land, and great inconvenience and confusion might result from having two separate texts for the same law, susceptible, as they necessarily would be from the imperfection of all languages, of different and perhaps opposite interpretations. (Lowrie & Franklin 1834, 71)

In the 1830s, Germans in Buffalo, NY, united to demand the publication of city council proceedings in German, a campaign led by the newly established newspaper the *Weltbürger* (Gerber 1984, 35).

Over the years some state constitutions and collections of state laws have been translated into various languages – German in Wisconsin, Iowa, Minnesota, Illinois, Texas, Missouri, Norwegian in Wisconsin and Minnesota, French in Minnesota and Illinois, Spanish and Czech in Texas

---

[1] This is apparently the source of the oft-repeated myth that German came within a vote of being named the official language of the United States.

(Kloss 1998, 100–103).[2] The legal value of translations has been contested: "A statute or ordinance has no legal existence except in the language in which it is passed."[3] However, in the early years of its statehood, Louisiana, in direct contradiction to the Congress' opinion concerning the laws of Michigan, granted both French and English equal status: "There are therefore two originals of the same strength and validity, neither can control the other – they must be taken as two laws on the same subject and construed together" (*Hudson* v. *Grieve* 1810, at 144).[4] After the 1812 constitution the French version could only be taken as advisory in the interpretation of the English, a role that has even been accepted at the US Supreme Court (*Viterbo* v. *Friedländer* 1877, at 725), noting "the greater precision of the French text." Still, "if the two texts cannot be reconciled, the English must prevail" (*ibid.*).[5]

Official notices could be published in English in foreign-language newspapers, but usually not in languages other than English.[6] In the 1850s, the city of Oshkosh, Wisconsin, designated the *Deutsche Zeitung* the newspaper of official record, though it published the official notices in English.[7] The 1898 statutes of Wisconsin provided that

The county board may order public notices relating to tax sales, redemption and other affairs of the county to be published in a newspaper printed in any other than the English language, to be designated in such order, whenever they shall deem it necessary for the better information of the inhabitants thereof, and it shall appear from the last previous census that one fourth or more of the adult population of such county are of a nationality not speaking the English language ... provided, that all such notices shall

---

[2] For a detailed record of the publication of laws in other languages in Indiana, Colorado, Pennsylvania, California, Louisiana, Ohio, and New Mexico, see Fedynskyj (1971).

[3] *North Baptist Church* v. *Mayor of Orange* (1891, at 117). The court went on to judge that "no translation, however accurate, can be adopted in the place of its original text for the purposes of construction in a legal proceeding ... a translation may be regarded as a proper explanatory adjunct of the English copy, but cannot be accepted as a legal substitute for it" (*ibid.*). However, in New Mexico, Spanish and English versions of the law were co-equal during the territorial period, with the English versions being the translations (Kloss 1998, 164).

[4] In the 1808 *Digest of Civil Laws*, the French version read "Si, dans quelqu'une des dispositions contenue dans ledit digest, il se trouve quelque obscurité ou ambiguïté, ou quelque faute ou omission, les deux textes Anglais et Français seront consultés pour s'interpréter mutuellement" (cited in *Viterbo* 1877, at 725 (footnote 1)).

[5] The Supreme Court observed in the matter under consideration (concerning a levee break on leased land) that the English text of the law was clearly a translation of the French (*Viterbo* 1877, at 727).

[6] In *Road in Upper Hanover* (1863, at 278), the court considering the official notice of road construction rejected the idea that "public notice may be given in any language that one of the parties may choose to employ." The court noted, however, a statute passed in the state assembly as the case was being considered, requiring, in certain counties, the publication of writs, orders, notices, and rules in a German-language newspaper, but only the English version had legal force. The text of the law is found in Kloss (1998, 186).

[7] This practice was upheld in *Kellogg* v. *Oshkosh* (1861), a case involving the collection of back taxes.

also be published in a newspaper published in the English language as provided by law. (Sec. 675, cited in *Hyman* v. *Susemihl* 1908, at 298–299)

However, a number of court decisions in other parts of the country specifically denied that the foreign-language press constituted a "newspaper of general distribution."[8]

The exception, as often, is New Mexico, which gave Spanish and English equal footing, requiring a Spanish version of the notice if the rest of the newspaper was overwhelmingly in Spanish (Kloss 1998, 167). The notice can be in Spanish only if 75 percent of the population within the legal district is Spanish-speaking.

The massive expansion of governmental services over the course of the twentieth century has sought to counterbalance the inherent inequalities of the market economy. One of those inequalities is language. The federal government, acting under civil rights guarantees under the Equal Protection Clause of the Fourteenth Amendment, has gradually expanded the rights of LEP persons to the assistance necessary to benefit from those services. Since the early 1980s, a contrary tendency to limit government services to the English language has been proposed but never passed at the federal level.[9] Following a pattern we have noted in other domains (see above Chapter 1), the proposed Official English legislation for protection against discrimination would consider English-speakers as the victim, offering "a private cause of action for anyone who believed that he or she had been injured by the federal government's communication in a language other than English" ("Language of Government Act of 1995," proposed by Senator Richard Shelby (R., Alabama; cited in Aka & Deason (2009, 63)).

At the state level, and occasionally at the local level, such constraints have been enacted, either as constitutional amendments or as statutes. The conflict between the levels of government takes us through the familiar ground of discriminatory intent and disparate impact.

Federal law (42 U.S. Code §1983) requires the equal protection of the laws:

Every person who, under color of any statute, ordinance, regulation, custom, or usage, of any State or Territory or the District of Columbia, subjects, or causes to be subjected, any citizen of the United States or other person within the jurisdiction thereof to the

---

[8] In *McCoy* v. *Chicago* (1889), the court upheld a taxpayer's complaint about publishing notices in a German-language newspaper, wondering "if the city may publish at public expense in German, why may it not pass ordinances and conduct its business in Greek?" (at 581). Similar rulings were issued in North Dakota (*Reuter* v. *Dickinson Building & Loan Association* (1933)) and in California (*Barony* v. *Ardery* (1934)).

[9] Almost every year since 1981, a bill has been submitted in one or both houses of Congress to declare English the official language of the United States. None has ever passed. In 2015, Senate Bill 678, English Language Unity Act of 2015, was introduced by Senator Inhofe (R., OK), and the matching H.R. 997 by Representative Steve King (R., IA).

deprivation of any rights, privileges, or immunities secured by the Constitution and laws, shall be liable to the party injured in an action at law, suit inequity, or other proper proceeding for redress.

The statute has been buttressed by President Clinton's Executive Order 13166, "Improving Access to Services for Persons with Limited English Proficiency,"[10] issued in 2000 shortly before he left office. The order equates language and national origin in demanding that "the programs and activities they [federally assisted programs] normally provide in English are accessible to LEP persons and thus do not discriminate on the basis of national origin." The measures mandated by that order were reaffirmed by President Obama and by Attorney General Eric Holder in 2011. In addition to requiring each federal agency to meet compliance standards established by the Department of Justice, the force of the order extends to programs that receive federal financial assistance, thus affecting almost all state and local governments. Compliance is necessary to avoid violation of Title VI of the Civil Rights Act of 1964 (see Chapter 1).

Some agencies recognized the need for language access quickly: the Department of Health, Education and Welfare and the Department of Justice issued regulations in 1964 and 1966, respectively (Rubin-Wills 2012, 474–475). The Department of Justice's four-factor approach to determining the necessity of accommodation has been generalized through Executive Order 13166 and subsequent guidelines.

A first requirement is that staff at the point of first contact with an individual determine the language required to serve that person best. LEP persons would then be best served (according to the priorities of the guidelines) by a bilingual staff member, or by qualified interpreters or translators.[11] All official correspondence and informational material should be readily available in the most common languages, with other procedures in place should a less common language be required. The degree of commonality can be determined by census data or by the history of requests within a given agency.

At the state level, thirty-three states confer some type of official status to English through statutory or constitutional means. In some cases it is a simple declaration that English is the official language, as in Illinois, where this

---

[10] The full text is available at www.gpo.gov/fdsys/pkg/FR-2000-08-16/pdf/00-20938.pdf. An interagency website provides information on the latest developments in access issues: www .lep.gov. Typically the federal agencies seek to avoid litigation and to work with state and local authorities in the form of "Voluntary Compliance Agreements," such as that between the Department of Housing and Urban Development and the Housing Authority of Independence, Missouri (April 2015), www.lep.gov/resources/Independence_07–13-R001-6_VCA_LE P_508_Signed.pdf?id=07–13-R001-6-VCASigned.pdf.

[11] The FAQ offered by the Justice Department correctly notes that just because a person is bilingual does not mean that s/he is competent to serve as an interpreter or translator.

statement is inserted in the State Designations Act, between the recognition of the monarch butterfly as the state insect and of fluorite as the state mineral.

A series of much more restrictive measures have been adopted in several states, some of which have been declared unconstitutional (Arizona, Oklahoma, Alaska) and reworked.[12] These measures, in similar language, mandated the use of English by the state and its subdivisions, listing several exceptions to this requirement (e.g., teaching of foreign languages in public schools, emergency services, court interpreting).

California led the way with Proposition 63 (1986), a ballot initiative driven by the then relatively new organization U.S. English, and growing out of antagonism toward bilingual or multilingual voting materials.[13] Proposition 63 was the culmination of a series of efforts to make English the official language of the state. In 1984, as soon as the Proposition 38 campaign opposing multilingual ballots was successfully concluded, Assemblyman Frank Hill introduced an official English measure in the California legislature. His initial proposal emphasized the symbolic nature, in terms similar to those in the Illinois constitution. It never made it out of committee in the Assembly, leading U.S. English to bypass the legislature with direct democracy, in Proposition 63. Sold as a means of helping immigrants to master English more quickly,[14] the ballot initiative passed overwhelmingly in 1986 (73.2 percent for, 26.8 percent against). However, the sentiments expressed by Proposition 63 were rejected by political leaders and the enacting legislation proposed by Mr. Hill never passed. Once passed Proposition 63 was invoked in an appeal of a complaint filed earlier (1984) by government employees. They believed that Proposition 63 imposed restrictions on the language they could use in the workplace (*Gutierrez* v. *Municipal Court* 1988). The Ninth Circuit disagreed, finding Proposition 63 to have only symbolic value (at 1043–1044).

Two years later Arizona chose more specific restrictions that clearly went beyond the symbolic. In 1988, Arizona voters approved with 50.5 percent of the vote Proposition 106, an amendment to the Arizona constitution (Article 28) requiring that English be "the language of the ballot, the public schools,

---

[12] The Oklahoma initiative was rejected by the Oklahoma Supreme Court before it could be placed on the ballot (*In re Initiative Petition No. 366* 2002). The Arizona constitutional amendment was approved by voters in 1998, leading to a long litigation that reached the US Supreme Court (see below).

[13] See Chapter 2. San Francisco passed Proposition O in 1983 and statewide a similar measure, Proposition 38, in 1984. These measures were advisory, because they could not contravene federal law and federal court decisions.

[14] For an analysis of the campaign strategy of Proposition 63, see HoSang (2010), especially Chapter 5 "How Can You Help Unite California? English Only and the Politics of Exclusion." Typical of this argument was campaign leader J. William Orozco's desire to prohibit sending messages to parents from school authorities in languages other than English, arguing that "if you continue to put crutches under people, they're never going to learn English." For a discussion from the perspective of a proponent of Proposition 63, see Diamond (1990).

and all government functions and actions." Section 3 stated that "this State and all political subdivisions of this State shall act in English and no other language." Exceptions were made for court interpreting, foreign-language instruction, "to protect public health and safety," and for compliance with federal laws, including assistance to LEP students insofar as the use of another language was necessary for them to make "as rapid as possible a transition to English."

Two days after the election, a state employee, Maria-Kelley Yniguez, sued to have the amendment ruled unconstitutional. The litigation over this initiative lasted ten years.[15] Ms. Yniguez worked for the state as an insurance claims manager. She frequently used her Spanish-language skills to communicate with those who came to her office, primarily to discuss medical malpractice claims against the state. She feared that the new amendment would prevent her from assisting state residents and claimed that the amendment was a content-based regulation of speech, in violation of the First Amendment, and discriminatory against non-English-speaking minorities, in violation of the Fourteenth Amendment.

The First Amendment claim was based on overbreadth, because the Official English Amendment could restrict protected speech, such as communication between elected officials and their constituents or state employees' commentary on matters of public concern (1990, at 314). The Attorney General of Arizona argued for a more narrow reading of the prohibition, distinguishing "official" communication from other communication, but his reading was not binding, just advisory. Furthermore, the court found his reading "a remarkable job of plastic surgery upon the face of the ordinance" (at 316, citing *Shuttlesworth* v. *City of Birmingham* 1969, at 153). The amendment was found to inhibit the "free discussion of governmental affairs" by denying access to information about governmental affairs to LEP persons and by denying to state employees the unfettered ability to communicate with the public. The District Court found the Arizona Amendment unconstitutional on the basis of these First Amendment issues and therefore did not pursue the claims based on the Fourteenth Amendment or the Civil Rights Act of 1964.

Governor Mofford declined to appeal, but the Attorney General and the association Arizonans for Official English pursued the matter. After a number of rulings concerning standing to file suit, a three-judge panel of the Ninth Circuit Court of Appeals and then the full court ruled in favor of Ms. Yniguez, who by that time had voluntarily ceased working for the state. The primary litigant became Armando Ruiz with several other government employees,

---

[15] The relevant decisions, in chronological order, are *Yniguez* v. *Mofford* (1990); *Yniguez* v. *Arizonans for Official English* (1995); *Ruiz* v. *Symington* (1996); *Arizonans for Official English* v. *Arizona* (1997); *Ruiz* v. *Hull* (1998).

working together in an association known as Arizonans Against Constitutional Tampering (AACT).

The Supreme Court found, unanimously, that the first interpretation of the constitutionality of Article 28 resided in the Arizona Supreme Court, not in the federal courts. The Ninth Circuit decision was vacated and the case moved to the Arizona Supreme Court. That court, in 1998, did rule Article 28 unconstitutional. Presented with the option to simply delete the offending portions of the Article (severability), the court declined, noting that without those portions the amendment was essentially meaningless (1998, at 459).

As the case in Arizona wended its way through the courts, three Alaska citizens organized a petition drive to place a ballot initiative declaring English the official language of the state and using wording almost identical to the Arizona amendment (Official English Initiative 1998, henceforth OEI). Their measure included a provision that allowed government entities to "use non-English languages ... to comply with federal law including the Native American Languages Act" (NALA, cited in *Alaskans for a Common Language, Inc. v. Kritz* 2000, at 909–910). The state's lieutenant governor excised that phrase from the final wording, which provoked a suit won by the lieutenant governor. The OEI went forward without reference to the NALA.

Voters in Alaska approved the OEI in 1998. Nine years later it was ruled unconstitutional by the state Supreme Court (*Alaskans for a Common Language, Inc. v. Kritz* 2007). The challenge was raised by several elected officials who spoke limited English or only their native language. Elected public officials and their staff could use another language "to communicate orally with constituents" (Sec. 44.12.340(a)(11)). Surprisingly, the only people protected were speakers of English: "No person may be denied services, assistance, benefits, or facilities, directly or indirectly provided by the government, because that person communicates only in English" (44.12.360(b)). As had the Arizona Attorney General, Alaskans for a Common Language argued that the law applied only to "official" language. The Alaska Supreme Court, as in the Arizona courts, rejected that interpretation, insisting on reading the text as it was written ("The English language is the language to be used by all public agencies in all government functions and actions" (44.12.320)). The second sentence of that section insists that English must be used in written documents but seems to leave the door open for publications in other languages: "The English language shall be used in the preparation of all official public documents and records, including all documents officially compiled, published or recorded by the government."

The constitutional dispute came over the obligation of state officials to use only English when communicating with residents of the state, an obligation found contrary to First Amendment free speech rights: "If all government communications must be in English, some voices will be silenced, some ideas will remain unspoken, and some ideas will remain unchallenged" (*Alaskans for a Common Language, Inc.* 2007, at 206). The Alaska Supreme Court took the option declined by the Arizona Supreme Court, using the principle of severability to decide that if the first sentence of 44.12.320 were removed, the rest of the Official English Initiative could stand.[16]

In 2014, Alaska passed a bill to name twenty native languages official alongside English, but it cautioned that this measure "does not require or place a duty or responsibility on the state or a municipal government to print a document or record or conduct a meeting, assembly, or other government activity in any language other than English" (H.B. 216). While it is not an obligation, it is now at least a possibility.

Alabama tried a different tactic. Its official English amendment (Amendment 509) did not ban outright the use of other languages, but it did require the legislature and state officials to "take all steps necessary to ensure that the role of English as the common language of the state of Alabama is preserved and enhanced" (adopted June 5, 1990). The Department of Public Safety interpreted this amendment as banning the use of any language other than English in driver's license exams, including the use of dictionaries or any aids. Martha Sandoval challenged this policy in 1996, claiming it was a violation of the national origin provisions of Title VI of the Civil Rights Act of 1964.[17] The US District Court and the Eleventh Circuit agreed, but the Supreme Court reversed, not based on the content of the law, but on the standing of Ms. Sandoval to pursue the suit.

This seemingly technical decision had nonetheless a far-reaching impact. At issue was the ability of a private party to bring suit through the judicial process. Instead, the slim majority held, private parties could sue only under the discriminatory intent standard, while administrative review – between the federal agency and the state agency it helps to fund – could proceed on the basis of disparate impact, the lower threshold of proof. Legislative efforts to allow private parties to sue under the disparate impact standard, such as the "Fairness and Individual Rights Necessary to Ensure a Stronger Society: Civil Rights Act of 2004" introduced in the Senate by Edward Kennedy, have not passed. In response the federal agencies' enforcement arms have acted more forcefully, while individuals have explored new strategies to prove intent (see *Almendares*, below).

Alabama ultimately reversed its policy and now offers the exam in Arabic, Chinese, Farsi, French, German, Greek, Japanese, Korean, Russian, Spanish,

---

[16] A dissent by Chief Justice Bryner felt that "because the initiative was carefully crafted in its entirety or impermissibly chill the right to free speech, I would hold that it must be declared invalid in its entirety" (at 226).

[17] The relevant cases are *Sandoval* v. *Hagan* (1998); *Sandoval* v. *Hagan* (1999); *Alexander* v. *Sandoval* (2001); *Cole* v. *Riley* (2007).

Thai, and Vietnamese. This accommodation was challenged by the association ProEnglish in *Cole* v. *Riley* (2007). The court ruled that Cole failed to prove that offering the tests in languages other than English diminished English's role as Alabama's common language or that offering the exam in English only would encourage immigrants to learn English more quickly. Instead, the court agreed with Governor Riley that taking the driver's license test in any language helps to integrate new immigrants into the community, which ultimately will encourage them to learn English. The issue remains a political issue,[18] but the legal dimension appears to have been resolved.

The language of driver's license exams is now all the more relevant because a valid driver's license or state identification card issued by the same agency is increasingly required for voting (see voter ID discussion in Chapter 2). Strict ID laws are now in effect in Arizona, Georgia, Indiana, Ohio, Kansas, Tennessee, Mississippi, North Carolina, Virginia, Texas, North Dakota, and Wisconsin.

The issues revolving around driver's licenses are not limited to states with little experience with LEP applicants. Hawaii recognizes Native Hawaiian as an official language, and through 2007 it provided written driver's license examinations in seven languages.[19] It stopped doing so even as the state enacted (2006) a revised statute requiring every state agency to establish a plan for improved language access by July 1, 2007. In 2007, over 4,000 people in the City and County of Honolulu took the exam in a language other than English. The state claimed that because of a change in the laws to be tested, specifically a law concerning leaving unattended children in a car, the translated tests were no longer valid and therefore the counties stopped offering them.

The Hawaii Department of Transportation (HDOT) claimed that it devoted all of its efforts to producing an access plan and did not have the resources to update the translations even though the update required only the translation of the one new question. To what extent do financial exigencies allow exceptions to compliance? Loretta King of the Department of Justice made clear that budgetary restrictions did not permit noncompliance: "Even in tough economic times, assertions of lack of resources will not provide *carte blanche* for failure to provide language access. Language access is essential and is not to be treated

---

[18] Tim James, a Republican candidate for Governor in 2010, promised that "we're only giving that test in English if I'm Governor" (a YouTube of that political advertisement is available at www.youtube.com/watch?v=eEPh_KlTyII). He came in third in the Republican primary.

[19] The original languages of translation were Tagalog, Mandarin, Korean, Vietnamese, Japanese, and Samoan, in addition to Native Hawaiian. The suit is *Faith Action for Community Equity* v. *Hawaii* (2015). After the suit was filed, the state created translations into Chinese, Japanese, Korean, Vietnamese, Tongan, Samoan, Tagalog, Ilocano, Hawaiian, Spanish, Chuukuse, and Marshallese.

as a 'frill' when determining what to cut in a budget."[20] At the time the financial exigency in Hawaii was minimal – each translation was estimated to cost $600.

The financial burden is limited by demographic considerations: the number of languages in which service must be offered depends on a four-factor analysis. Language access is more urgent if the LEP population of a given region (municipality, county, state) exceeds 5 percent or 1,000 persons,[21] and then it depends on the frequency of need, the impact of the service on people's lives, and only after these the cost of the language assistance.

In 2014, HDOT made available translations into ten languages. The question remained whether the six-year absence of such tests constituted a violation of §1983, as a supposedly neutral law motivated by discriminatory intent and with discriminatory impact. Did the failure to produce a translated exam when one could expect several thousand applicants per year to need an exam in a language other than English constitute a violation of the Equal Protection Clause?[22] Knowledge of the problem and the ability to foresee the conse-quences of a failure to act are considered circumstantial evidence of intentional discrimination. HDOT's intent to translate indicates an awareness of the problem. The Department of Justice found HDOT's explanations for the five-and-a-half-year delay in translating the tests "unworthy of credence" (p. 28 of the Statement of Interest, January 13, 2015). At the time of this writing no resolution had been reached.

Official English ordinances have been passed in counties and municipalities as well as states. Dade County, Florida, passed a language ordinance in 1980, four years after declaring the county officially bilingual. In between the Mariel boatlift increased the Cuban population in the county, unleashing the backlash ordinance that required all county meetings, hearings, and publications be in English only, and prohibited the county from spending money "for the purpose of utilizing any language other than English" (Section 1(b)). The ordinance was rescinded in 1993, by which time Latinos and African-Americans held the majority of seats in the county commission.

California passed Proposition 63, making English the official language of the state in 1986 (see above p. 150); several suburbs of Los Angeles passed their own ordinances in the next few years. After the change in immigration laws in 1965, allowing equal access to Asian immigrants, the eastern suburbs of Los

---

[20] Remarks to the Federal Interagency Working Group on Limited English Proficiency, April 20, 2009, cited in Jung et al. (2013, 43). The full text of her remarks is available at www.lep.gov /Kingremarks4_20_09.pdf.

[21] See, for example, the Nebraska Department of Economic Development "Four Factor Analysis Assessing Limited English Proficiency and Language Assistance Plan," June 2014, available at www.neded.org/files/crd/consolidated_plan/Four_Factor_Analysis_and_LAP_07212014.pdf.

[22] A federal Department of Justice "Statement of Interest" regarding the history of this case and the legal issues involved is available at www.justice.gov/crt/about/cor/cases/HI_SOI/11315_DO J_SOI_FACE_v_HDOT_DHaw.pdf.

Angeles transitioned rapidly to majority-Asian populations: by 1990, 60 percent of the population of Monterey Park was Asian-American. The unease of the earlier residents expressed itself in two related movements, the "Slow Growth" movement and the Official English movement. City Councilman, and then mayor, Barry Hatch led the Official English movement in Monterey Park, until he was voted out in 1990 (he had survived a recall election in 1987). He aligned with Patricia Reichenberger and Chris Houseman to promote English as the official language (repealed in 1990 but revived in 2013) and to place restrictions on the use of foreign languages in all business signs. They also tried to stop the Bruggemeyer Memorial Library from accepting a gift of Chinese books, disbanding the library's independent board of commissioners and slashing the budget for foreign-language materials from $11,000 to $3,000 (Fong 1994, 144; see also Horton 1995).

In 1988, the city of Pomona, California, passed a similar ordinance requiring that at least half of any public sign in a business be in English. Safety concerns were proffered as the compelling state interest for mandating English: if at least half of the signs visible from the street were in English, it would be easier for police and fire officials to locate a business. US District Court Judge Robert M. Takasugi ruled against the city, finding that the proof of such a necessity was lacking. Today, most emergency responders use global positioning systems (GPS) rather than signs to locate their destination.[23] When Carpentersville, Illinois, considered an official English ordinance, the police and fire chiefs opposed it, claiming the restrictions would endanger public safety. In 2013, the issue re-emerged in Monterey Park when an ordinance was proposed that required some text in a Latin alphabet in public signs; once again safety issues were cited. After receiving unanimous approval in a first reading in July, it was unanimously rejected in the second reading in December.

Other towns around the country have passed official English ordinances. Hazleton, Pennsylvania, passed two, one on immigrant housing and employment, the other on official English, in 2006. The housing and employment ordinance was declared unconstitutional by the federal courts, but the official English one remains in effect, as it explicitly makes exceptions for all areas where use of another language is mandated by federal law. Frederick County, Maryland, passed an official English ordinance in 2012, which was challenged in a countermeasure proposed in 2015. The opponents cited the need to encourage "multi-linguistic acceptance, tolerance and multi-cultural diversity in an increasingly global economy."[24]

---

[23] For the subsequent developments in this issue, see Chang and Killion (2015).

[24] "An Act to Repeal Ordinance No. 12–03-598 (Frederick County Official English Ordinance)," submitted June 16, 2015. The full text of the proposed repeal is available at www .frederickcountymd.gov/documentcenter/view/280941.

Generally speaking then, declaring English the official language of a state has not had severe repercussions on the provision of services to LEP residents. Federal law has supremacy over state and local law: the Executive Orders and the Civil Rights Act require accommodations for LEP residents under penalty of losing federal funding, on which all states are dependent. To pass constitutional muster the official English laws, amendments, and ordinances must include so many exceptions that they end up having mostly symbolic value. What is the symbolism? Proponents of such laws have claimed that they seek only to help immigrants participate more fully in American society. Opponents, however, view these measures as ill-disguised expressions of racism and xenophobia.

A second area of legal intervention in the language of services concerns the provision of "meaningful notice": governments and certain private enterprises must provide notice of legal action, such as foreclosure or termination of benefits, in a language understood by the recipient. Although mentioned in earlier court cases,[25] this requirement dates only to the Civil Rights Act, and even after that bill was passed in 1964, the legal implications have been determined only slowly. Until the Civil Rights era, the notion that the government had an obligation to provide multilingual materials was considered so foolish it did not merit consideration. In *Carmona* v. *Sheffield* (1971), the California Department of Human Resources Development was sued because services relating to unemployment benefits were not offered in languages other than English. In dismissing the suit the court leapt to the worst-case scenario – all services in all possible languages – to reach the conclusion that "the breadth and scope of such a contention is so staggering as virtually to constitute its own refutation. If adopted . . . it would virtually cause the processes of government to grind to a halt" (*Carmona* 1971, at 1342). A number of factors are at play: the nature of the government agency, the foreseeability of difficulties encountered by LEP individuals or communities, and the expectation that recipients of a legal notice will find a translator/interpreter to help them understand its contents.

Several of these factors combined in the case of *Soberal-Perez* v. *Heckler* (1983), in which several residents, natives of Puerto Rico but living on the mainland, claimed that they had been illegally denied Social Security

---

[25] "An elementary and fundamental requirement of due process in any proceeding which is to be accorded finality is notice reasonably calculated, under all the circumstances, to apprise interested parties of the pendency of the action and afford them an opportunity to present their objections . . . When notice is a person's due, process which is a mere gesture is not due process. The means employed must be such as one desirous of actually informing the absentee might reasonably adopt to accomplish it. The reasonableness and hence the constitutional validity of any chosen method may be defended on the ground that it is in itself reasonably certain to inform those affected" (*Mullane* v. *Central Hanover Bank & Trust* 1950, at 314–315).

retirement income or disability insurance. The initial question was one of jurisdiction: does the Civil Rights Act impose antidiscrimination constraints only on non-federal recipients of federal funding, or does it apply equally to those federal agencies that are funded directly? Enforcement of the Civil Rights Act is dependent on the threat of withdrawal of funding, but this is not possible on a directly funded agency like the Social Security Administration.

Other federal agencies that fund state and local programs, such as Health and Human Services, Housing and Urban Development, and Education (as seen in the previous chapter), have written regulations applying antidiscrimination laws to their programs and have established units to ensure compliance. While litigation is possible, voluntary consent decrees are preferred.[26] Individuals can file complaints with federal agencies at no cost, and federal agencies are required to investigate every complaint. Voluntary consent decrees between a federal funding agency and a state receiving agency have the potential advantages of cooperative compromise over adversarial confrontation and of comprehensive plans of language access over piecemeal accommodations. The drawback is that the federal agencies' commitment to enforcement varies widely according to the party in power, and agencies proceed with cases at their own discretion. Speed of action is an issue, even in the best of circumstances: relief may come too late to help the aggrieved individual. Finally, the end result for the individual victim is less appealing, as a consent decree does not provide for attorney's fees and for punitive damages.

The standard for private litigation, since a 5–4 Supreme Court decision in *Guardians Association* v. *Civil Service Commission of the City of New York* (1983),[27] confirmed by *Sandoval*, is proof of discriminatory intent, a much higher standard than disparate impact. However, individual agencies can invoke the less onerous requirement of disparate impact.

Proving discriminatory intent is not impossible. *Almendares* v. *Palmer* (2003) concerned the Food Stamp program, a Department of Agriculture service that is administered by the individual states. According to the Food Stamp Act of 1964 (7 U.S.C.S. § 2020(e)(1)(B)), participating state agencies must "comply with regulations of the Secretary requiring the use of appropriate bilingual personnel and printed material in the administration of the program in those portions of political subdivisions in the State in which a substantial number of members of low-income households speak a language other than English." Spanish-speaking recipients alleged

---

[26] For a discussion of the relative benefits of the different approaches, see Rubin-Wills (2012, 488–508).

[27] The Supreme Court cited *Regents* v. *Bakke* (1978). The initial decisions, at the District Court level (1977 & 1979), required only disparate impact. The Second Circuit held that Title VI relief required intent (1980). We will revisit this case in the next chapter, concerning workplace discrimination.

discriminatory intent on the part of Ohio's administrators of the program. The Lucas County Department of Human Resources had entered into consent decrees to provide translation assistance (1997, 1999) but had not done so. As in the HDOT case (above), knowledge and failure to act on that knowledge were found to constitute discriminatory intent.

State laws can require more than the federal law. When an individual state has an official policy specifying the situations in which accommodation is necessary, the state is expected to follow its own policy (*Wai Po Leung* v. *Employment Department* 2014). Wai Po Leung is a native speaker of Cantonese who has lived and worked in the United States for thirty years and can understand spoken English but reads it with difficulty. He filed a claim for unemployment insurance benefits in 2009, and then for an extension; when the extension was denied, the notice was sent in English, including the information necessary to file an appeal of that decision. The Employment Department's own policy requires that "All written communication mailed to LEP customers regarding agency services and programs . . . including benefits, information, adjudication, or hearings decisions – will include a multi-language service insert offering language services at no cost to the LEP customer" (at 800). The Department claimed that Mr. Leung failed to express a language preference, a contention rejected by the Oregon Court of Appeals.

Are special accommodations implied, even if not explicitly addressed? New Mexico has consistently granted rights to its Spanish-speaking population that exceed the federal minimum. Several articles of the New Mexico constitution provide for special consideration of the Spanish speakers. In *Maso* v. *State Taxation & Revenue Dept.* (2004), Raphael Maso, a monolingual Spanish speaker, was stopped for driving with more than double the legal blood–alcohol level. He received from the arresting officer an English-language notice that his driving privileges would be revoked automatically in twenty days if he did not submit a written request for a hearing within ten business days. He submitted his request almost a month after the arrest, and therefore it was rejected as too late. He claimed that given New Mexico's special accommodations for Spanish speakers, he should have received a notice in Spanish: if the constitution or the relevant statute did not guarantee a Spanish-language notice, it should have. The court disagreed, following many years of precedents ruling that people receiving a notice they do not understand have an obligation to find out what it means.

Inequality in medical care is perhaps the feature that most distinguishes American society from other countries in the developed world. While much of that inequality is financial, linguistic barriers contribute to problems in delivering effective care. In 2000, the Office of Minority Health (OMH) in the Department of Health and Human Services issued national standards for "culturally and linguistically appropriate services" in health care.[28] The need for such standards was documented by several reports compiled by the Institute of Medicine (Geiger 2003; Perez 2003) describing racial and ethnic differences in health care and its effects. Seven states have passed legislation encouraging cultural competency in health care (California, Oregon, Washington, New Mexico, Maryland, New Jersey, and Connecticut).[29]

Most medical facilities in the United States receive, directly or indirectly, federal funds and therefore are required to comply with regulations concerning accommodations for LEP patients.[30] The regulations are based on the principles of informed consent and of illegal discrimination. Since *Canterbury v. Spence* (1972), informed consent has depended on the patient's understanding of the risks involved in any treatment, rather than the physician's opinion.[31] Patients must be able to communicate effectively with health-care providers, collaborating in the diagnostic procedures and care choices. For LEP patients, the goal has been "culturally competent care."[32]

Intentional discrimination in health care is perhaps even harder to prove than in other domains as much of the evidence is hidden in private consultations. As in education, the most obvious intentional discrimination was in segregation, de jure in the South, de facto in some northern cities, for example, Chicago where African-Americans were primarily channeled to Cook County Hospital

---

[28] The OMH was created in 1990, the same year as the passage of the Disadvantaged Minority Health Improvement Act. The full document and other related materials are available at http://minorityhealth.hhs.gov/omh/browse.aspx?lvl=2&lvlid=53.

[29] www.thinkculturalhealth.hhs.gov/Content/LegislatingCLAS.asp. The Connecticut law, passed in 2013, merely requires physicians renewing their licenses to take one hour of continuing education in each of six areas, one of which is cultural competency.

[30] "Guidance to Federal Financial Assistance Recipients Regarding Title VI Prohibition Against National Origin Discrimination Affecting Limited English Proficient Persons," 68 *Federal Register* 47311 (2003), lists the following potential recipients of Department of Health and Human Services assistance, all of which would be subject to the non-discrimination policies of HHS: (1) hospitals, nursing homes, home health agencies, and managed care organizations; (2) universities and other entities with health or social service research programs; (3) state, county, and local health agencies; (4) programs for families, youth, and children; (5) head start programs; (6) public and private contractors, subcontractors, and vendors; (7) physicians and other providers who receive federal assistance from HHS.

[31] *Canterbury v. Spence* (1972). Jerry Canterbury was a 19-year-old typist for the FBI when Dr. W. T. Spence recommended surgery to relieve back pain. Canterbury was subsequently paralyzed. The Circuit Court stated that "due care normally demands that the physician warn the patient of any risks to his well-being which contemplated therapy may involve" (at 781). See Teitelbaum, Cartwright-Smith, and Rosenbaum (2012) for a discussion of the history of the concept of informed consent and the implications of patient-centered health care of the Affordable Care Act (commonly referred to as Obamacare) for effective communication concerning qualifying health plans and exchanges.

[32] In 1995, the Office of Minority Health established the Center for Linguistic and Cultural Competency in Health Care. Note also Georgetown University's National Center for Cultural Competence, http://nccc.georgetown.edu/.

or Provident Hospital. One of the motivations for Title VI of the Civil Rights Act of 1964 was to deny federal funding to segregated hospitals, thus contravening the "separate but equal" provisions of the Hill-Burton Act (1946) and confirming the lesson of *Simkins* v. *Moses H. Cone Memorial Hospital*.[33] One example of intentional discrimination in treatment was pursued by the Office for Civil Rights within the Department of Health and Human Services, the policy of a South Carolina hospital to deny epidurals to pregnant women with limited English proficiency. Disparate impact is clearer, as evidenced in a number of studies indicating that heart catheterization was more likely to be offered to white patients than to patients of color (cited in Perez 2003, 632–633).

The most common failure is the lack of adequate interpretation/translation. The standards issued by the Office of Minority Health include the advice that "the use of untrained individuals and/or minors as interpreters should be avoided." The specific qualifications of interpreters and translators are enumerated in the Health and Human Services (HHS) "Guidance" document (see above), noting in particular the domain-specific vocabulary and the regional variation of many languages (e.g., Puerto Rican Spanish does not use the same word for "mumps" as does Central American Spanish (cited in Flores *et al.* 2003)).[34] For oral interpretation a number of options are possible: bilingual staff, staff interpreters, contracting for outside interpreters, telephone and internet interpreter services, community volunteers, family members, and friends. The patient has the choice and may prefer the comfort of a familiar face, but that advantage has to be balanced against the ability to translate complex scientific vocabulary, the desire for privacy and confidentiality, and potential conflicts of interest.

Flores *et al.* (2003) offer examples of the pitfalls of interpretation by unqualified persons. This research team recorded and transcribed thirteen encounters with Spanish-speaking patients at a pediatric outpatient clinic. In these thirteen patient–physician encounters, 396 errors of interpretation were identified. Surprisingly, hospital interpreters committed slightly more errors than did ad hoc interpreters (family, friends, nonclinical hospital employees, etc.), but the errors made by the ad hoc interpreters were significantly more likely to have potential clinical consequences, such as omitting information about prior history and future treatment. A follow-up study in an Emergency Department (Flores *et al.* 2012) found that professional interpreters with more

---

[33] For more details on this landmark case, see Smith (2003).

[34] The National Council on Interpreting in Health Care offers standards for medical translators. California has instituted a certification examination for medical interpreters and maintains a registry of those who have passed (California Assembly Bill 1263, passed September 11, 2013). The full text of the law is available at http://leginfo.legislature.ca.gov/faces/billNavCli ent.xhtml?bill_id=201320140AB1263.

than 100 hours of training committed far fewer errors of clinical significance (roughly one-sixth the errors identified in other interpreters).

Courts have not been sensitive to the difference between interpretation and direct communication. In *Trejo-Perez* v. *Arry's Roofing/Builders Ins. Group* (2014), a worker who suffered a head injury after a fall from a ladder while working as a roofer was denied access to a Spanish-language psychologist, even though his physician specifically recommended such treatment. The employer/carrier instead selected a monolingual English physician, a decision the initial doctor rejected at trial because "you could get the wrong information [working with a translator]. You have to communicate with the patient" (*Trejo-Perez* 2014, at 222). Justice Thomas in his dissent took note of the medical testimony "that the presence of a non-psychiatric interpreter would interfere in the sensitive nature of the psychotherapist-patient relationship" (*Trejo-Perez* 2014, at 227). Justice Makar (concurring with the majority) concluded that "not a single law or program, federal or state, appears to create an entitlement for LEP patients to a health care provider who speaks the patient's primary language. Instead, it appears that the governing standard is that an interpreter is used when required to ensure non-discrimination in the delivery of medically necessary health care services" (*Trejo-Perez* 2014, at 225).

Written documents that should be translated into the languages of the commonly served LEP population include consent and complaint forms, written notices concerning benefits and services offered both by government agencies and by the health-care provider (including notification of eligibility criteria and rights to hearings in the case of denial or reduction in benefits), and an explanation of the right to free language assistance. Translation of essential forms into commonly served languages and the explanation of the availability of free language assistance to speakers of other less common languages constitute evidence of compliance, a qualification that grants the health-care providers with a "safe harbor" status.

Cost remains an issue. The American Medical Association asked that the HHS guidelines not be implemented because they imposed an undue burden on individual physicians. Thirteen states and the District of Columbia provide direct reimbursement for interpreter services used with Medicaid and Children's Health Insurance Program patients. However, other patients are often not covered in this way, and the cost of an interpreter, paid by the health-care provider, may exceed the fee a physician can charge. In his concurring opinion in *Trejo-Perez*, Justice Makar invoked the "cost and supply of health care resources" to justify selecting a physician plus a translator/interpreter over a physician fluent in the patient's language, though it is not clear that this was, in the Tampa (FL) area, a cheaper solution. He continued: "Claimants justifiably want medical providers with whom they can communicate effectively in their primary languages, but the supply of and cost for meeting this demand can be limited and prohibitive" (*Trejo-Perez* 2014, at 225).

The motivation for absorbing such costs lies in the liability risk for health-care providers who fail to make a bona fide effort to ensure adequate patient–provider communication. Kelvin Quan of the University of California, Berkeley's School of Public Health, studied thirty-five malpractice cases between 2005 and 2009, with over $5 million in damages and legal fees. The issue is often one of informed consent, a requirement for proceeding with treatment and an impossibility without understanding. A complicating factor is the use of children as interpreters. When a 9-year-old serves as interpreter for her parents, the minor cannot give informed consent, nor do the parents have the information necessary to do so.[35] In many of the cases described (Quan's publication pp. 10–12), patients with little or no knowledge of English signed consent forms and/or discharge instructions written entirely in English.

Since the passage of the Civil Rights Act of 1964, failure to accommodate the needs of LEP individuals has been considered illegal discrimination. However, after *Sandoval* it is much harder for individuals to obtain justice, as private claims of national origin discrimination are not permitted, and working through the federal funding agencies does not necessarily provide satisfaction. "Adequate notice," "meaningful access," "informed consent" – all of these require not just the presentation of information but its comprehension by the recipients. Equality of service depends on the quality of communication, and quality of communication depends on a mutual language. LEP residents pay taxes and have a reasonable expectation of services. The "Official English" approach, equality through uniformity, has simplicity on its side but not reality.

---

[35] The National Health Law Program website has the full report at www.pacificinterpreters.com /docs/resources/high-costs-of-language-barriers-in-malpractice_nhelp.pdf.

6   Language in the Workplace

All are created equal, but clearly individuals are different. Linguistic differences are one of the many such distinguishing characteristics. Language is a necessary component of the relationship between the employer and the employees, between employees, and between the place of business and the public it serves. Because language is so crucial to these relationships, courts have granted businesses wide latitude in employment decisions relating to language, both in hiring and firing, and in the maintenance of a safe, efficient, and peaceful workplace. Nonetheless, there are limits to this discretion when irrational application constitutes illegal discrimination, or, in case of safety, failure to warn. The employment decisions can depend on knowledge of English, or on the English-language accent of the employee. Warning of danger depends on the ability to foresee potential users and to inform them in a language they understand of the harmful consequences of misuse.

A peaceful and efficient workplace depends on the mutual respect of employees and employers and on safety issues that can have a linguistic component. As we have seen in many other areas, language itself is not protected, but language as a marker of national origin or race may be. Protections may involve the employee's choice of language, or the divergence of the employee's English from standard English. Concerns about safety, efficiency, and about the creation of a hostile workplace environment can motivate both English-only rules in the workplace and employees' rejection of such rules. Equal opportunity in the workplace depends on the resolution of these issues. Targeting explicitly discriminatory practices in the 1960s gave way to the identification of seemingly neutral barriers to equality in the 1970s and to the effects of a hostile working environment for protected classes.

The empowering legislation for protecting equality in the workplace is Title VII of the Civil Rights Act of 1964.

§ 1606.1 Definition of national origin discrimination.

   The Commission defines national origin discrimination broadly as including, but not limited to, the denial of equal employment opportunity because of an individual's, or his or her ancestor's, place of origin;[1] or because an individual has the physical, cultural or linguistic characteristics of a national origin group. The Commission will examine with particular concern charges alleging that individuals within the jurisdiction of the Commission have been denied equal employment opportunity for reasons which are grounded in national origin considerations ... In examining these charges for unlawful national origin discrimination, the Commission will apply general Title VII principles, such as disparate treatment and adverse impact.

The enforcement of this legislation falls primarily on the Equal Employment Opportunity Commission, which produced a series of guidelines to help employers and legal authorities in its application.[2] The first challenge is defining national origin (see Chapter 1, pp. 11), and then determining what constitutes illegal discriminatory behavior. Title VII claims can be based on disparate treatment or on disparate impact. Disparate treatment requires proof of discriminatory intent, prior to the employer's action, while disparate impact targets discriminatory effect, after the employer's action. Disparate treatment requires proof that the employer applied different standards and different punishments according to the national origin of the workers. The worker may choose to demonstrate that national origin was the sole reason for disparate treatment (single-motive theory) or, more realistically, that it was a contributing factor to disparate treatment (mixed-motive theory).[3]

The framework for disparate treatment litigation was established by *McDonnell-Douglas Corp.* v. *Green* (1973). The worker must establish a prima facie case of discrimination. The employer then is asked to provide a legitimate, non-discriminatory, work-related explanation for the disparate treatment. The worker can then counter by demonstrating that the explanation proffered by the employer is a pretext for engaging in impermissible discriminatory behavior. Alternatively, the employee can produce direct evidence of a discriminatory animus against a protected class, sometimes a single remark. In this case employees need to prove that the remark demonstrating impermissible prejudice was made, that it was made by a person with authority to

---

[1] The initial wording was "country of origin," amended in 1980 (Guidelines on Discrimination Because of National Origin, 45 Fed. Reg. 85632 (December 29, 1980), codified at 29 C.F.R. pt. 1606). See further discussion below concerning the definition of protected origins.

[2] The EEOC guidelines first appeared in 1970, with subsequent revisions. For a discussion of the importance of such guidelines in administrative law, see Chen (2014). Chen contrasts the Office of Civil Rights, which has rulemaking authority, to the EEOC, which does not. Ultimately, the power of the OCR in the field of bilingual education derives from the ability to cut off federal educational funding to those who do not comply, generally local school districts and institutions of higher education. The EEOC has much less powerful weapons at its disposal: the adversaries are individual corporations and the penalties much less severe.

[3] The mixed-motive approach, more realistic in most circumstances, has been permitted since the amendment of Title VII in 1991. The trade-off is that employers can then claim that they would have acted in the same way based on permissible reasons.

influence their employment, and that the remark was tied to the employment decision.

Disparate impact claims do not require proof of intent. Instead, the employee must show that a policy that seems neutral at first glance, for instance the use of a standardized test in hiring or promotions, has a discriminatory effect. In this case the employee must show that the policy or practice, seemingly unrelated to impermissible discrimination, is discriminating against qualified members of protected groups. For example, if language skills are not important in a job, but success in a test used to screen applicants for that job requires English-language competencies,[4] then the effect will be the exclusion of candidates with limited linguistic abilities in English. Because those limited abilities correlate to national origin outside the United States, the rejection of those candidates could be considered illegal discrimination.

In a disparate impact claim using Title VII, following congressional amendments to the law in 1991, the employees can specify a particular employment practice or show that a combination of practices has disparate impact on a protected class. The employer can argue that the practices are job-related and driven by a business necessity (the Business Necessity Defense (BND) so defined in the Fifth Circuit's decision in *Garcia* v. *Gloor*, discussed in the following). The employees can counter either by showing that the reasons given are a pretext, or that the employer could address the same issues in a manner that would not be discriminatory against the protected class.

We will follow the issue of legitimate business necessity and discrimination through the path of employment in hiring, promotion and demotion, and firing. Starting with hiring, employment decisions are sometimes the work of a single individual or can be made by committees or human resources personnel. The more people involved, the more complicated it is to prove a clear case of discrimination; in larger firms statistical patterns may serve to demonstrate a discriminatory process. The hiring process might involve interviews, tests, or other evaluative procedures. Under disparate impact the potential employee might contest decision-making factors which seemingly have nothing to do with the job advertised but systematically exclude members of a protected class.

A frequent non-linguistic complaint concerns physical requirements that prevent women or members of certain ethnic groups from competing for jobs, a height requirement, for example. Other jobs that have a limited language component, for instance a position as janitor, should not have a linguistic job qualification. However, the EEOC allows considerable latitude to employers,

---

[4] The landmark case for pretextual job qualifications is *Griggs* v. *Duke Power* (1971), in which African-American workers were confined to menial jobs by requirements for testing and a high school diploma which did not "bear a demonstrable relationship to successful performance of the jobs" (*Griggs* 1971, at 431).

as virtually every occupation has some communicative requirement. The linguistic qualification can be knowledge of English or, in public service positions, the comprehensibility of the candidate's English (accent). Language is a business necessity "bona fide occupational qualification" (BFOQ) if it "materially interferes with the ability to perform job duties."[5] In the case of accent discrimination cases, the decision is extraordinarily subjective, sometimes dependent on the individual judge's opinion of comprehensibility.

A much-cited case is *Fragante* v. *City of Honolulu* (1987, 1989). Manuel Fragante's education in the Philippines was entirely in English; he had worked with the US Army in Vietnam and had advanced training at military bases in Kansas and Indiana. Upon retirement from the Philippine Army, he moved to Hawaii.

Fragante applied for an entry-level clerk position at the Department of Motor Vehicles (DMV) and was placed first among 721 who took the Civil Service Examination for the position. Invited for an interview, the Department's hiring committee found his English difficult to understand, and another candidate was selected. The District Court agreed, as the judge also found him hard to understand, and the Ninth Circuit refused to intervene, though it worried that "it would ... be an easy refuge in this context for an employer unlawfully discriminating against someone based on national origin to state falsely that it was not the person's national origin that caused the employment or promotion problem, but the candidate's inability to measure up to the communications skills demanded by the job" (*Fragante* 1989, at 596).

His communication skills were supported by a linguistic expert witness. Fragante imputed the comprehension problems to "listener prejudice" (1989, at 598). Indeed, a large part of understanding is goodwill. A study of student reaction to teachers who appear Asian demonstrated that the students' assumptions about comprehensibility colored their comprehension even when the actual voice had no foreign accent[6] (Rubin 1992; we will return to comprehension issues in our discussion of language in academic employment in the following). Even in the best of circumstances, prejudice may color understanding.

The particular circumstances of the Honolulu DMV, where many of the clients come in angry, may be even more lacking in the goodwill necessary to understand a foreign accent. Since the passage of Civil Rights legislation in the

---

[5] EEOC FAQ at www.eeoc.gov/policy/docs/qanda-nationalorigin.html.

[6] In the study students listened to a short lecture recorded by a native speaker of English from central Ohio. At the same time, an image was projected representing the instructor: in some cases the photograph was of a Caucasian woman; in others it was an Asian (Chinese) woman. Though the tape was identical, students who thought the speaker was Asian performed significantly less well on follow-up quizzes: "participants stereotypically attributed accent differences – differences that did not exist in truth – to the instructors' speech ... listening comprehension appeared to be undermined simply by identifying (visually) the instructor as Asian" (Rubin 1992, 519).

1960s, consumer prejudices have not been a defense against charges of discrimination: an employer cannot, for example, refuse to hire African-Americans because white customers might not like it. Court cases have rejected customer preference in the gender of flight attendants (*Diaz* v. *Pan. Am.* 1971). However, courts have readily accepted customer preference arguments for accent.[7] Thus, the district judge's own "honest assessment" that Fragante "has a difficult manner of pronunciation" took the place of scientific evidence of comprehensibility[8] (*Fragante* 1989, at 593), an off-the-cuff evaluation arrived at even though the judge asked Fragante to clarify his testimony only one time in two days of direct and indirect interrogation.

The same issues can arise after hiring in promotion, demotion, layoff, or dismissal decisions. The importance of communication skills in job performance and safety is again the standard defense against charges of discrimination. According to its lawyers, the Nibco factory in Fresno, California, was having trouble with quality control and plant safety, problems it attributed to poor communication between supervisors and workers, and between workers on the plant floor. The workers came from many different language backgrounds.

To solve this communication problem, the company tested its employees for English proficiency. Most passed but some failed even after two or three attempts. Martha Rivera and twenty-two co-workers found the test discriminatory because their work had no language-specific duties; they had been working at the factory between two and nineteen years with no complaints about linguistic ability. The workers had limited proficiency in English (of Latin American, Hmong, Lao, and Khmer origin) and performed poorly on the test. Subsequently, they were either moved to lesser jobs or fired. In 1998, the workers sued, claiming that a test conducted entirely in English and bearing no relation to job performance is discriminatory against LEP workers, because of their national origin.

This case had many twists and turns.[9] In the first instance the court ruled that the company used impermissible questions in the discovery phase, inquiring

---

[7] See Nguyen (1993) and Smith (2005). Both Matsuda (1991) and Nguyen suggest more scientific ways to determine comprehensibility, while Smith focuses on ways of encouraging wider acceptance of diverse accents. The connection of accent to national origin discrimination is demonstrated by the fact that certain foreign accents (mainly Western European accents) are accepted while those from the developing world are not. For a scientific approach, see Lindemann (2005). She found that students characterized French-accented English as poetic (2005, 205), Chinese-accented English as "choppy" (2005, 200). For a non-scientific approach, see Brian Williams' "The 16 Sexiest Accents in the World" available at http://thoughtcatalog .com/brian-m-williams/2014/07/the-16-sexiest-accents-in-the-world/.

[8] Ultimately, Fragante took another job with the state of Hawaii; much of his work in the new position involved telephone interviews (Matsuda 1991, 1339).

[9] The relevant decisions are *Rivera* v. *Nibco, Inc.* 2001, 2004, 2006, 2010 (9th Cir.), and 2010 (U.S. District Court). The Supreme Court denied *certeriori* in January of 2011, and a settlement was reached.

about the employees' immigration status. This was found to have an impermissibly chilling effect on testimony.[10] The case finally went to a jury trial in 2008, at the conclusion of which the jury unanimously found for the company. However, the company's lawyers had used discriminatory tactics in jury selection (see Chapter 3, p. 76), which led the 9th Circuit to reverse the decision and send it back to the lower court. Subsequent legal maneuvering concerning back-pay issues further delayed a settlement, finally reached in 2011. The issue of workplace discrimination by the use of tests that may or may not be related to job performance was never, in this case, decided by a legitimate jury.

English-only rules in the workplace have been a common source of friction, though often imposed, at least theoretically, to reduce conflict and improve safety.[11] In *Long* v. *First Union Bank,* the Spanish speakers acknowledged that "fellow employees were talked about in Spanish because the plaintiffs [the Spanish speakers] did not want others to understand what they were saying" (*Long* 1995, at 942). Employers and courts have often acted on the assumption that the employees consciously choose their language for every utterance or that they could choose to express themselves solely in English. A disparate impact claim is based on the fact that the burden of English-only rules falls on a protected class, employees from a particular national origin.

In the landmark case of *Garcia* v. *Gloor* (1980), Hector Garcia, 24 years old with a 10th-grade education, worked in a lumber yard in Brownsville, Texas, at the Mexican–US border. He worked in the stocking department, but assisted sales people. He received compliments for his work and in May 1975 a bonus. Garcia had, however, been reprimanded for a variety of deficiencies (failure to replenish stock, keep inventory current, etc.).

Gloor had a rule prohibiting employees from speaking Spanish on the job unless communicating with a Spanish-speaking customer. The rule did not apply to workers away from public contact, in the lumber yard or during break times. The English-only policy was not strictly enforced, but Garcia had frequently violated it (according to his own testimony). In June 1975, Garcia was asked by another Spanish speaker about an item requested by a customer;

---

[10] Elizabeth Kristen described this as an example of "Rambo-like tactics in discovery" in which lawyers and their clients from marginalized communities are subjected to belligerent and/or inappropriate questioning. www.americanbar.org/content/dam/aba/administrative/labor_law/meetings/2011/ethics/60_kristen.authcheckdam.pdf.

[11] English-only rules are of course not limited to the workplace. They have been instituted in schools (see Chapter 4, and for recent examples, *Silva* v. *St. Anne Catholic School* (2009) and *Rubio* v. *Turner Unified School District* (2006)). For a discussion of English-only rules in schools, see Bent (2012). English-only rules have also been imposed and contested in prisons (*Sisneros* v. *Nix* 1995), objecting to a rule that all letters sent from prisoners to outsiders be in English, and in *Diaz-Wassmer* v. *Ferriter* (2011). See also *Ortiz* v. *Fort Dodge Correctional Facility* (2004) for a more nuanced policy.

he responded in Spanish. When Gloor heard this it was the final straw and he fired Garcia.

Gloor defended the English-only policy because (1) English-speaking customers objected to communications between employees that they could not understand; (2) pamphlets and trade literature were in English, so it was important for employees to develop their skills in English; (3) supervisors who did not speak Spanish needed to be able to evaluate their work. The court found that Garcia could have spoken English but chose to speak Spanish:

> Our opinion does not, of course, impress a judicial imprimatur on all employment rules that require an employee to use or forbid him from using a language spoken by him at home or by his forebears. We hold only that an employer's rule forbidding a bilingual employee to speak anything but English in public areas while on the job is not discrimination based on national origin. (*Gloor* 1980, at 165)

The court, holding that employment is a privilege, denied that employees had "a right to speak any particular language while at work" (*Gloor* 1980, at 161), nor would it equate national origin with "the language an employee prefers to use" (*Gloor* 1980, at 162). In the process of deciding this case, the court lamented the failure of the EEOC guidelines to address specifically the questions raised by English-only rules in the workplace. Those were addressed in the revised guidelines (1980), finding that English-only rules are prima facie evidence of discrimination. However, guidelines are not statutes, and the courts could still use their discretion in following them.[12]

The courts have thus established limits to the employer's discretion, though different courts to different extents. Premier Operator Services in DeSoto, Texas, offered services to Spanish-speaking customers in connecting long-distance telephone calls. Speaking Spanish as well as English was a required qualification for employment. The company instituted a blanket policy of English-only that covered all conversations in the building, even when employees were on break, or off work.

Employees were required to sign an agreement to follow the policy or face dismissal. Six employees who refused to sign were immediately fired. Two others who signed under protest and then filed charges with the EEOC were fired in retaliation as soon as the EEOC complaint was received. Five others who expressed their opposition to the policy were "laid off" or "taken off the schedule" within three months. All were replaced by non-Hispanic operators.

Dr. Susan Berk-Seligson, a sociolinguist specializing in issues related to court interpreting (see Chapter 3), served as an expert witness on the phenomenon of code-switching, in which bilingual speakers pass back and forth

---

[12] The revised guidelines were issued in Guidelines on Discrimination Because of National Origin, 45 Fed. Reg. 85,635 (December 29, 1980). See Chen (2014, 326) for discussion of this issue.

between two languages in informal conversation. She testified that denying two bilinguals the right to code-switch "not only makes the individual feel uncomfortable, but is tantamount to intimidating him or her and being punitive with such a constraint" (*EEOC* v. *Premier* 2000, at 1070).

The company president's use of the term "wetbacks," a derogatory term for Mexican-American immigrants, established a link between a national origin animus and the English-only policy. In *EEOC* v. *Premier Operator Services, Inc.* (2000), the District Court rejected the policy that applied the rule at all times on the company's premises. Given the employer's "malice" and "reckless indifference to an employee's rights" (*EEOC* v. *Premier* 2000, at 1076), punitive damages were added to the back-pay plus interest awarded to the former employees, even though the company had declared bankruptcy.

The employers in *Gloor* argued that the English-only rule was necessary in the public access part of the business because non-Hispanic customers might be offended[13] and to facilitate oversight by monolingual supervisors. *Premier Operator Services* offered no reason for its policy. In *Garcia* v. *Spun Steak* (1993), there was no customer-service component, but the employer cited one of the most frequent justifications for an English-only policy: maintaining a peaceful atmosphere between monolingual and bilingual employees. An African-American and a Chinese-American working alongside Spanish-speaking employees in a meat factory felt they were victims of derogatory, racist comments in Spanish. In response the company required all workers to speak only English while on the production line. They were free to speak other languages during breaks but were implored not to use linguistic difference to "lead other employees to suffer humiliation" (*Spun Steak* July 1993, at 1483).[14]

The Spanish-speaking employees filed a complaint with the EEOC claiming that they were adversely affected by the policy because it denied them the opportunity to express their cultural heritage on the job, a privilege enjoyed by monolingual English speakers, thus creating an "atmosphere of inferiority, isolation, and intimidation" (at 1487, citing the wording used in the guidance provided by the EEOC). The Ninth Circuit discerned in Title VII no right to the expression of one's culture. Nor did it find disparate privileges granted to monolinguals and bilinguals, as the bilinguals could still converse in English:

---

[13] Similarly, in *Pacheco* v. *New York Presbyterian Hospital* (2009), hospital patients complained that Spanish-speaking staff were laughing at them. Jose Pacheco's supervisor asked that he not speak Spanish when patients were present. The court found no problem with such a request. In *EEOC* v. *Sephora USA, LLC* (2005), the court ruled that "when salespeople speak in a language customers do not understand, the effects on helpfulness, politeness and approachability are real and are not a matter of abstract preference" (at 417).

[14] Ainsworth (2010, 247–248) claims that "In none of the reported appellate cases was there any evidence whatsoever that bilingual workers were in fact making insulting or mocking comments about their English-speaking co-workers," but a number of cases, including *Spun Steak*, contradict this statement. Such comments were admitted in *Long*.

"Title VII is not meant to protect against rules that merely inconvenience some employees, even if the inconvenience falls regularly on a protected class" (*Spun Steak* July 1993, at 1488). Finally, the court found no evidence to support the claim that the English-only policy created a hostile environment; in fact, it was imposed to remedy a hostile environment situation. English-only policies cannot be presumed discriminatory, but the court left open the possibility that such a policy might be discriminatory against employees with limited proficiency in English.[15]

This then was the question in *EEOC* v. *Synchro-Start Products, Inc.* (1999). In *Gloor*, *Spun Steak* (for the most part), and *Premier Operator Services*, the employees were bilingual and assumed capable of following an English-only rule. The unreasonable extension of the rule to employees on break combined with the expert linguist's testimony about the involuntary nature of code-switching made all the difference in *Premier Operator Services*. But what if the employees speak so little English that the English-only rule essentially renders them mute? The court found theirs a viable Title VII claim (*EEOC* v. *Synchro-Start* 1999, at 913).

What if the English-only rule is a personal quirk of a supervisor, but not authorized by policy? In *Rodriguez* v. *City of Rochester* (2014), eight city employees sued because they claimed the city forbade them to speak Spanish in casual, non-work-related conversations. A jury trial awarded each plaintiff $2,500 in damages and $2,500 in punitive damages, plus $69,000 in legal fees (July 12, 2013). The jury trial exonerated the City and Commissioner Paul Holohan, but did find that City Manager Karen St. Aubin had "impaired the liberty interest" of the plaintiffs by using her supervisory authority to require employees not to use their native language. In this case the plaintiffs were unable to prove that the City of Rochester had an English-only policy, or that it directed the City Manager to enforce such a policy. Furthermore, the behavior described was confined to a relatively short period and stopped as soon as the plaintiffs brought the matter to the attention of the City Commissioner. The District Court found that the rapid action by the city excluded claims not only against the city but also against Ms. St. Aubin.

---

[15] In a scathing dissent by Judge Reinhardt, who wished the case to be heard not by a three-judge panel but by the entire 9th Circuit, he lamented: "Once again, a civil rights principle is the loser at the hands of an unsympathetic court. In this case, by a divided vote, a three-judge panel invalidated an Equal Employment Opportunity Commission (EEOC) Guideline of national scope, upheld an employment rule that discriminates against national-origin minorities without requiring any showing of business justification, and challenged the EEOC's ability to enact rules codifying its findings regarding specific discriminatory practices. The two judges in the majority were able to do so only by improperly substituting their policy judgments for those of the EEOC and by misconstruing, or, in one instance, completely disregarding, prior case law" (*Spun Steak* December 1993, at 296).

As is often the case, protection of minorities soon was invoked to protect majorities, where the use of other languages in the workplace is considered discriminatory against monolinguals. In *McNeil* v. *Aguilos* (1993), a case heard by future Supreme Court Justice Sotomayor when she was a District Court Judge,[16] Juanita McNeil, a clerk at Bellevue Hospital, sued her supervisor, the chief nurse, a woman of Filipino origin (Marie Aguilos). McNeil claimed that Aguilos spoke Tagalog with fellow Filipino nurses, creating a hostile work environment, and caused McNeil such distress that she had to resign ("constructive discharge"). A lower-level court ruled in favor of McNeil, but the District Court vacated that judgment, a ruling affirmed by the Second Circuit (1996). The Supreme Court chose not to consider it.

English-only rules are also justified as part of marketing. The Ladies Professional Golf Association in 2008 proposed a rule that would require all players on its tour to speak only English in media interviews, victory speeches, and with amateur partners in pro-am events that are a standard part of the tour's program. Interpreters were not enough. At the time 121 international golfers were part of the tour, including 45 South Koreans, a group that is rapidly establishing its dominance in women's golf.[17] After much public outcry, the LPGA did not pursue this policy.

Accent in English has been a frequent matter of dispute in education, particularly salient in promotion and tenure decisions at universities. Typically, an American university evaluates an assistant professor after five years of service, reaching a decision whether to promote the faculty member to the rank of associate professor and to grant indefinite tenure, that is, lifetime job security. There are many variations on this pattern. A candidate for promotion and tenure is evaluated on teaching, research, and service, with the emphasis varying according to the type of university (with or without MA or PhD programs, etc.). Additionally, the university usually requests several external reviews from scholars at other universities who are competent to judge the candidate's scholarship. The first evaluation is at the departmental level, the second at the level of the college, and the final one at the level of the university.

---

[16] Subsequently, McNeil demanded that Judge Sotomayor recuse herself because of her prior position on the Board of Directors of the Puerto Rican Legal Defense and Education Fund, which opposed the *Spun Steak* ruling. McNeil felt *Spun Steak* was relevant to her case, and questioned Judge Sotomayor's impartiality, even though Judge Sotomayor had resigned from the Board before *Spun Steak* was decided. Judge Sotomayor recognized that the questions raised by McNeil were "on the cutting edge of civil rights law," but lamented that McNeil's insistence on being her own lawyer made it impossible to pursue the case as presented (*McNeil* 1993, at 1087).

[17] In July 2015, Inbee Park was rated No. 1 in the world and Korean-born players had won thirteen of nineteen events on the 2015 LPGA tour. For more discussion, see Lloyd (2009).

Student reaction is often part of a teaching evaluation, including student judgments of comprehensibility based on accent. As we have seen above, comprehensibility is a subjective matter, dependent to some extent on the goodwill of the listener. When accent is mentioned as a factor in a negative promotion decision, foreign-born faculty members have sometimes filed claims based on national origin discrimination. Several scholars have proposed using more objective manners to determine comprehensibility, such as the Test of Spoken English (Nguyen 1993) or the OPI of the ACTFL, which are evaluated by well-trained graders to ensure uniformity (as for the determination of the need for interpreters, cited in Chapter 3).

Haile Larebo was hired by the Department of History at Clemson University, South Carolina. A native of Ethiopia, he obtained his PhD at the University of London in 1991 and in the fall of that year began his career at Clemson. From the beginning his teaching was a matter of concern, with specific reference to his "pattern of speech and pronunciation" and a need "to continue work on diction." His students gave him the lowest teaching evaluations in the department. When he was denied tenure he sued the university, claiming the comments on his accent were motivated by impermissible animus. However, he had no proof of discriminatory motivations for the teaching evaluations, which dogged him throughout his time at Clemson.[18]

Sometimes the employees in these cases call on expert witnesses to support their claims of comprehensibility. Dr. Shu-Hui Wu sued Mississippi State University when she was denied promotion to the rank of (full) professor in the Department of History and received lower salary increases than her colleagues.[19] One of the factors in her negative evaluation was her teaching, affected by her accent. To pursue her case, she called on Dr. Donald Rubin, who had conducted the widely cited studies of student attitudes toward accented English in the early 1990s (see above, p. 167). Dr. Rubin found that her intelligibility was "in the desirable range for college instructors" (at 29–30) and that stereotyping by students might contribute to negative evaluations. However, the court found that jurors could decide for themselves if she was intelligible and that in any case accent had not been the primary motivation for the adverse decision. The court therefore barred Dr. Rubin's testimony.

---

[18] Dr. Larebo is now at Morehouse College in Atlanta, Georgia. The "Rate My Professor" website includes several student comments about his accent. www.ratemyprofessors.com/ShowRatings .jsp?tid=1053172.

[19] The case is Wu v. *Mississippi State University* (2014). The University's website indicates that she was promoted to full professor. A student rating site includes several comments about her English, www.koofers.com/mississippi-state-university-msstate/instructors/wu-804419/, including one that states "she bearly [sic] speaks English."

Accent issues arise at other levels of education as well. Olga Forsythe, a native of Cuba, was not reappointed in the Hays, Kansas, school district, in part because students found her accent difficult to understand. That she had a Spanish-speaker's accent when speaking English was not disputed, but she was hired to teach Spanish. The court ruled in favor of the district (*Forsythe v. Board of Education* 1997).

Accent discrimination is not necessarily directly related to geographic origin: it can be a case of racial discrimination (African-American) or, more recently, sexual orientation.[20] In *US* v. *Habersham Properties*, an apartment complex was accused of racial discrimination on the basis of accent: when potential renters with an African-American accent called to inquire about available apartments, they were told that none were available; when potential renters with "white" accents called, they were invited to visit available units. The agent claimed it was just "poor salesmanship" (at 1373); the government found it racial discrimination through linguistic stereotyping.

Sounding gay is associated with sounding feminine, and the association of discrimination with behaving like a woman opens the door for a claim of sex discrimination: "Sex stereotyping is central to all discrimination: Discrimination involves generalizing from the characteristics of a group to those of an individual, making assumptions about an individual because of that person's gender, assumptions that may or may not be true" (*Henderson* 2013, at 16, citing *Centola* 2002). Brian Prowel worked as a machine operator for Wise Business Forms in Butler, Pennsylvania. He claimed that his high voice along with other traits associated with femininity led to harassment by his co-workers and ultimately to his layoff. The District Court found no basis in Title VII for protecting sexual orientation, but the Third Circuit vacated most of this ruling and remanded it to the lower court for a jury to decide.

In employment decisions, it is extremely difficult to overcome the employer's prerogatives relating to language. Unlike other areas of discrimination law, customer preference or, in the case of education, student preference – even if it might be an expression of prejudice – is not excluded, in the spirit of the business maxim, "the customer is always right." Communication barriers can usually be overcome with an accommodating attitude on both sides, but when that fails it is the speaker who is expected to bend, not the listener, the bilingual not the monolingual.[21]

Language is rarely the sole issue in such cases. In *Gloor*, Hector Garcia already had a couple negative comments in his work record. In *Spun Steak*,

---

[20] For African-American accent, see *U.S.* v. *Habersham Properties* (2003). For gay accent discrimination, see Castle (2013). A key case is *Prowel* v. *Wise Business Forms* (2007, 2009).

[21] Rodriguez (2006, 1714) argues that "the process of absorbing the cultural consequences of immigration must involve shared burdens" and specifically calls for burden shifting between the majority and the minority.

Priscilla Garcia and Maricela Buitrago were accused of using their non-English language to mock fellow workers; rudeness was really the issue. In *Wu,* the quality of placement of her publications was questioned. In *Prowel*, the company attributed his layoff to his inefficiency as a worker along with a downturn in business. After the *Price-Waterhouse*[22] decision (1989), the courts ask "would the employer have made the same adverse employment decision without the language/national origin component?" Stray comments that reflect the employer's prejudice are not enough. The comments must be made at a time close to an adverse decision by someone with authority to make such a decision. Proving causation is the key requirement, a standard, like proving intent, that is difficult to meet.

Workplace safety is frequently invoked as one reason for an English-only law. Such a policy might have saved the tragedy described in *Exxon* v. *Roberts* (1986).[23] However, an English-only policy has no effect if the employees hired speak no English and yet are given instructions only in that language. An employer has an obligation to warn of dangers in a language the worker understands.

Armando Campos was raised in Portugal and emigrated to the United States in 1971. He worked for Theurer Atlantic, assembling tires for truck trailers, placing a tire plus inner tube on a three-piece rim assembly, and then putting the assembled tire in a steel safety cage to prevent injuries in case the assembled parts separated under pressure. Then he would insert air into the tire.

---

[22] Ann Hopkins was a senior manager in the accounting firm of Price-Waterhouse, working at their Office of Government Services in Washington. In the process of being considered for partner, some voting partners commented on her interpersonal skills: overly aggressive, unduly harsh, difficult to work with, impatient with staff. Some of these comments seemed to come from the perspective that she behaved "too much like a man." She was described as "macho" and used too much profanity. To improve her chances for partnership she was told "to walk more femininely, talk more femininely, dress more femininely, wear make-up, have her hair styled, and wear jewelry." The District Court judge in the case found that the firm's decision was based on too narrow a definition of proper behavior by a woman, and thus constituted sex discrimination. Sexual stereotyping is not permissible: "an employer who acts on the basis of a belief that a woman cannot be aggressive, or that she must not be, has acted on the basis of gender" (at 250). The Court of Appeals ruled that if the firm could demonstrate that it would have reached the same conclusion even without the impermissible comments, then it could proceed as it wished. Only if the discriminatory comments were decisive could the court favor the plaintiff; mere presence of such discriminatory comments was insufficient. The question for the Supreme Court was the nature of the necessary evidence. Ultimately (1990), she was awarded partnership and back pay, retiring from the company in 2002. See Hopkins (2005).

[23] Two oil drilling teams needed to collaborate in the removal of some heavy tools. One team spoke only Spanish, the other only English: "Proper communication between the crews was essential for them to understand and coordinate their actions. It was Exxon's responsibility to coordinate the two crews' actions but Exxon's representative . . . did not know if the two crews could communicate and did nothing to ensure that they could" (*EXXON* 1986, at 867). Twenty-three-year-old David Roberts was killed; his widow and daughter sued and were awarded over $1 million for pecuniary loss, loss of companionship, and mental anguish.

He was injured on November 1, 1978. He noticed that a locking element on the rim components was opening and feared a big accident. He reached in to the steel cage to try to disengage the hose. The assembly exploded as he did so and he was injured. Firestone had manufactured the rim assembly. Theurer had made the protective cage. Firestone had delivered manuals concerning correct usage to Theurer. Firestone also provided a chart that was hung on the wall at Theurer, recommending the use of a remote valve. The written warnings were of no use to Campos, who was illiterate in both Portuguese and English.

Campos had received some oral instructions from his supervisor. A previous accident, in July 1972, under similar circumstances, had occurred. Campos thought Firestone was liable on two counts: improper design and failure to warn. The improper design argument was rejected by the jury. Inadequate warning was accepted by the jury and he was awarded $255,000. Firestone appealed and won the appeal from a divided appeals court. It was then forwarded to New Jersey's Supreme Court (*Campos v. Firestone* 1984).

The expert witness for the defendant claimed that some type of graphic or symbolic warning should have been created, in anticipation that illiterate people would be working with such machines. The expert admitted that such a warning was hardly foolproof, even if backed up with an oral explanation of the symbolic warning.[24] The company claimed that there is no duty to warn when the danger is obvious and the user is knowledgable.

The role of language in workplace safety is, in such cases, not ruled by civil rights legislation but by the law of torts. Torts law covers injuries and other harm, inflicted intentionally, by negligence, and by product liability. The linguistic element enters in the nature of the warnings. In testing the need and the adequacy of a warning, the manufacturer is deemed to know the dangerousness of the product and is responsible for making a reasonable guess about the possible users. How obvious a danger is it to the people who are likely to be using it? "In view of the unskilled or semi-skilled nature of the work and the existence of many in the work force who do not read English, warnings in the form of symbols might have been appropriate, since the employee's 'ability to take care of himself' was limited" (at 208).

In another case, Jesus Favala operated a plastic cutting machine known as a pelletizer. His hands got caught in the pelletizer, resulting in injury. No warning labels were present on the machine. The manufacturer of the

---

[24] "We note that although symbols and pictograms can be used effectively to warn that a substance is flammable or toxic, or to explain its preparation and use (see C.F.R. 107.20(b) (1993) [preparation of infant formula]), it is doubtful that they are at present able to convey the more complex warning information typically required for nonprescription drugs" (*Ramirez* 1993, at 545).

machine contested a jury award to Favala,[25] in part because Favala was illiterate in English, rendering English-language warnings on the machine useless. The judge thought of other solutions that might have been pursued, such as having someone translate the warnings or providing multilingual warnings, and denied the company's request.

In a country where a fifth of the population speaks a language other than English at home, many unable to read English at all, it is likely that most products will reach at least some limited-English-proficient users or consumers. While there are several hundred languages spoken by these people, the overwhelming majority of the LEP population could be served by warnings in just a few languages (Spanish, Chinese, Vietnamese, Korean, French/Haitian Creole).[26] The obligation becomes all the more pressing when the company advertises its products in a given language but fails to provide warnings in that language.

Designing an adequate warning in one language is already a murky area of the law, as adequacy has many components. Adequacy is partly addressed by the quantity of information and the design of warning, partly by consideration by the characteristics of potential users or consumers, an expectation of "reasonableness." Latin (1994, 1195) argues instead that actual consumer behavior rather than a notion of rational or reasonable behavior should be the standard: "Product warnings and other disclosure mechanisms can be effective only when the intended recipients are able to receive, comprehend, and act upon the information imparted." Warning in other languages is generally welcomed but not required, as in the Food and Drug Administration's (FDA) guideline that labeling must be in English, and "labeling to meet the needs of non-English speaking or special user populations" is encouraged, "so long as such labeling fully complies with agency regulations" (cited in Cox 1993, 524).

One of the most commented cases in labeling standards is *Ramirez* v. *Plough* (1993).[27] On March 12, 1986, Jorge Ramirez was less than 4 months old. He had a cold and his mother gave him Saint Joseph's Aspirin for Children (SJAC),

---

[25] *Favala* v. *Cumberland Engineering* (1995). Two juries had come to the same conclusion. The company asked that the judge overrule the second jury verdict, a procedure that requires the judge to give all benefit of the doubt to the plaintiff (Favala). Sealing (2001) cites a number of other cases with similar concerns.

[26] The American National Standards Institute issued ANSI Z535.4 (2011), which describes acceptable formats for labels, suggesting but not requiring multilingual labels:

The selection of additional languages for product safety signs is an extremely complex issue. Experts suggest that nearly 150 languages are spoken in the United States and millions of Americans speak a language other than English in their homes. If it is determined that additional languages are desired on a safety sign, the following formats should be considered. In all examples, the use of symbols is strongly encouraged in order to better communicate the sign's hazard information across language barriers.

[27] For extended discussion of this case, see Dillard (1994), Cox (1993), Baldwin (1995), Sealing (2001), Labadie-Jackson (2008).

even though the warning label stated that children under two should take this medication only under direction from a doctor. His mother gave him three tablets. On March 16 the mother took him to the hospital. The doctor recommended that she use Dimetapp or Pedialyte (non-aspirin products), but she continued to give her son SJAC. As a result he developed Reye's syndrome, resulting in severe neurological damage, blindness, spastic quadriplegia, and developmental disabilities.

An English-language warning appeared on the package received by Jorge's mother, Rosa Rivera. She was from Mexico and could not read English, although she could read Spanish. She did not ask anyone to read the warnings, although there were people in the household who could read English. She had learned about SJAC from a friend and had not been influenced by advertising, either in Spanish or in English. The pharmaceutical company claimed that it had no duty to warn of the dangers of aspirin in languages other than English. Lawyers for the boy claimed that it did have this obligation, since it was advertising in Spanish to Hispanic markets in New York and Los Angeles, and was particularly popular in the Latino population (twice the sales of non-Hispanic neighborhoods according to the company's own surveys).

The dispute then hinges on the adequacy of the warning. Since Plough knew that non-English-literate Hispanics would be using the product, the court had to determine if the failure to warn in Spanish constituted an unreasonable failure to act. The standard is that of a "reasonably prudent person in similar circumstances."

The company claimed that meeting FDA standards was enough. The FDA states that it "encourages the preparation of labeling to meet the needs of non-English-speaking or special user populations so long as such labeling fully complies with agency regulations."[28] Only products distributed in Puerto Rico are required to have non-English labeling. If any part of the label is in a foreign language, then all the required elements of the label, including warnings, must be in the foreign language.

California law already required foreign-language warnings and information in a number of circumstances (unemployment insurance, emergency telephone systems, etc.). Certain types of commercial transactions between private citizens also require information in languages other than English (consumer credit, door-to-door salesmen). By defining those areas clearly, the legislature limited

---

[28] The FDA had required Spanish in some materials, but had abandoned this because accurate translations were too hard to obtain. "The burden of including warnings in so many different languages would be onerous, would add to the costs and environmental burdens of the packaging, and at some point might prove ineffective or even counterproductive if the warning inserts became so large and cumbersome that a user could not easily find the warning in his or her own language."

its mandate, implicitly stating that in other circumstances foreign languages were not required.

Multilingual labeling for prescription drugs is not required nationally, but it is offered in some areas. Bailey *et al.* (2009) performed a four-state survey of pharmacies to determine factors in offering multilingual labels. More than half of the pharmacies had no or little translation capacity, and a majority of those that did used computer translation services. In general, computer translation services are notoriously inaccurate, though with the limited vocabulary of pharmaceutical transactions, the record might be better. Sharif and Tse (2010) found an unacceptably high risk of mistranslation. Computer translation programs continue to improve, but they are still far inferior to human translations.

Better options are offered by translation services that have online compilations of translated instructions for thousands of prescription drugs. New York City (Language Access Pharmacies Act 2009) requires that chain pharmacies offer translations of medical instructions in seven languages other than English: Spanish, Chinese, Korean, Russian, Haitian Creole, Italian, and Polish. A New York state-wide "SafeRX" program, instituted in 2013, offers similar protections for speakers of four languages (Chinese, Italian, Russian, and Spanish).

The dangers of monolingual warnings are not just physical/medical: the potential for consumer fraud through linguistic means was illustrated by the subprime mortgage crisis, in which some companies specifically targeted non-English speakers, misrepresenting orally in the client's language the mortgage products and their dangers and providing the clients the real information in forms written only in English.[29] The Government Accountability Office issued a report in 2010 noting the higher dependence of limited English speakers on non-bank financial services, with a corresponding vulnerability to fraud in unregulated or underregulated transactions.[30]

Throughout this volume we explore the extent to which linguistic differences create inequalities. The workplace requires communication, between the employer and the employee, between employees, and between companies and consumers. Communication in a single language is simpler for the native

---

[29] See, for example, *Bojorquez* v. *Gutierrez* (2010). Bojorquez, who could not read English and had limited literacy in Spanish, was issued a subprime mortgage in 2005. All of the oral interactions were in Spanish, but all the documentation was in English. After his default, collection letters were sent in Spanish. For further discussion of how African-Americans and Latinos were especially affected by the subprime crisis, see Rugh (2012).

[30] "Factors Affecting the Financial Literacy of Individuals with Limited English Proficiency," May 2010, available at www.gao.gov/new.items/d10518.pdf.

speaker of the dominant language, but it can cause varying degrees of discomfort, miscomprehension, or uncomprehension for others. The legal system tries to determine the boundaries of permissible and impermissible constraints on language choice, invoking reasonableness to people who are not always so inclined; goodwill is in short supply. A single language can divide as well as unite a multilingual economy.

7   Conclusions

In his first inaugural address (1801),[1] Thomas Jefferson enunciated what to him was a "sacred principle" of republican government, "that tho' the will of the majority is in all cases to prevail, that will, to be rightful, must be reasonable; that the minority possess, their equal rights, which equal laws must protect, and to violate would be oppression." In the same address, Jefferson speaks of "our equal right to the use of our own faculties, to the acquisitions of our own industry, to honor and confidence from our fellow citizens, resulting not from our birth, but from our actions and their sense of them." He foresees many of the issues we have dealt with in the preceding pages, the relationship between the majority and minorities, the veneration of equality, for all (as liberty to pursue our individual happiness), for minorities (as rights that protect the minority), and procedurally (through a respect for laws). This equality does not deny material difference, as acquisitions earned through effort are natural, as are the differences in our innate faculties.

From the earliest days of the Republic, equality and liberty have been supreme virtues in American ideology, necessary components of a legitimate democracy. Both are served by justice, a process of rational decision-making. Equality has natural constraints: we are all born unequal in one manner or another. Justice is a matter of deciding rationally the ways in which we *should* be equal, and by what procedures we should pursue the redistributions necessary to create equality in those domains.[2] Liberty also has natural constraints: our freedom does not extend to committing crimes. Justice is a matter of

---

[1] This text went through several versions, which themselves are instructive. The initial manuscript: "The succesful majority too will keep in mind that tho' their will is to prevail, that will, to be rightful, must be reasonable: the minority retain their equal rights, which equal law must protect, and to violate would be tyranny." In a second attempt he phrased it this way: "all too will bear in mind this sacred principle, that tho' the will of the majority is in all cases to prevail, that will, to be rightful, must be reasonable; that the minority possess their equal rights, which equal laws must protect, & to violate would be oppression."

[2] Rawls (1971, 7): "justice is ... the way in which the major social institutions distribute fundamental rights and duties and determine the division of advantages from social cooperation." As Allingham (2014) points out, contemporary Western theories of justice are based on laissez-faire capitalism and differ according to which factors of differentiation between individuals are deemed morally arbitrary.

deciding rationally the limits of our liberty. The rationality of justice depends on a sense of fairness, a confidence in an impartiality born of higher principles. Reason, in a social context, is a perception rather than a reality, a term whose meaning is constantly negotiated. So too are the meanings of equality, liberty, and justice.

The negotiation of meaning takes place in language. There is no level playing field of language, as we judge others by their language and through our language. Language is a fundamental inequality of any society. This is all the more so in a multi-ethnic society at a time of mass migrations. The inability to use one's native language is a substantial disadvantage to any member of a given society, a liberty denied and an inequality imposed in the name of efficiency. Differences in the majority language, English, likewise create inequalities that education tries, with only limited success, to overcome. By confronting the foundation of equal participation in a society – in a real society not a utopia – this study of linguistic inequalities challenges philosophical visions of equality, liberty, and justice.

The achievement of equality, given historical and natural inequalities, requires some redistribution, but what is redistributed and how are matters of great contention. Many goals have been proposed: equality of property, equality before the law, equality of opportunity, equality of welfare (in the sense of well-being), equality of happiness among others. Each type of equality is subjective. The negotiation between subjective conceptions of equality is necessarily political. The way to achieve goals of equality, supposing that agreement on the goals is possible (a utopian vision), requires a procedure dependent, for its success, on agreement concerning what constitutes fairness. Politics, the participation in the negotiation of these agreements, is necessarily linguistic. The redistribution of linguistic capital, effected through court cases, statutes, executive orders, and other legal means, is a necessary first step toward all the other equalities.

Linguistic inequality is a blind spot of contemporary political philosophy. The social contract assumes a linguistic equality that does not exist, a fatal flaw in much political philosophy. In a volume on deliberative democracy and public discourse in America (Rodin & Steinberg 2003), leading public intellectuals say nothing about linguistic inequality or linguistic communities, though language is the medium of all deliberation.

John Rawls, in his *Theory of Justice* (1971, 44), posits an "original position" in which rational people in a contractual situation come to common agreement.[3] Later he acknowledges the problems created by this assumption:

---

[3] "It seems reasonable to suppose that the parties in the original position are equal. That is, all have the same rights in the procedure for choosing principles; each can make proposals, submit reasons for their acceptance, and so on" (1971, 19). It is hard to imagine that such equality existed even in the dawn of human existence, and certainly it was absent in the framing of the

"since the ideas of justice regard persons as normal and fully cooperating members of society over a complete life, and having the requisite capacities to do this, there arises the problem of what is owed to those who fail to meet this condition, either temporarily or permanently." The social primary goods that constitute his measure of justice, both the means (freedom, liberty) and the ends (wealth, self-respect), require negotiation that can only happen through language (Rawls 2001, 58–61).

The basis for agreement on justice and fairness, Rawls states, is to start from some fixed points, such as rejection of religious intolerance and racial discrimination, and then to find the principles that will incorporate those fixed points and can be applied to less certain questions. But religious intolerance and racial discrimination have hardly been fixed points of agreement, either historically or even in the present day.[4] The fixed points are further destabilized by language and linguistic difference. The social contract as conceived in the philosophical tradition depends on linguistic equality.

Brian Barry has taken a very different approach to equality and justice, following his philosophical preference for universality. He fears that

> In advocating the reintroduction of a mass of special legal statuses in place of the single status of uniform citizenship that was the achievement of the Enlightenment, multiculturalists seem remarkably insouciant about the abuses and inequities of the *ancien régime* which provoked the attacks on it by the Encyclopedists and their allies. It is not so much a case of reinventing the wheel as forgetting why the wheel was invented and advocating the reintroduction of the sledge. (2001, 11)

He would prefer a kind of ahistorical universalism. In particular, he advocates pragmatic solutions to inequality based on classifications, but not on classes (as

American political system. Only adult white males with property could participate in the fashioning of the Constitution and, for well over a century, in the jurisprudence that followed.

[4] The French example of a "facially neutral" policy of secularism in fact driven by religious intolerance and American examples of racial profiling and of religious freedom as a license for intolerance cast serious doubt on the ability of reasonable people to agree to be rational, or to agree on what constitutes rationality. A most recent example is a decision in Chalon-sur-Saône to ban alternatives to pork in school lunches. To recognize group difference, the Jewish and Moslem interdiction of eating such meat is perceived as against the Republican ideal of strict equality. The president of the political party UMP (and former president of the French Republic) Nicolas Sarkozy supported this policy stating "Il y a une crise républicaine grave. La République, c'est la laïcité, et la laïcité ne doit pas souffrir d'exception" [There is a serious crisis of the Republic. The Republic is secular, and secularism can admit no exceptions]. We will never know if Catholic students in Chalon will be required to eat meat on Good Friday, because, in the secular Republic, Good Friday is a school holiday. ("Laïcité à l'école: du vivre-ensemble à l'exclusion," an article by Aurélie Collas in *Le Monde*, March 24, 2015, http://abonnes.lemonde.fr/religions/article/2015/03/24/laicite-a-l-ecole-du-vivre-ensemble-a-l-exclusion_4600133_1653130.html). The anticlericalism of the French Enlightenment has been transformed, by a linguistic sleight of hand, into religious prejudice. Similarly, in the United States, state Religious Freedom Restoration Acts have attempted to legalize anti-gay discrimination, though negative publicity and economic threats have occasioned a retreat from this type of legislation.

we discussed in Chapter 1, p. 12). Redistribution in the name of equality requires recognition of groups. The way Barry defines egalitarianism refuses such recognition. In this he follows closely the French definition of equality, one that denies any minority group recognition. Such majoritarianism masks prejudice behind lofty philosophical principles.

Even those who grant a larger importance to historical context and allow for individual difference rarely if ever consider the problems raised by language. The "seriously problematic exclusions" Amartya Sen (2009, 90) finds in Rawls do not mention language. Sen, following Arrow (1951), notes how little information is involved in democratic political decision-making. It is surprising, therefore, that he does not follow up on the role of language and linguistic difference in contributing to the disconnect between rationality and democracy that presents such a challenge to justice in contemporary America (2009, 92–93).[5] In a more optimistic vein, also within the "capabilities" approach to justice, Martha Nussbaum (2006) lists three problems for social contract theory (disabilities, nationality,[6] and species), but linguistic equality is not mentioned among the "Central Human Capabilities" even though it is crucial to her seventh category, affiliation.[7]

Alasdair MacIntyre acknowledges that every individual has constructed a (more or less) coherent way of judging from "an amalgam of social and cultural fragments," of which language is an element. He addresses rhetorical skill as an element of linguistic power, noting that one of the attractions of blind faith is a suspicion that those who engage in rational argument "exercise a kind of power which favors their own interests and privileges, the interests and privileges of a class which has arrogated the rhetorically effective use of argument to itself for its own purposes" (1988, 5).[8] Language as a weapon thus divides even speakers of the same language, all the more so speakers of different languages within the same political community.

---

[5] Sen (2009, 119–122) does address the conflict between the conformity that is the foundation of linguistic structures and the creativity of expressing new ideas. He focuses primarily on the difficulty of establishing objectivity through language, and thus on the ability to convince another of the reasonableness of one's argument.

[6] Under nationality Nussbaum considers only transnational law (between states), not national origin as understood in American jurisprudence.

[7] Nussbaum (2006, 76–78). Earlier, she notes exclusions from the social contract of people thought not to be productive: the elderly, children, even women (2006, 33). This would not exclude speakers of languages other than English in the United States, as these are frequently extremely productive, if also frequently undercompensated, members of our society.

[8] People of faith are equally capable of the rhetorically effective use of argument. Abuse of rhetorical devices was the central point of Orwell's *Animal Farm* (1945). He catalogues the particular deficiencies of political language in "Politics and the English Language," attributing the misuse of language to an aversion, on the part both of politicians and of their constituents, to confronting the brutality of their thoughts, to the opposition between stated political goals and the means to achieve them: "political language has to consist largely of euphemism, question-begging, and sheer cloudy vagueness" (1946, 261).

MacIntyre's solution to the problem of finding a common rationality is to go beyond the fragmented universality of the Enlightenment[9] into historical traditions in which the standards of rational justification are transmitted and improved upon by succeeding generations. In contemporary societies, however, there is not one historical tradition but many,[10] and each is expressed in a different linguistic tradition. Through the study of these traditions, MacIntyre proposes, one can resolve the differences between seemingly incompatible traditions, and the first step in understanding these traditions is learning their language, which leads him to consider issues of translation.

He opposes his traditions-based approach to what he terms "cosmopolitan modernity," which he defines as "the confident belief that all cultural phenomena must be potentially translucent to understanding, that all texts must be capable of being translated into the language which the adherents of modernity speak to each other" (1988, 327). This linguistic hubris has three bad outcomes: (1) the belief that one does not need to understand a foreign language to understand a foreign culture (both as a student and as a teacher); (2) the confidence that one can negotiate without understanding the language of the interlocutor; and (3) "the willingness to allow internationalized versions of such languages as English, Spanish and Chinese to displace both the languages of minority cultures and those variants of themselves which are local, dialecticized languages-in-use" (1988, 328).

When he gets around to discussing translatability, however, he takes this issue out of the political realm, out of the relationship of minorities to majorities, and away from the use of languages as weapons of domination ("Tradition and Translation," 1988, 370–388). Language, as we have seen, is an essential part of the relationship between communities within a given political unit and also a key component in "distributive justice." MacIntyre's example of Protestant and Catholic names for a single town in Northern Ireland illustrates the incommensurability of linguistic traditions; naming is often included in international treaties that mention linguistic rights.

The equality of linguistic capital is also fundamental to Jürgen Habermas' discursive and intersubjective determination of reason. Here the emphasis is on the process of forming a common will, rather than on a belief in a universal reason. This approach to reason assumes free and equal people participating in the process, even as Habermas wonders if "the discursive social relations

---

[9] The Enlightenment's promise of universal rationality is belied by the variety of "principles ... which would be found undeniable by all rational persons" proposed by its successors: "One kind of answer was given by the authors of the *Encyclopédie*, a second by Rousseau, a third by Bentham, a fourth by Kant, a fifth by the Scottish philosophers of common sense and their French and American disciples" (MacIntyre 1988, 7).

[10] MacIntyre acknowledges that "not all traditions ... have embodied rational enquiry as a constitutive part of themselves" (*ibid.*).

assumed for an association of free and equal citizens ... are at all possible under the conditions for the reproduction of a complex society" (1996, 302–303).[11] In his early years Habermas spoke of the "liberal model of the bourgeois social sphere" ([1962] 1989, xx). Habermas is thus aware of the disparity between reality and such democratic ideals, but the focus is on manipulation of political opinion through mass media rather than on linguistic difference within the community. Thus, he counts on a "suspicious, mobile, alert, and informed public" (1996, 441–442) to intervene against corporatist decision-making, but he does not address the foundation for such intervention in linguistic equality.

Focusing on feminist issues Nancy Fraser (1990) noted a number of short-comings in Habermas' model, shortcomings that often apply equally well to linguistic inequities. The creation of the bourgeois public sphere involved the exclusion of women, racial and ethnic minorities, and had a class element as well. Access to public life was limited, giving rise to what Fraser describes as counter-publics (though she omits non-dominant-language communities as one of the important counterpublics). While acknowledging the importance of "protocols of style and decorum" and the ability to find the "right voice and words" in status inequality, she does not proceed to recognize the importance of linguistic issues in participatory parity (1990, 63–64). But it is not hard to extend her vision to incorporate linguistic inequality among those inequalities that need to be elimi-nated in order to create a true participatory democracy and to imagine linguistic "arrangements that accommodate contestation among a plurality of competing publics" which then "better promote the ideal of participatory parity than does a single, comprehensive, overarching public" (1990, 66).

She presents two models, a stratified society and an egalitarian multicultural society. We would add a "stratified multicultural society" in which linguistic difference is an element of social stratification. If "participation means being able to speak 'in one's own voice'" (1990, 69), the first component of that voice is the language in which one expresses oneself best. Recognizing that funda-mental inequality is step one in rendering "visible the ways in which social inequality taints deliberation within publics" (1990, 77).[12]

---

[11] Subsequently, he cites John Dewey's call for an "improvement of the methods and conditions of debate, discussion and persuasion" (Habermas (1996, 304), from Dewey, *The Public and Its Problems* (1927), Dewey himself quoting Samuel Tilden).

[12] Fraser does mention issues of language in the context of the transnational expansion of the public sphere, noting that "language issues compromise both the *legitimacy* and the *efficacy* of public opinion in a postwestphalian world" (2009, 91; italics in the original). Westphalian here refers to the Treaty of Westphalia that ended the Thirty Years War in 1648 and favored a world political system based on independent sovereign states. This had linguistic repercussions that have subsequently contributed to many wars. The treaty put German-speaking Alsace under the French king, but with an agreement that German could continue to be the language of the law and administration in that region. Louis XIV later reneged on those promises and attempted to impose French.

Ronald Dworkin defines equality in terms of the distribution of property,[13] a process decided upon by equal participants in a community.[14] This process requires a "substantial" or "ample" degree of liberty. It is a utopian vision, like much of philosophical thought, as equality of participation depends on conditions, economic, social, and linguistic, that simply do not exist. Through the simplification of complex problems philosophers as well as ordinary citizens imagine stereotypical and simplified scenarios from which supposedly rational conclusions can be drawn.[15]

Participation in a deliberative democracy within a liberal economic framework, as espoused by Amartya Sen and discussed by numerous other philosophers, requires, like justice and fairness, linguistic equality, or at least measures to counteract the inevitable inequalities of language. Sen does not so much

---

[13] Dworkin first distinguishes political from distributional equality, assuming for unexplained reasons that equality should be approached in a piecemeal fashion: "it seems likely that a full theory of equality, embracing a range of issues including political and distributional equality, is best approached by accepting initial, even though somewhat arbitrary, distinctions among these issues" (1981a, 186). He then subdivides distributional equality into equality of welfare and equality of resources before abandoning the idea of equality of welfare, the definition of which people would have a very hard time agreeing on (see his 1981a and 1981b). He returns to political equality in later work (2011, 388–392), acknowledging that it "requires the distribution of political power be distributed so as to confirm the political community's equal concern and respect for all its members" (391). He concedes here the importance of a group's historical record of discrimination, but limits the discussion to racial injustice. This "partnership conception of democracy" must necessarily consider questions of linguistic inequality, but Dworkin does not mention this barrier.

[14] Dworkin (1987, 2–3): "these liberties [freedom of speech, religion, conviction, privacy] must be protected according to the best view of what distributional equality is, the best view of when a society's distribution of property treats each citizen with equal concern." This is a procedural definition: how distribution is effected, "a *process* of coordinated decisions in which people who take responsibility for their own ambitions and projects, and who accept, as part of that responsibility, that they belong to a community of equal concern, are able to identify the true costs of their own plans to other people, and so to design and redesign these plans so as to use only their fair share of resources in principle available to all."

[15] The imaginary part can reside in the scenarios themselves, or in the claim that the stereotype is typical. The philosophical literature is replete with thought experiments – for example, "suppose that a man of some wealth has several children … " (Dworkin 1981a, 186) – that, like much science fiction, oversimplify reality while trying to provide a "real" example. Barry similarly posits extreme examples that have simply not occurred, for example a Spanish-speaking community in the United States that has no interest in learning English. Of course, there will be individuals that fit this stereotype, but it is not true of the vast majority of immigrants. This canard of U.S. English and similar organizations has been repeatedly disproven (e.g., Portes and Schauffler's (1994) research demonstrates that even in the heart of the highest concentration of Spanish speakers, in South Florida, 99 percent of second-generation children of Spanish speakers not only have a high degree of fluency in English, but 80 percent prefer speaking English to speaking Spanish). Even in isolated rural settings immigrant communities "Americanized" much more rapidly than has generally been acknowledged, as Kuyper shows in her 1980 dissertation about German communities in Wisconsin in the second half of the nineteenth century. Similarly, Ronald Reagan in the Republican primary campaign of 1976 invoked the image of "welfare queens" as typical of poor women on public assistance. The woman he described was a real person, but her abuse of the system was not typical.

define democracy as establish the ground rules under which it can operate in a morally justifiable manner:

Democracy has complex demands, which certainly include voting and respect for election results, but it also requires the protection of liberties and freedoms, respect for legal entitlements, and the guaranteeing of free discussion and uncensored distribution of news and fair comment. (1999, 9–10)

Democracy is intrinsically good as a means to preserve individuals' freedom of agency, sometimes through group identity. That agency is the means to attenuate the inevitable inequalities of society.[16] Through this agency individuals combine to determine the values of their society and the policies that will create concrete expression of those values. The combination of individuals' agency is achieved through language. The agency is expressed through language, in deliberative processes that use language, in institutions acting through language.

In the United States, 20 percent of the population speaks a language other than English at home. Additionally, language is a weapon of discrimination used against many native speakers of English through accent stereotyping.[17] Linguistic inequality plays an important part in other inequalities of political, judicial, and economic participation.

Is linguistic uniformity the only path to linguistic equality? This has been the contention of the French state since soon after the French Revolution of 1789[18] and of organizations such as U.S. English in their campaigns for English-only laws. Universality through uniformity solves many philosophical issues, which helps to explain why philosophers are loath to confront the sociolinguistic reality of multilingualism in virtually every nation on earth. Brian Barry has dismissed multiculturalism as an elitist dream, but other

[16] Scanlon (2000, 46) presents five goals achievable by the elimination of inequalities: (1) relieve suffering or severe deprivation; (2) prevent stigmatizing differences in status; (3) avoid unacceptable forms of power or domination; (4) preserve the equality of starting places which is required by procedural fairness; (5) procedural fairness sometimes supports a case for equality of outcomes. While he mentions many types of inequalities, language is not one of them. His chapter was originally delivered in 1996 as the Lindley Lecture at the University of Kansas.

[17] See in particular the work of Dennis Preston (1996, 2011) for attitudes toward native English varieties in the United States and Podberesky, Deluty, and Feldstein (1990) on foreign accents in the United States. We have treated these findings in our discussion of accent discrimination, in Chapter 6.

[18] Initially, the new state in France tried to accommodate linguistic difference through an ambitious translation program. By 1793 that program was viewed with considerable suspicion, and the pitiful quality of the translations was decried both in Southern France (the varieties of Occitan) and in Alsace (German). Subsequently, the state settled on a program of enforced assimilation to the dominant language. The Convention established state-supported primary education in the hope that French would be the common language everywhere in the Republic, through an insistence that all instruction be given in French alone (Articles 6 and 7 of the decree of October 26, 1793). For further detail on the experiment with multilingualism, see Schlieben-Lange (1996) and, for Alsace, Lüsebrink (1986).

philosophers have embraced the sociolinguistic reality: Will Kymlicka has argued for "multicultural citizenship." Kymlicka's "culture" is the social realization of MacIntyre's philosophical "tradition":

MacIntyre: tradition is a system of rational enquiry that determines the themes to be discussed and the basis for rational justification, set in an evolving historical context in which the resolution of new problems requires changes over time to the themes and the justifications. (paraphrased from 1988, 7–8)

Kymlicka: [culture is] an intergenerational community, more or less institutionally complete, occupying a given territory or homeland, sharing a distinct language and history. (1995, 18)

When multiple cultures inhabit a single territory, the universalist approach based on the dominant language group entails an institutionalization of linguistic inequality.

Kymlicka would distinguish polyethnic states, in which the diversity of cultures is a result of immigration, from multinational states, in which several cultures have equal claim to indigenous rights within the given territory (e.g., Switzerland). However, this distinction requires some historical cut-off point, as every cultural group has immigrated at some point to the territory they now inhabit. German speakers have inhabited the region now designated "Alsace" for more than 1,500 years, but the language of the French Republic is based on the Roman invasion that occurred 500 years before that. This historical priority, in the eyes of the Republic, excludes the use of German as an official language. Most countries, including the United States and France, are both polyethnic and multinational. In the United States, Native Americans preceded English speakers, as did Spanish and French speakers in many regions. Many other Spanish and French speakers, as well as speakers of hundreds of other languages from all over the world, have immigrated after English was established as the dominant language. In terms of equality, the synchronous situation in any modern state makes the distinction between polyethnic and multinational irrelevant to most aspects of language policy, affecting primarily cultural reproduction through language maintenance.

For Barry, the distinction is irrelevant because he sees no reason to accommodate the minority cultures, believing that the universalization of the dominant group in society promises more equality for minority groups than does accommodation. Barry devotes several pages of his attack on multiculturalism to language issues (2001, 103–109) and later on bilingual education and multiculturalism (2001, 292–328). The premises of his arguments, unfortunately, demonstrate an unfortunate ignorance of the realities we have discussed in the preceding chapters. For instance, he assumes that monolingual minority language speakers demand jobs that require majority language competence.

Similarly, he uses outdated and clearly biased information to rail against bilingual education as it has been pursued in the United States. Citing studies performed by conservative think tanks in the mid-1970s, he ignores the subsequent research and policy changes (2001, 298–299).[19]

The devil is in the details, details that Barry has not explored. These details, listed in the preceding chapters, force us to consider political philosophy in a different light. How large a percentage of the society is one willing to exclude from participation in the name of the ancestral privilege of the English language? The legitimacy of the social contract is at stake. What types of participation are rights, and what types are based on practicalities? By positing the most extreme case – a minority-language speaker demanding employment for a position that requires mastery of English (Barry uses the example of banking) – he attacks a judicial and political position that has never been endorsed in this country.

By using such an example, he dismisses or ignores the many more legitimate questions about language's effect on participation in American society. In the name of universality, he abandons equality and embraces an unbridled power of the majority.[20] Majoritarian impositions play an important part in minority groups' recourse to identity.[21] Over and over again we have seen in the preceding chapters how minority-language group organizations have spearheaded challenges to majoritarian English-only inequalities: PROPA, LULAC, MALDEF, and the Asian-American Justice Center, among many others.[22]

The determination of equality of any sort is necessarily a political decision: equality necessarily means an agreement of two or more. This is why political equality is a necessary precondition to any other attempt at equality, and any sort of equality is defined through a constant negotiation with respect to specific

[19] Barry loses credibility by his one-sided choice of sources; indeed, all his information on bilingual education seems to come from one book chapter by Noel Epstein, an education writer for the *Washington Post*, published in 1980, a resume of his monograph published in 1977. The sociolinguist Joshua Fishman (1978, 16) described Epstein's book as "an ignorant critique ... heaps bias upon bias, suspicion upon suspicion, misinterpretation upon misinterpretation." While not excusing the sloppiness of Epstein's work, Fishman recognized weaknesses in educational research. Probabilistic measurements in educational research will always have exceptions that an opposing viewpoint can cite. The variability in humankind renders the relationship of the generalization to the particular case problematic. Furthermore, findings depend on the questions asked, and the questions depend on the researchers' ideology.

[20] "Where a minority is constituted out of those who are on the losing side in a disagreement about the future of institutions they share with the majority, there appears to be no case for building in special protections for the minority" (2001, 300). Rights of all sorts and the principles of equal protection and due process that have come up repeatedly in the preceding chapters show precisely why, in certain circumstances, the power of majorities can and must be constrained.

[21] As Fraser (1990, 62) notes, the bourgeois masculinist conception of the public sphere assumes "that the proliferation of a multiplicity of competing publics is necessarily a step away from, rather than toward, greater democracy, and that a single comprehensive public sphere is always preferable to a nexus of multiple publics."

[22] Just as other organizations have highlighted other inequities (NAACP, NOW, etc.).

circumstances. Any equality is a perception; perception is a temporary and ephemeral reality. Equality is subject to perpetual revision.[23] Perception itself and the resolution of different perceptions is a linguistic activity. The a priori exclusion of linguistic inequality in the name of social cohesion embraces historical prejudice.

We opened this book with a discussion of the history of human rights. Rights can be a means of limiting the dangers of democratic rule, the tyranny of the majority and the manipulation of public opinion. Rights can also create a tyranny of the minority, a refusal of some, particularly religious, minorities to accede to the majority's vision of civic virtues. They can establish parameters of equality in the face of natural difference and a society oriented toward inequality through the ideology of economic liberalism. They are the minimum settings for systems of redistribution in the name of equality. They are granted to individuals, but in some domains they depend on the individuals' identity as a group.

The spectrum of rights runs from the universal and eternal to historical accident, but even the universal and eternal are interpreted through the prism of history and expressed with language that eludes precision and fixity. The resulting picture, like most human endeavors, is not always clear and never finished. Throughout this book we have traced ways in which language colors the realization of democracy, equality, fairness, and justice in our society.

The right to vote is essential to political equality. This is a procedural equality that provides at least the illusion of equal influence in determining how equality of welfare or equality of resources might be pursued. Equality of access to the ballot box is a relatively recent development, and now it is once again under siege with voter ID requirements. Even equality of access is not the same as equality in the power of the vote. In our bicameral system of government all votes are inherently not equal, but even more so all votes are not equally effective. The will of certain minority voters will never be realized by the election of their preferred candidate or the passage of their preferred ballot initiative. A minority vision of equality of welfare or equality of resources, whatever its philosophical or practical merits, is unlikely ever to be successful.

The disparity between the adult population of the United States and the rolls of eligible voters is the first challenge to the principles of democracy. Residents

---

[23] Dworkin (1981a, 194) recognizes but dismisses the importance of the constant changes in conceptions of equality, however it is defined: "I do not believe the temporal problems affect the various points I shall make, but readers who do should consider whether my arguments hold against alternate versions." I would counter that the ephemerality of any conception of equality is essential to the idea. The perception of equality or inequality is a negotiation, with oneself (psychologically) or with others (politically or socially). One's feeling that one is "equal enough" is essential to a democratic society; the equilibrium of equal enough and the unbalanced state of too unequal are in constant flux.

who are not citizens and those who have been convicted of a felony are systematically excluded. Past laws have restricted participation in the electoral process through literacy tests, poll taxes, and other means. Much like property requirements and the exclusion of women, English literacy tests were presented as neutral – a guarantee of an informed electorate. This assumed that the information necessary for voting intelligently was accessible only in English, and that English speakers took advantage of the information available to vote more intelligently. Since 2000 the favored means of restricting minority participation in the electoral process has been the implementation of strict voter identification laws.

Voter identification and voter registration drive restrictions serve to suppress minority participation in the electoral process. The illusion of rationality – the limitation of suffrage to informed and engaged voters, and the protection of the integrity of elections – has served anti-democratic (and partisan anti-Democratic) purposes.

Once registered, voters want to use their franchise effectively. Receiving the ballot and other voting assistance in a language understood by the voter would be one reasonable way to encourage informed voting, the proffered reason for literacy tests. Some contend that such election materials are unnecessary because new citizens must pass an English test to be naturalized. Others argue that monolingual English ballots encourage new immigrants to make a more rapid transition to English. The factors affecting the speed of that transition are numerous, but voting with a monolingual English ballot is not one of them. Others argue that the financial burden of producing multilingual ballots is too heavy, but the cost of fundamental rights has usually not been a successful argument when such services have been challenged in the courts. Since 1975 the Voting Rights Act and its successors have required bilingual voting materials if certain factors relating to the population density of the language minority are met. Those LEP voters who live in electoral districts that do not meet these requirements must find their own way to ensure that the mark they put on the ballot will reflect their real choice.

The delimitation of voting districts determines whether those real choices will result in the representation of minority groups in elected bodies. Reapportionment determines if various "suspect classes" will have a direct voice in towns, counties, states, and the federal government. Does a principle of equality require such a presence, even if it is achieved only by oddly configured circumscriptions? Or is a principle of geographic uniformity, come what may, more important? All votes are equal, but some votes are more equal than others. The argument is never innocent, as the political ramifications are too obvious. Reason is in the eyes of the beholder.

Voting law conditions democracy by limiting and shaping participation in fundamental democratic processes. "Official English" provisions, so far restricted to individual states, threaten equality by limiting the access of LEP residents to governmental programs. The most restrictive of these have accordingly been declared unconstitutional.[24] The protection of freedom of speech and the encouragement of citizen interaction with government have been held to preclude requirements that all governmental business be conducted and/or recorded solely in English. The effectiveness of governmental programs crucial to equality in a democratic society is dependent on the language of the citizen, not on the language of the government.

This principle applies equally well to the justice system, government's fundamental contribution to an orderly society. The legal system depends on language. Establishing meaning essential to the pursuit of justice is difficult enough in one language. The complexity grows exponentially when two or more languages are involved. In the hope of establishing a fixed and precise legal language, French terms remained in English law for centuries after French ceased to be a native language to the overwhelming majority of English subjects.[25] Statutes and legal arguments frequently, and increasingly, feature definitions or references to dictionaries in the vain hope of establishing incontrovertible meaning.[26] Even within English, linguistic issues are crucial to justice.

For linguistic minorities two issues in the legal system come to the fore. First is the use of interpreters from the very first contact with officers of the law through an eventual judgment, either at trial or in some other agreement. Only in the 1970s were strict guidelines established, both for the use of interpretation and for the qualifications of certified interpreters. The determination of the need for and the quality of interpretation are still largely in the hands of the original trial judge, who must also take into account the costs associated with interpretive services.

The second controversial area within the legal system is the composition of the jury. An impartial jury is guaranteed by the Sixth Amendment, but concerns about the equality of input have been used to exclude systematically jurors who might understand testimony given in a language other than English. Even if all the testimony is in English, jury selection excludes the LEP potential juror, a category that numbers over 10 million members. Some states have taken limited steps to address that issue, but in general the ability to be a member of a jury is not considered a right. A jury of one's peers requires a definition of

---

[24] See above, concerning English-only laws in Arizona and Alaska.

[25] Just to cite a few terms still in the American legal vocabulary, *parole, torts, voir dire*.

[26] For more detail on the Supreme Court's increasing reliance on dictionaries, see Brudney and Baum (2013), and Calhoun (2014). Lexicography, despite the best efforts of its practitioners and the resources provided by the internet, is an imprecise science that depends on a limited range of sources. The interpretive value of dictionaries in a legal setting is further compromised by the conflict between "ordinary" meaning and what the writers of statutes, regulations, guidelines, or court decisions "meant to say" within a specific historical context.

"peers," an area of discrimination that the courts have been reluctant to consider; impartiality is assumed through semi-random selection procedures, combined with the use of juror challenges, both "for-cause" and "peremptory." Abuses of the *venire* selection procedure and of peremptory challenges have been addressed for racial discrimination, but not for language per se.

Education is an important role of the state in the preparation of future participants in civic society, either as the provider of instruction in the public schools or as the monitor of private education. Language is both the medium of education and the subject of education. Nancy Fraser (2009, 16) describes two obstacles to participatory parity: the denial of resources necessary to interact with others as peers and "institutionalized hierarchies of cultural value that deny them requisite standing." The education of those whose primary language is not the dominant language concerns both of these obstacles. Immigrants speaking languages other than English have long attempted to guide their children along the fine line between assimilation to the dominant culture and preservation of their heritage culture.

Bilingual education in the United States is primarily a means to help students reach full parity in the dominant language. The best means to achieve this goal are constantly being tested and revised. At the most elementary grades, teaching monolingual students to read and write in their native language and then to apply those skills to the learning of English has apparently had the most success. At higher grades, other approaches may help the student reach parity more rapidly. Applying the generalization to any individual is problematic: at all levels and in all contexts individual students will react best to different approaches.

The method preferred by groups like U.S. English and in much recent legislation passed by English-only supporters is "sink-or-swim," that is, total immersion in the English-speaking classroom. Total immersion has the allure of not costing any extra money to financially starved school districts and can under specific circumstances work efficiently. If the parents of the students are English speakers and are committed to assisting their children in English acquisition, immersion may in fact be the best way. But those are two very big "ifs," conditions rarely met.

The biggest fear of English-only proponents is that bilingual education might encourage LEP students to maintain their native language. The economic pressures to learn English make this an unlikely outcome, and indeed all studies have demonstrated an ever-more rapid transition to English. Even if first-language maintenance were one of the outcomes of bilingual education, given the nature of global competition in the modern world, discouraging true bilingualism seems counterproductive.

The fear of language maintenance has also fueled an over-reaction to attempts to apply bilingual education methods to speakers of non-standard

English, in particular African-American children. The goal has been to help teachers understand the nature of African-American Vernacular English, some-times called Ebonics, so that they might better guide students toward mastery of standard English. The "institutionalized hierarchies of cultural values" have served to inflame public opinion by deforming the original intent of such initiatives and thus to deny resources that might contribute to fuller participa-tion in society. While the focus has been on African-American children's learning success, the same principles could be applied to any number of stigmatized varieties of English.

Not all speakers of other language varieties are immigrants. As we noted earlier (see above, p. 132), indigenous cultures are generally recognized to retain certain cultural rights that are not granted immigrant cultures. This interpretation of indigenous rights is a fairly recent development, so for the first two centuries of the American Republic forced assimilation, sometimes to the point of child abduction and removal, decimated Native American linguis-tic communities. Only since the 1990s has government policy pursued main-tenance of these languages, though for many it is too little, too late.

Education is just one of many services offered by the modern state. To what extent do equal taxpayers get equal services when their knowledge of the majority language is weak or non-existent? This was the question President Clinton hoped to resolve at the federal level through his Executive Order 13166. At the state and local levels, the provision of services in languages other than English is one of the primary targets of "English-only" constitutional amendments and statutes, and subsequently of court decisions. As in education, many state and local programs are funded at least in part by the federal government, and therefore subject to federal requirements.[27] The issue is equality before the law, tempered by the reasonableness of service given the demography of the minority language.

The boundary between legal and illegal discrimination in employment is blurry, a constant negotiation between legitimate occupational needs and illegitimate prejudices. The courts have elaborated procedures to test legiti-macy in hiring, firing, assessment, and punishment, and to combat the intimi-dation of a hostile environment in the work situation. The burden of proof is higher for subaltern groups than it is for the dominant, as broad latitude is offered employers in occupational requirement explanations. Just as size and height standards in some professions have been challenged as discriminatory against women and certain ethnicities, so language requirements have been contested as irrelevant for some jobs. The courts have generally accepted the

---

[27] Funding cut-offs are in fact rare for a variety of reasons. Pasachoff (2014) argues that this weapon should be used more frequently.

demand that all workers speak only English as long as such policies only pertain to working time, and not to breaks or lunch hours. A hospitable environment for the LEP worker has been interpreted as creating a hostile work environment for those who speak only English.

The issues become murkier when the language is another variety of English. Accent has frequently been a determining factor in employment, though scientific means of establishing comprehensibility are unconvincing. In the university setting, negative teacher evaluations based on the instructor's accent and subsequent employment decisions based on such evaluations have been contested, but rarely successfully. Comprehensibility depends significantly upon context and goodwill. The listener who anticipates what the speaker is trying to say may be less affected by the speaker's accent. Open-mindedness on the part of the listener in the work situation, and then on the part of the judge or jury if a case goes to trial, can also play an important role in assuring communication. Can goodwill, or ill will, be proven in a court of law?

Safety for workers is one of the reasons proffered for linguistic uniformity in the workplace. It also comes into play in consumer protection. Companies are expected to be able to foresee dangers, to prevent them when possible (duty to care), and to inform users when dangers cannot be avoided (duty to warn). As we have often seen, the requirements for LEP Americans can be transposed more generally into requirements for those who consider themselves fully competent in English, in the "plain English" movement for legal warnings. Once again, the concept of reasonableness is crucial, and reason is subject to negotiation.

In the fundamental procedures of governmental and economic action, we have observed time and again the confrontation of philosophical principles and the everyday reality of linguistic difference. The ideal universal of rationality is contingent on local conditions, history, and language, an ever-shifting conception of the reasonable. What is perceived as arbitrary shifts constantly as social mores change and as we become more aware of the effects of seemingly neutral decisions on equality and justice. Such decisions are all the more difficult because the concerned parties are transforming themselves as the process unfolds: immigrants, and especially immigrants' children, are improving their English skills, but at the same time new immigrants arrive, starting the process all over again. Limited English proficiency is a temporary state for individuals but characterizes a segment of the population that is constantly being renewed.

Language is both the medium and target of our deliberations on equality and justice. Power has always been a component of language. The words of a given language are in origin mostly arbitrary (aside from onomatopoeia), imposed by relations of power among human beings. The Bible gives Adam the power to name things, Plato speaks of the *nomothetes*,[28] the creator of words; today we have "spin-doctors" and lawyers to try to fix meaning. The meaning of words, however, is ever-changing and dependent on context: in some circumstances and in some dialects of English *bad* is good. Words and meanings are imposed, but the success, short- and long-term, of these impositions is entirely unpredictable, as the Académie Française and French terminological commissions can attest.[29] Legal vocabulary is thus also subject to constant reinterpretation and redefinition, a constant site for renegotiation, rendering originalism as a legal method[30] and the recourse to dictionaries now so popular in legal argumentation as vain as the work of the terminological commissions (see above p. 194).

As if the meaning of words were not already complex enough, the relations between words are also dependent on historical and random connections. Rorty (1999, 60) notes that language being human, all attempts to create fixity in language are doomed.[31] Every language has been created over long periods of time. Each element of language, whether it be a distinction between aspirated and unaspirated consonants, gender assignment for nouns, a morphological representation of future tense or imperfective aspect, agreement between a subject and a verb, is a historical creation, one that came into being because a particular linguistic community, or a particularly influential part of a particular linguistic community, found it useful. Subsequent generations made the distinction habitual, through imitation or imposition.[32] Sometimes,

---

[28] For an extended and very insightful analysis of name-giving, and more generally of the concepts of "natural" and its opposites, through the history of Western linguistic thought, see Joseph (2000).

[29] France, after a couple false starts, established terminological commissions in the 1970s attached to each governmental ministry. The avowed purpose of these commissions was to permit French citizens to talk about the latest developments in many fields without reverting to English vocabulary. There have been some successes, such as *logiciel* for "software", and subsequent derivatives such as *ludiciels* "computer games," but many of the substitutes created, particularly in science and engineering, are outdated before they reach the concerned publics. For a general history of the commissions, see Chansou (2003); for five studies of the success in implanting the new terms, see Depecker (ed.) (1997). These efforts have generally seemed more successful in Québec, where there is a much stronger political will to follow the recommendations of the commissions.

[30] Originalism itself is a term with many meanings. The scholarly literature on originalism is vast and divided. We use the term here to mean placing special importance on the intentions of the framers of the Constitution. For a recent attempt to describe the phenomenon in all its complexity, see Berman (2009).

[31] Rorty (2007) considers attempts to transcend our humanity and the relations imposed by our human language "the project of escaping from time and chance." But language being bound by time and chance, these constraints are inescapable.

[32] Imposition can be informal, such as a parent correcting a child, or formal through education or such institutions as the terminological commissions mentioned above. The study of prescriptive linguistic behavior has come under more scrutiny in recent years, after years of neglect because it was considered unnatural.

but equally unpredictably, a distinction loses importance and is mostly dropped, such as gender of common nouns in English or the second-person singular (*thou*), though each subsists in limited form, a reminder of history. Unpredictability is the common thread in the elaboration of distinctions and in their demise.

Logic rarely has anything to do with the development of a language, or rather, competing linguistic logics are resolved by various types of linguistic power, which might be based on class, or race, or artistic prestige, or any number of other factors in multiple combinations. Linguistic power affirms other social, economic, and political powers. Competing dialects and competing languages reproduce other competitions within and between communities. "We, the people" in the United States, the residents of its states and territories, includes numerous linguistic divisions, between speakers of the dominant language themselves and between English speakers and those more comfortable in other languages. To the extent that the role of linguistic power in perpetuating or even promoting inequality is ignored or dismissed, our theories of justice, democracy, and fairness are fatally flawed.

Issues are almost never resolved once and for all. Some types of discrimination are perceived as rational, others as irrational, but the application of those terms to specific social situations depends on ever-changing social contexts. Justice, democracy, and fairness are constantly negotiated, negotiations that are rarely conducted between equals. How our laws and government address difference is thus crucial to the realization of the ideals to which we aspire.

Bibliography

Abbott, Edith (1931) *Report on Crime and the Foreign Born*. Washington, DC, Government Printing Office.

Abdelall, Brenda Fathy (2005) "Not Enough of a Minority? Arab Americans and the Language Assistance Provisions (Section 203) of the Voting Rights Act." *University of Michigan Journal of Law Reform* 38, 911–939.

Abellera Cruz, Eugenio (1998) "Unprotected Identities: Recognizing Cultural Ethnic Divergence in Interpreting Title VII's 'National Origin' Discrimination." *Hastings Women's Law Journal* 9, 161–187.

Ahmad, Muneer I. (2007) "Interpreting Communities: Lawyering Across Language Difference." *UCLA Law Review* 54, 999–1086.

Ainsworth, Janet E. (1993) "In a Different Register: Powerlessness in Police Interrogation." *Yale Law Journal* 103, 259–322.

Ainsworth, Janet E. (2010) "Language, Power and Identity in the Workplace: Enforcement of 'English-Only' Rules by Employers." *Seattle Journal for Social Justice* 9, 233–257.

Aka, Philip C. & Lucinda M. Deason (2009) "Culturally Competent Public Services and English-Only Laws." *Howard Law Journal* 53, 53–131.

Alduy, Cécile & Stéphane Wahnich (2015) *Décryptage du nouveau discours frontiste*. Paris, Seuil.

Alfredsson, Gudmundur & Erika Ferrer (1998) *Minority Rights: A Guide to United Nations Procedures and Institutions*. London, Minority Rights Group International.

Ali, Farida (2013) "Multilingual Prospective Jurors Assessing California Standards Twenty Years after *Hernandez v. New York*." *Northwestern Journal of Law and Social Policy* 8, 236–273.

Allingham, Michael (2014) *Distributive Justice*. London/New York, Routledge.

Ancheta, Angelo (2010) "Language Assistance and Local Voting Rights Law." *Indiana Law Review* 44, 161–199.

Arriola, Christopher (1995) "Knocking on the Schoolhouse Door: *Mendez v. Westminster*. Equal Protection, Public Education and Mexican Americans in the 1940s." *La Raza Law Journal* 8, 166–207.

Arrow, Kenneth (1951) *Social Choice and Individual Values*. New York, Wiley.

Asato, Noriko (2003) "Mandating Americanization: Japanese Language Schools and the Federal Survey of Education in Hawai'i, 1916–1920." *History of Education Quarterly* 43 (1), 10–38.

Asturias, María-Daniel (2012) "Burden Shifting and Faulty Assumptions: The Impact of *Horne v. Flores* on State Obligations to Adolescent ELLs after the EEOA." *Howard Law Journal* 55, 607–642.

Atkinson, Carroll (1947) "The Foreign-Language School Controversy in Hawaii." *The Modern Language Journal* 31 (3), 153–156.

August, Diane, Claude Goldenberg, & Robert Rueda (2010) "Restrictive State Language Policies: Are They Scientifically Based?" In *Forbidden Language: English Learners and Restrictive Language Policies*, Patricia Gándara & Megan Hopkins (eds.), 139–158. New York/London, Teachers College Press.

Badillo, David A. (2011) "Litigating Bilingual Education: A History of the *Gomez* Decision in Illinois." In *Latinos in the Midwest*, Rubén O. Martinez (ed.), 207–226. East Lansing, MI, Michigan State University Press.

Bagnato, Christopher F. (2010) "Change Is Needed: How Latinos Are Affected by the Process of Jury Selection." *Chicana/o-Latina/o Law Review* 29, 59–67.

Bailey, Stacy C., Anjali U. Pandit, Laura Curtis, & Michael S. Wolf (2009) "Availability of Spanish Prescription Labels: A Multi-State Survey." *Medical Care* 47 (6), 707–710.

Baker, Keith & Adriana de Kanter (1981) *Effectiveness of Bilingual Education: A Review of the Literature*. Washington, DC, U.S. Department of Education.

Baldwin, Linda M. (1995) "*Ramirez v. Plough, Inc.*: Should Manufacturers of Nonprescription Drugs Have a Duty to Warn in Spanish?" *University of San Francisco Law Review* 29, 837–874.

Barbas, Terin M. (2009) "We Count Too! Ending the Disenfranchisement of Limited English Proficient Voters." *Florida State University Law Review* 37, 189–214.

Baron, Dennis E. (1990) *The English-Only Question: An Official Language for Americans?* New Haven, CT, Yale University Press.

Barrett, James R. (2012) *The Irish Way: Becoming American in the Multiethnic City*. New York, Penguin.

Barry, Brian (2001) *Culture and Equality: An Egalitarian Critique of Multiculturalism*. Cambridge, MA, Harvard University Press.

Baugh, John (2000) *Beyond Ebonics: Linguistic Pride and Racial Prejudice*. Oxford, Oxford University Press.

Beaver, R. Pierce (1962a) "Church, State, and the Indians: Indian Missions in the New Nation." *Journal of Church and State* 4, 11–30.

Beaver, R. Pierce (1962b) "The Churches and President Grant's Peace Policy." *Journal of Church and State* 4, 174–190.

Benson, Jocelyn F. (2007) "!Su voto es su voz! Incorporating Voters of Limited English Proficiency into American Democracy." *Boston College Law Review* 48, 251–329.

Bent, Scott J. (2012) " 'If You Want to Speak Spanish, Go Back to Mexico'?: A First-Amendment Analysis of English-Only Rules in Public Schools." *Ohio State Law Journal* 73, 343–394.

Berk-Seligson, Susan (1990) *The Bilingual Courtroom. Court Interpreters in the Judicial Process*. Chicago/London, University of Chicago Press.

Berk-Seligson, Susan (2002) "The Miranda Warnings and Linguistic Coercion: The Role of Footing in the Interrogation of a Limited-English-Speaking Murder Suspect." In *Language in the Legal Process*, Janice Cotterill (ed.), 127–143. Basingstoke, Palgrave-Macmillan.

Berk-Seligson, Susan (2009) *Coerced Confessions: The Discourse of Bilingual Police Interrogations*. Berlin/New York, Mouton de Gruyter.

Berman, Mitchell (2009) "Originalism Is Bunk." *New York University Law Review* 84, 1–96.

Birdsong, David (ed.) (1999) *Second Language Acquisition and the Critical Period Hypothesis*. Mahwah, NJ, Lawrence Erlbaum Associates.

Birman, Beatrice F. & Alan L. Ginsburg (1983) "Introduction: Addressing the Needs of Language Minority Children." In *Bilingual Education: A Reappraisal of Federal Policy*, Keith A. Baker & Adriana A. de Kanter (eds.), ix–xxi. Lexington, MA, D. C. Heath & Co.

Blanton, Carlos K. (2004) *The Strange Career of Bilingual Education in Texas, 1836–1981*. College Station, TX, Texas A & M University Press.

Breen, Timothy H. (2001) *The Lockean Moment: The Language of Rights on the Eve of the American Revolution: An Inaugural Lecture Delivered Before the University of Oxford on May 15, 2001*. Oxford, Oxford University Press.

Bridges, Khiara M. (2013) "The Dangerous Law of Biological Race." *Fordham Law Review* 82, 21–80.

Brière, Eugene (1978) "Limited English Speakers and the Miranda Rights." *TESOL Quarterly* 12, 235–245.

Brigham, Carl C. (1923) *A Study of American Intelligence*. Princeton, NJ, Princeton University Press.

Browne, Kingsley (2001) "Zero Tolerance for the First Amendment." *Ohio Northern University Law Review* 27, 563–605.

Brudney, James J. & Lawrence Baum (2013) "Oasis or Mirage: The Supreme Court's Thirst for Dictionaries in the Rehnquist and Roberts Eras." *William and Mary Law Review* 55, 483–580.

Buntin, Jennifer T. (2011) "Reaching across Borders: The Transnationalizing Effect of Mexican Migration on Public Schools on the Outskirts of Chicago." In *Latinos in the Midwest*, Rubén O. Martinez (ed.), 227–255. East Lansing, MI, Michigan State University Press.

Bureau of Education (1902) *Report of the Commissioner of Education, Volume 1*. Washington, DC, Government Printing Office.

Bureau of Education (1920) *A Survey of Education in Hawaii*. Washington, DC, Government Printing Office.

Calderón, Carlos (1950) "The Education of Spanish-speaking Children in Edcouch-Elsa Texas." Unpublished MA Thesis, University of Texas-Austin.

Calhoun, John (2014) "Measuring the Fortress: Explaining Trends in Supreme Court and Circuit Court Dictionary Use." *Yale Law Journal* 124, 484–526.

California Judicial Branch (2014) "Strategic Plan for Language Access in the California Courts" (Draft, July 29, 2014) Proposal SP14-05.

Callagy, Maeve (2013) "'My English is Good Enough' for San Luis: Adopting a Two-Pronged Approach for Arizona's English Fluency Requirements for Candidates for Public Office." *Journal of Law and Policy* 22, 305–339.

Cartagena, Juan (2004) "Latinos and Section 5 of the Voting Rights Act: Beyond Black and White." *Columbia University National Black Law Journal* 18, 201–223.

Cassin, Barbara (ed.) (2014) *Dictionary of Untranslatables: A Philosophical Lexicon*, translated by Emily Apter, Jacques Lezra, & Michael Wood. Princeton, NJ, Princeton University Press.

Castle, Ryan (2013) "The Gay Accent, Gender, and Title VII Employment Discrimination." *Seattle University Law Review* 36, 1943–1965.

Chang, Cyndie M. & Paul J. Killion (2015) "Sign Languages: The Regulatory Authority of Municipalities Over Commercial Signage Does Not Trump the First Amendment." *Los Angeles Lawyer* 37, 28–33.

Chansou, Michel (2003) *L'aménagement lexical en France pendant la période contemporaine (1950–1994). Étude de sociolexicologie.* Paris, H. Champion.

Charles, Patrick J. (2011) "Restoring 'Life, Liberty and the Pursuit of Happiness' in Our Constitutional Jurisprudence: An Exercise in Legal History." *William and Mary Bill of Rights Journal* 20, 457–532.

Chávez, Edward L. (2008) "New Mexico's Success with Non-English Speaking Jurors." *Journal of Court Innovation* 1, 303–327.

Chavez, Hilda Lyssette (2012) "Examining the Effects of the Inclusion of Non-English Speaking Jurors on Jury Verdicts and Juror Experiences." Unpublished PhD dissertation, University of Nevada, Reno.

Chemerinsky, Erwin (1992) "The Supreme Court and the Fourteenth Amendment: The Unfulfilled Promise." *Loyola of Los Angeles Law Review* 25, 1147–1157.

Chen, Ming Hsu (2014) "Governing by Guidance: Civil Rights Agencies and the Emergence of Language Rights." *Harvard Civil Rights-Civil Liberties Law Review* 49, 291–342.

Clinton, DeWitt (1815) *An Introductory Discourse, Delivered Before the Literary and Philosophical Society of New York, On the Fourth of May, 1814.* New York, Longworth.

Cochrane, Diana K. (2009) "'¿Como se dice?, ¿Necessito a un interprete?' The Civil Litigant's Right to a Court-Appointed Interpreter in Texas." *The Scholar: St. Mary's Law Review on Minority Issues* 12, 47–94.

Cogley, Richard W. (1999) *John Eliot's Mission to the Indians before King Philip's War.* Cambridge, MA, Harvard University Press.

Collins, James (1999) "The Ebonics Controversy in Context: Literacies, Subjectivities, and Language Ideologies in the United States." In *Language Ideological Debates*, Jan Blommaert (ed.), 201–234. Berlin, Walter de Gruyter.

Commission on Naturalization (1905) *Report to the President of the Commission on Naturalization.* Washington, DC, Government Printing Office.

Commons, John R. (1907) *Race and Immigrants in America.* New York, The Macmillan Company.

Cox, Kelly (1993) "The Duty to Warn: Should California Extend the Duty to Include Foreign Language Warnings?" *San Diego Justice Journal* 1, 517–540.

Crawley, Cheryl & Kay Schultze (2008) "Cultures Out of Sync: Bilingual Education on the Crow Indian Reservation." Unpublished PhD dissertation, University of California, Berkeley.

Cullinane, Michael P. (2014) "The 'Gentlemen's Agreement' – Exclusion by Class." *Immigrants and Minorities* 32 (2), 139–161.

Curtis, Michael Kent (2000) "Historical Linguistics, Inkblots, and Life After Death: The Privileges and Immunities of Citizens of the United States." *North Carolina Law Review* 78, 1071–1150.

Davidson, Chandler, Tanya Dunlap, Gale Kenny, & Benjamin Wise (2008) "Election Law: Vote Caging as a Republican Ballot Security Technique." *William Mitchell Law Review* 34, 533–562.

Deák, Julia (2007) "African-American Language and American Linguistic Cultures: An Analysis of Language Policies in Education." *Working Papers in Education Linguistics* 22 (1), 105–134.

de Jongh, Elena M. (2008) "Court Interpreting: Linguistic Presence v. Linguistic Absence." *The Florida Bar Journal* 82 (7), 21–32.

De la Trinidad, Maritza (2008) "Collective Outrage: Mexican-American Activism and the Quest for Educational Equality and Reform, 1950–1990." Unpublished PhD dissertation, University of Arizona.

Del Valle, Sandra (2003) *Language Rights and the Law: Finding Our Voices.* Basingstoke, Multilingual Matters.

Denton, Douglas (2007) "Procedural Fairness in the California Courts." *Court Review* 44, 44–54.

Department of the Interior, Bureau of Education (1919) *The Rural School in Nebraska.* Washington, DC, Government Printing Office.

Depecker, Loïc (ed.) (1997) *La mesure des mots. Cinq études d'implantation terminologique.* Rouen, Publications de l'Université de Rouen.

Diamond, Stanley (1990) "English – the Official Language of California – 1983–1988." In *Perspectives on Official English: The Campaign for English as the Official Language the USA*, Karen L. Adams & Daniel T. Brink (eds.), 111–119. Berlin, Walter de Gruyter.

Diaz, Jacqueline Grace (2014) "The Divided States of America: Reinterpreting Title VII's National Origin Provision to Account for Subnational Discrimination within the United States." *University of Pennsylvania Law Review* 162, 649–681.

Dillard, R. Geoffrey (1994) "Multilingual Warning Labels: Product Liability, 'Official English', and Consumer Safety." *Georgia Law Review* 29, 197–244.

Dolson, David P. & Jan Mayer (1992) "Longitudinal Study of Three Program Models for Language-Minority Students: A Critical Examination of Reported Findings." At www.ncela.us/files/rcd/BE018850/Longitudinal_Study_of_Three_Program_ Models.pdf.

Dolson, Lee S. (1964) "The Administration of the San Francisco Public Schools, 1847–1947." Unpublished PhD dissertation, University of California, Berkeley.

Dorsey, Dana (2013) "Segregation 2.0: The New Generation of School Segregation in the 21st Century." *Education and Urban Society* 45 (5), 533–547.

Downes, Randolph C. (1945) "A Crusade for Indian Reform, 1922–1934." *Mississippi Valley Historical Review* 32 (3), 331–354.

Dunnigan, Timothy & Bruce T. Downing (1995) "Legal Interpreting on Trial: A Case Study." In *Translation and the Law*, M. Morris (ed.), 93–113. Amsterdam/ Philadelphia, John Benjamins .

Dupleix, Scipion (forthcoming (1651)) *La liberté de la langue françoise dans sa pureté.* Douglas Kibbee & Marcus Keller (eds.), Paris, Garnier.

Dussias, Allison M. (1999) "Waging War with Words: Native Americans' Continuing Struggle against the Suppression of their Languages." *Ohio State Law Journal* 60 (3), 901–994.

Dussias, Allison M. (2001) "Let No Native Child Be Left Behind: Re-Envisioning Native America Education for the Twenty-First Century." *Arizona Law Review* 43, 819–903.

Dussias, Allison M. (2008) "Indigenous Languages under Siege: The Native American Experience." *Intercultural Human Rights Law Review* 3, 5–78.

Dworkin, Ronald (1981a) "What Is Equality? Part 1: Equality of Welfare." *Philosophy and Public Affairs* 10, 185–246.

Dworkin, Ronald (1981b) "What Is Equality? Part 2: Equality of Resources." *Philosophy and Public Affairs* 10, 283–345.

Dworkin, Ronald (1987) "What Is Equality? Part 3: The Place of Liberty." *Iowa Law Review* 73, 1–54.

Dworkin, Ronald (2011) *Justice for Hedgehogs*. Cambridge, MA, The Belknap Press of Harvard University Press.

Edwards, I. N. (1923) "The Legal Status of Foreign Languages in the Schools." *The Elementary School Journal* 24 (4), 270–278.

Eggington, William G. & Tony Cox (2013) "Using Elicited Oral Response Testing to Determine the Need for an Interpreter." *Harvard Latino Law Review* 16, 127–146.

Einesman, Floralynn (1999) "Confessions and Culture: The Interaction of 'Miranda' and Diversity." *Journal of Criminal Law and Criminology* 90, 1–48.

Ellis, Frances H. (1954a) "Historical Account of German Instruction in the Public Schools of Indianapolis, 1869–1919." *Indiana Magazine of History* 50, 119–138.

Ellis, Frances H. (1954b) "German Instruction in the Public Schools of Indianapolis, 1869–1919 II." *Indiana Magazine of History* 50, 251–276.

Ellis, Frances H. (1954c) "German Instruction in the Public Schools of Indianapolis, 1869–1919 III." *Indiana Magazine of History* 50, 357–380.

Epstein, Noel (1977) *Language, Ethnicity and the Schools: Policy Alternatives for Bilingual-Bicultural Education*. Washington, DC, Institute for Educational Leadership, George Washington University.

Eskridge, William N., Jr. (2001) "Social Movements and Law Reform: Channeling: Identity-Based Social Movements and Public Law." *University of Pennsylvania Law Review* 150, 419–525.

Eskridge, William N., Jr. (2002) "Some Effects of Identity-Based Social Movements in the Twentieth Century." *Michigan Law Review* 100, 2062–2407.

Evren, Lisa T. (1986) "When Is a Race not a Race?: Contemporary Issues under the Civil Rights Act of 1866." *New York University Law Review* 61, 976–1002.

Fass, Paula (1989) *Outside In: Minorities and the Transformation of American Education*. Oxford, Oxford University Press.

Fedynskyj, Jurij (1971) "State Session Laws in Non-English Languages: A Chapter of American Legal History." *Indiana Law Journal* 46, 463–478.

Ferguson, George O. (1916) "Psychology of the Negro, an Experimental Study." PhD Dissertation, Columbia University. Printed in *Archives of Psychology* 36.

Fishman, Joshua (1978) "A Gathering of Vultures: The 'Legion of Decency' and Bilingual Education in the USA." *NABE Journal* 2, 13–16.

Fiss, Owen (1976) "Groups and the Equal Protection Clause." *Philosophy and Public Affairs* 5, 107–177.

Flores, Glenn, M., Barton Laws, Sandra J. Mayo, Barry Zuckerman, Milagros Abreu, Leonardo Medina, & Eric J. Hardt (2003) "Errors in Medical Interpretation and Their Potential Clinical Consequences in Pediatric Encounters." *Pediatrics* 111, 6–14.

Flores, Glenn, Milagros Abreu, Cara Pizzon Barone, Richard Bachur, & Hua Lin (2012) "Errors of Medical Interpretation and Their Potential Clinical Consequences: A Comparison of Professional Versus Ad Hoc Versus No Interpreters." *Annals of Emergency Medicine* 60 (5), 545–553.

Flores, Nelson & Jonathan Rosa (2015) "Undoing Appropriateness: Raciolinguistic Ideologies and Language Diversity in Education." *Harvard Educational Review* 85 (2), 149–171.

Fong, Timothy (1994) *The First Suburban Chinatown: The Remaking of Monterey Park, California*. Philadelphia, PA, Temple University Press.

Fraga, Luis R. & Maria L. Ocampo (2007) "More Information Requests and the Deterrent Effect of Section 5 of the Voting Rights Act." In *Voting Rights Act Reauthorization of 2006: Perspectives on Democracy, Participation, and Power*, Ana Henderson (ed.), 47–82. Berkeley, CA, Berkeley Public Policy Press.

Fraser, Nancy (1990) "Rethinking the Public Sphere: A Contribution to the Critique of Actually Existing Democracy." *Social Text* 25, 56–80.

Fraser, Nancy (2009) *Scales of Justice. Reimagining Political Space in a Globalizing World*. New York, Columbia University Press.

Friedman, Lawrence (2011) *The Human Rights Culture. A Study in History and Context*. New Orleans, LA, Quid Pro Books.

Friendly, Henry J. (1975) "Some Kind of Hearing." *University of Pennsylvania Law Review* 123, 1267–1317.

Fukuda, Tonan (1923) "Some Data on the Intelligence of Japanese Children." *American Journal of Psychology* 34 (4), 599–602.

Fukurai, Hiroshi (1999) "A Collaborative Work with *La Raza Law Journal*: Social De-construction of Race and Affirmative Action in Jury Selection." *African-American Law & Policy Report* 4, 17–72.

Gándara, Patricia & Megan Hopkins (eds.) (2010) *Forbidden Language. English Learners and Restrictive Language Policies*. New York/London, Teachers College Press.

Garcia, Mario T. (1991) *Mexican Americans: Leadership, Ideology and Identity, 1930–1960*. New Haven, CT, Yale University Press.

Garth, Thomas R. (1923) "A Comparison of the Intelligence of Mexican and Mixed and Full Blood Indian Children." *Psychological Review* 30 (5), 388–401.

Gaulding, Jill (1998) "Against Common Sense: Why Title VII Should Protect Speakers of Black English." *University of Michigan Journal of Law Reform* 31, 637–706.

Gehrke, William H. (1935) "The Transition from the German to the English Language in North Carolina." *North Carolina Historical Review* 12 (1), 1–19.

Geiger, H. Jack (2003) "Racial and Ethnic Disparities in Diagnosis and Treatment: A Review of the Evidence and Consideration of Causes." In *Unequal Treatment: Confronting Racial and Ethnic Disparities in Health Care*, Brian D. Smedley,

Adrienne Y. Stith, & Alan R. Nelson (eds.), 417–454. Washington, DC, The National Academies Press.

Gellman, David N. & David Quigley (eds.) (2003) *Jim Crow New York. A Documentary History of Race and Citizenship, 1777–1877*. New York, New York University Press.

Gerber, David A. (1984) "Language Maintenance, Ethnic Group Formation, and Public Schools: Changing Patterns of German Concern, Buffalo, 1837–1874." *Journal of American Ethnic History* 4 (1), 31–61.

Gerhardt, Michael J. (1990) "The Ripple Effects of Slaughter-House: A Critique of a Negative Rights View of the Constitution." *Vanderbilt Law Review* 43, 409–450.

Gonzales Rose, Jasmine (2014) "Language Disenfranchisement in Juries: A Call for Constitutional Remediation." *Hastings Law Journal* 65, 811–864.

Gould, Stephen J. (1996) *The Mismeasure of Man*. Revised and Expanded Edition. New York, W. W. Norton.

Graham, Virginia T. (1925) "The Intelligence of Italian and Jewish Children in the Habit of Clinics of the Massachusetts Division of Mental Hygiene." *Journal of Abnormal and Social Psychology* 20 (4), 371–376.

Green, Christopher R. (2008) "The Original Sense of the (Equal) Protection Clause: Pre-Enactment History." *George Mason University Civil Rights Law Journal* 19, 1–76.

Green, Gordon C. (1963) "Negro Dialect, the Last Barrier to Integration." *Journal of Negro Education* 32 (1), 81–83.

Griffith, Elmer C. (1907) *The Rise and Development of the Gerrymander*. Chicago, Scott, Foresman and Company.

Grofman, Bernard & Gary King (2006) "The Future of Partisan Symmetry as a Judicial Test for Partisan Gerrymandering after *LULAC v. Perry*." *Election Law Journal* 6, 2–35.

Gross, Ariela J. (2007) "The 'Caucasian Clock': Mexican Americans and the Politics of Whiteness in the Twentieth-Century Southwest." *Georgetown Law Journal* 95, 337–392.

Guo, Qian & Daniel Koretz (2013) "Estimating the Impact of the Massachusetts English Immersion Law on Limited English Proficient Students' Reading Achievement." *Educational Policy* 27 (1), 121–149.

Haakonssen, Knud (1991) "From Natural Law to the Rights of Man." In *A Culture of Rights. The Bill of Rights in Philosophy, Politics and Law – 1791–1991*, Michael J. Lacey & Knud Haakonssen (eds.), 19–61. Cambridge, Cambridge University Press.

Habermas, Jürgen (1989[1962]) *The Structural Transformation of the Public Sphere: An Inquiry into a Category of Bourgeois Society*. Translated by Thomas Burger & Frederick Lawrence. Cambridge, MA, MIT Press.

Habermas, Jürgen (1996) *Between Facts and Norms. Contributions to a Discourse Theory of Law and Diplomacy*. Translated by William Rehg. Cambridge, MA, MIT Press.

Hakuta, Kenji, Ellen Bialystok, & Edward W. Wiley (2003) "Critical Evidence: A Test of the Critical-Period Hypothesis for Second-Language Acquisition." *Psychological Science* 14, 31–38.

Hamburger, Phillip (2011) "Privileges or Immunities." *Northwestern University Law Review* 105, 61–147.

Handschin, Charles H. (1913) *The Teaching of Modern Languages in the United States. Bulletin of the Bureau of Education* 3. Washington, DC, Government Printing Office.

Harrison, Gordon S. (2007) "Alaska's Constitutional 'Literacy Test' and the Question of Voting Discrimination." *Alaska History* 22 (1/2), 23–38.

Healey, Melina A. (2014) "Montana's Rural Version of the School-to-Prison Pipeline: School Discipline and Tragedy on American Indian Reservations." *Montana Law Review* 75, 15–66.

Herrnstein, Richard J. & Charles Murray (1994) *The Bell Curve. The Reshaping of American Life by Difference in Intelligence.* New York, Free Press.

Higbee, Jay A. (1966) *Development and Administration of the New York State Law Against Discrimination.* University, AL, University of Alabama Press.

Hirsch, Eric D., Jr. (1988) *Cultural Literacy. What Every American Needs to Know.* New York, Vintage Books.

Hobbes, Thomas (1651) *Leviathan, or the Matter, Forme, & Power of a Common-Wealth Ecclesiasticall and Civill.* London, Andrew Crooke.

Hobbes, Thomas (1681) "A Dialogue Between a Phylosopher and a Student of the Common Laws of England." In *The Art of Rhetoric, with a Discourse of the Laws of England.* London, William Crooke.

Hollander, Jocelyn A. & Miriam J. Abelson (2014) "Language and Talk." In *Handbook of the Social Psychology of Inequality,* Jane D. McLeod *et al.* (eds.), 181–206. Dordrecht, Springer.

Holoszyc-Pimental, Raphael (2015) "Reconciling Rational-Basis Review: When Does Rational Basis Bite?" *New York University Law Review* 90, 2070–2117.

Hopkins, Ann (2005) "*Price Waterhouse v. Hopkins:* A Personal Account of a Sexual Discrimination Plaintiff." *Hofstra Labor and Employment Law Journal* 22, 357–416.

Horton, John (1995) *The Politics of Diversity: Immigration, Resistance, and Change in Monterey Park, California.* Philadelphia, PA, Temple University Press.

HoSang, Daniel (2010) *Racial Propositions: Ballot Initiatives and the Making of Postwar California.* Berkeley, CA, University of California Press.

Hoxie, Frederick E. (1984) *A Final Promise: The Campaign to Assimilate the Indians, 1880–1920.* Lincoln, NE, University of Nebraska Press.

Hrbková, Šárka (1919) *Bridging the Atlantic. A Discussion of the Problems and Methods of Americanization.* Lincoln, NE, State Council of Defense.

Hsieh, Marina (2001) "Language-qualifying Juries to Exclude Bilingual Speakers." *Brooklyn Law Review* 66, 1181–1206.

Huntington, Samuel P. (2004) *Who Are We? The Challenges to America's National Identity.* New York, Simon & Schuster.

Institute for Social Research, California State University, Sacramento (2010) *2010 Language Need and Interpreter Use in California Superior Courts.* Sacramento, Judicial Council of California/Administrative Office of the Courts.

Jackman, William J., *et al.* (1911) *History of the American Nation.* Chicago, Western Press Association.

Jackson, Jeffrey D. (2011) "Be Careful What You Wish For: Why *McDonald v. City of Chicago*'s Rejection of the Privileges and Immunities Clause May Not Be Such a Bad Thing for Rights." *Penn State Law Review* 115, 561–606.

Jensen, Richard (1971) *The Winning of the Midwest. Social and Political Conflict, 1888–1896.* Chicago/London, University of Chicago Press.

Jensen, Richard J. (2002) "'No Irish Need Apply': A Myth of Victimization." *Journal of Social History* 36 (2), 405–429.

Joseph, John E. (2000) *Limiting the Arbitrary: Linguistic Naturalism and Its Opposites in Plato's Cratylus and Modern Theories of Language.* Amsterdam/Philadelphia, PA, John Benjamins.

Jung, David, Noemi Gallardo & Ryan Harris (2013) "A Local Official's Guide to Language Access Laws." *Hastings Race & Poverty Law Journal* 10, 31–68.

Ka'awalowa, L. Kaipoleimanu (2014) "Translation v. Tradition: Fighting for Equal Standardized Testing ma ka 'ōlelo Hawai'i." *University of Hawai'i Law Review* 36, 487–527.

Karlan, Pamela S. (1995) "Our Separatism? Voting Rights as an American Nationalities Policy." *University of Chicago Legal Forum* 1995, 83–109.

Keyssar, Alexander (2000) *The Right to Vote. The Contested History of Democracy in the United States.* New York, Basic Books.

King, Thomas A. (2014) "How 11 Boston Transitional Bilingual Teachers Implemented and Resisted Sheltered English Immersion Following a Ballot Initiative Eliminating Bilingual Education on [sic] Massachusetts." Unpublished EdD dissertation, University of Massachusetts, Boston.

Kloss, Heinz (1998[1977]) *The American Bilingual Tradition.* McHenry, IL, Delta Systems/Center for Applied Linguistics.

Kracum, John (2014) "Comment: The Validity of *United States v. Nazemian* following *Crawford* and Its Progeny: Do Criminal Defendants Have the Right to Face their Interpreters at Trial?" *Journal of Criminal Law and Criminology* 104, 431–456.

Kuyper, Susan J. (1980) "The Americanization of German Immigrants: Language Religion and Schools in Nineteenth Century Rural Wisconsin." Unpublished PhD Dissertation, University of Wisconsin-Madison.

Kymlicka, Will (1995) *Multicultural Citizenship: A Liberal Theory of Minority Rights.* Oxford, Oxford University Press.

Labadie-Jackson, Glenda (2008) "Warning: Silence Can Cause Severe Harm: Spanish Language and Civil Liability for Inadequate Warnings and Instructions." *Harvard Latino Law Review* 11, 85–101.

Landreth, Natalie & Moira Smith (2007) "Voting Rights in Alaska: 1982–2006." *Southern California Review of Law and Social Justice* 17, 79–129.

Latin, Howard (1994) "'Good Warnings', Bad Products, and Cognitive Limitations." *UCLA Law Review* 41, 1193–1295.

Lenneberg, Eric H. (1967) *Biological Foundations of Language.* New York, Wiley.

Levitt, Justin (2012) "Election Deform: The Pursuit of Unwarranted Electoral Regulation." *Election Law Journal* 11, 97–117.

Lindemann, Stephanie (2005) "Who Speaks 'Broken English'? US Undergraduates' Perceptions of Non-Native English." *International Journal of Applied Linguistics* 15 (2), 187–212.

Lloyd, Aaron T. (2009) "You're Next on the Tee, Just Remember to Speak English! Could the LPGA Really Force Players to Learn and Speak English?" *Virginia Sports and Entertainment Law Journal* 9, 181–217.

Lo, Lily (2011) "The Right to Understand Your Doctor: Protecting Language Access Rights in Healthcare." *Boston College Third World Law Journal* 31, 377–401.

Lomawaima, K. Tsianina & Teresa L. McCarty (2002) "When Tribal Sovereignty Challenges Democracy: American Indian Education and the Democratic Ideal." *American Educational Research Journal* 39 (2), 279–305.

Lowrie, Walter & Walter S. Franklin (1834) *American State Papers. Documents, Legislative and Executive, of the Congress of the United States.* Washington, DC, Gales and Seaton.

Lüsebrink, Claire (1986) "Un défi à la politique de la langue nationale: La lutte autour de la langue allemande en Alsace sous la Révolution française." *Linx* 15, 146–168.

MacIntyre, Alasdair (1988) *Whose Justice? Whose Rationality?* Notre Dame, IN, University of Notre Dame Press.

Matsubayashi, Yoshihide (1984) "The Japanese Language Schools in Hawaii and California from 1892 to 1941." Unpublished EdD dissertation, University of San Francisco.

Matsuda, Mari (1991) "Voices of America: Accent, Antidiscrimination Law, and a Jurisprudence for the Last Reconstruction." *Yale Law Journal* 100, 1329–1407.

McGovern, Shannon K. (2011) "A New Model for States as Laboratories for Reform: How Federalism Informs Education Policy." *New York University Law Review* 86, 1519–1555.

McGowan, Miranda O. (2004) "Gay Rights After *Lawrence v. Texas*: From Outlaws to Ingroup: *Romer, Lawrence,* and the Inevitable Normativity of Group Recognition." *Minnesota Law Review* 88, 1312–1345.

Mead, Margaret (1926) "Methodology of Racial Testing: Its Significance for Sociology." *American Journal of Sociology* 31 (5), 657–667.

Mead, Margaret (1927) "Group Intelligence Testing and Linguistic Disability among Italian Children." *School & Society* 25, 465–468.

Messina, Elizabeth G. (2010) "Perversions of Knowledge. Confronting Racist Ideologies behind Intelligence Testing." In *Anti-Italianism. Essays on a Prejudice*, William J. Connell & Fred Gardaphé (eds.), 41–65. Basingstoke, Palgrave Macmillan.

Miller, Maxwell A., Lynn Davis, Adam Prestidge, & William Eggington (2011) "Language in the Law: Finding Justice in Translation: American Jurisprudence Affecting Due Process for People with Limited English Proficiency Together with Practical Suggestions." *Harvard Latino Law Review* 14, 117–154.

Misaki, Hisakichi (1927) "The Effect of Language Handicap on Intelligence Tests of Japanese Children." MA thesis, Stanford University.

Moran, Rachel F. (1988) "The Politics of Discretion: Federal Intervention in Bilingual Education." *California Law Review* 76, 1249–1352.

Mourgeon, Jacques (2003) *Les droits de l'homme.* Paris, Presses universitaires de France.

Muñoz, Laura K. (2001) "Separate but Equal? A Case Study of *Romo v. Laird* and Mexican American Education." *OAH Magazine of History* 15 (2), 28–35.

National Education Association (1966) *The Invisible Minority: Report of the NEA-Tucson Survey on the Teaching of Spanish to the Spanish-Speaking.* Washington, DC, NEA.

Nepper, John A. (1919) "School Legislation in Nebraska." *Catholic Educational Association Bulletin* 15 (4), 268–278.

Newman, JoNel (2007) "Ensuring that Florida's Language Minorities Have Access to the Ballot." *Stetson Law Review* 36, 329–364.

Nguyen, Beatrice B. (1993) "Accent Discrimination and the Test of Spoken English: A Call for an Objective Assessment of the Comprehensibility of Nonnative Speakers." *California Law Review* 81, 1325–1361.

Nussbaum, Martha (2006) *Frontiers of Justice. Disability, Nationality, Species Membership.* Cambridge, MA, The Belknap Press of Harvard University Press.

Nu'uhiwa, Breann (2015) "'Language Is Never about Language': Eliminating Language Bias in Federal Education Law to Further Indigenous Rights." *University of Hawai'i Law Review* 37, 381–427.

Oh, Reginald C. (2004) "Vision and Revision: Exploring the History, Evolution, and Future of the Fourteenth Amendment: A Critical Linguistic Analysis of Equal Protection Doctrine: Are Whites a Suspect Class?" *Temple Political and Civil Rights Law Review* 13, 583–610.

Orwell, George (1945) *Animal Farm: A Fairy Story.* London, Secker and Warburg.

Orwell, George (1946) "Politics and the English Language." *Horizon: A Review of Literature and Art* 13 (76), 252–265.

O'Sullivan, Matthew P. (2015) "Laboratories for Inequality: State Experimentation and Educational Access for English-Language Learners." *Duke Law Journal* 64, 671–715.

Otto, William N. (1919) "Better American Speech Week." *The Educator Journal* 20, 15–18.

Pasachoff, Eloise (2014) "Agency Enforcement of Spending Clause Statutes: A Defense of the Funding Cut-Off." *Yale Law Journal* 124, 248–335.

Peal, Elizabeth & Wallace Lambert (1962) "The Relation of Bilingualism to Intelligence." *Psychological Monographs: General and Applied* 76 (27), 1–23.

Penfield, Wilder & Lamar Roberts (1959) *Speech and Brain Mechanisms.* Princeton, NJ, Princeton University Press.

Perea, Juan F. (1994) "Ethnicity and Prejudice: Reevaluating 'National Origin' Discrimination under Title VII." *William and Mary Law Review* 35, 805–870.

Perez, Thomas E. (2003) "The Civil Rights Dimension of Racial and Ethnic Disparities in Health Status." In *Unequal Treatment: Confronting Racial and Ethnic Disparities in Health Care*, Brian D. Smedley, Adrienne Y. Stith, & Alan R. Nelson (eds.), 626–663. Washington, DC, The National Academies Press.

Petrzela, Natalia M. (2010) "Before the Federal Bilingual Act: Legislation and Lived Experience in California." *Peabody Journal of Education* 85 (4), 406–424.

Pintner, Rudolf (1923) "Comparison of American and Foreign Children on Intelligence Tests." *Journal of Educational Psychology* 14 (5), 292–295.

Podberesky, Rosita, Robert H. Deluty, & Stanley Feldstein (1990) "Evaluations of Spanish- and Oriental-Accented English Speakers." *Social Behavior and Personality* 18 (1), 53–63.

Pollvogt, Susannah (2014) "Beyond Suspect Classifications." *University of Pennsylvania Journal of Constitutional Law* 16, 739–803.

Portes, Alejandro & Richard Schauffler (1994) "Language and the Second Generation: Bilingualism Yesterday and Today." *International Migration Review* 28 (4), 640–664.

Powers, Jeanne M. & Lirio Patton (2008) "Between *Mendez* and *Brown*: '*Gonzales v. Sheely*' (1951) and the Legal Campaign Against Segregation." *Law & Social Inquiry* 33 (1), 127–171.

Preston, Dennis (1996) "Where the Worst English Is Spoken." In *Focus on the USA*, Edgar Schneider (ed.), 297–360. Amsterdam/Philadelphia, PA, John Benjamins.

Preston, Dennis (2011) "The Power of Language Regard – Discrimination, Classification, Comprehension, and Production." *Dialectologia*, Special issue II, 9–33.

Prucha, Francis P. (ed.) (2000) *Documents of United States Indian Policy*. Lincoln, NE, University of Nebraska Press.

Purnell, Thomas, William Idsardi, & John Baugh (1999) "Perceptual and Phonetic Experiments on American English Dialect Identification." *Journal of Language and Social Psychology* 18, 10–30.

Radmann, Jana A. (2005) "Do You Speak English? A Study on English Language Proficiency Testing of Hispanic Defendants in U.S. Criminal Courts." Unpublished MA Thesis, Louisiana State University.

Ramsey, Paul J. (2010) *Bilingual Public Schooling in the United States. A History of America's "Polyglot Boardinghouse."* Basingstoke, Palgrave Macmillan.

Rangel, Jorge C. & Carlos M. Alcala (1972) "Project Report: De Jure Segregation of Chicanos in Texas Schools." *Harvard Civil Rights-Civil Liberties Law Review* 7 (2), 307–391.

Raskin, Jamin B. (1993) "Legal Aliens, Local Citizens: The Historical, Constitutional and Theoretical Meanings of Alien Suffrage." *University of Pennsylvania Law Review* 141, 1391–1470.

Rawls, John (1971) *A Theory of Justice*. Cambridge, MA: The Belknap Press of Harvard University Press.

Rawls, John (1993) "The Law of Peoples." In *On Human Rights*, Stephen Shute & Susan Hurley (eds.), 41–68. New York, Basic Books.

Rawls, John (2001) *Justice as Fairness: A Restatement*. Cambridge, MA, Harvard University Press.

Re, Richard M. (2011) "Jury Poker: A Statistical Analysis of the Fair Cross-Section Requirement." *Ohio State Journal of Criminal Law* 8, 533–552.

Reardon, Sean F., Ilana Umansky, Rachel Valentino, Ritu Khanna, & Christina Wong (2014) "Differences Among Instructional Models in English Learners Academic and English Proficiency Trajectories." Findings from the SFUSD/Stanford Research Partnership. www.edpolicyinca.org/sites/default/files/PACE%20slides %20feb2014.pdf.

Reyhner, Jon (1993) "American Indian Language Policy and School Success." *Journal of Educational Issues of Language Minority Students* 12, 35–59.

Richardson, James D. (1902) *A Compilation of Messages and Papers of the Presidents, 1789–1902*. New York, Bureau of National Literature and Art.

Richardson, John G. (1984) "The American States and the Age of School Systems." *American Journal of Education* 92 (4), 473–502.

Rickford, John R. (1999) "The Ebonics Controversy in My Backyard: A Sociolinguist's Experiences and Reflections." *Journal of Sociolinguistics* 3 (2), 267–275.

Rivera, Jenny (2007) "An Equal Protection Standard for National Origin Subclassifications: The Context Matters." *Washington Law Review* 82, 897–965.

Rochmes, Daniel A. (2007) "Blinded by the White: Latino School Desegregation and the Insidious Allure of Whiteness." *Texas Hispanic Journal of Law and Policy* 13, 7–22.

Rodin, Judith & Stephen P. Steinberg (eds.) (2003) *Public Discourse in America. Conversation and Community in the Twenty-First Century.* Philadelphia, PA, University of Pennsylvania Press.

Rodriguez, Cristina M. (2006) "Language Diversity in the Workplace." *Northwestern University Law Review* 100, 1689–1774.

Rorty, Richard (2007) *Philosophy as Cultural Politics.* Cambridge, Cambridge University Press.

Rose, Mary R. (1999) "The Peremptory Challenge Accused of Race or Gender Discrimination? Some Data from One County." *Law and Human Behavior* 23, 695–702.

Ross, William G. (1994) *Forging New Freedoms. Nativism, Education and the Constitution, 1917–1927.* Lincoln, NE/London, University of Nebraska Press.

Rubert, Joel (2014) "Analyzing Calcrim 121: Are Bilingual Jurors 'Triers of Fact' or 'Triers of Language'?" *Orange County Lawyer* 56, 32–34.

Rubin, Donald L. (1992) "Nonlanguage Factors Affecting Undergraduates' Judgments of Nonnative English-Speaking Teaching Assistants." *Research in Higher Education* 33 (4), 511–531.

Rubin-Wills, Jessica (2012) "Language Access Advocacy after *Sandoval*: A Case Study of Administrative Enforcement Outside the Shadow of Judicial Review." *New York University Review of Law and Social Change* 36, 465–511.

Rugh, Jacob S. (2012) "Betrayal of the American Dream: Why Blacks and Latinos Were Hit Hardest by the U.S. Housing Crisis." Unpublished PhD dissertation, Princeton University.

Rumbaut, Rubén G., Douglas S. Massey, & Frank D. Bean (2006) "Linguistic Life Expectancies: Immigrant Language Retention in Southern California." *Population and Development Review* 32 (3), 447–460.

Rush, Benjamin (1806 [1798]) *Essays Literary, Moral and Philosophical.* 2nd Ed. Philadelphia, Thomas and William Bradford.

Russell, Thomas D. (2011) "Keep Negroes Out of Most Classes Where There Are a Large Number of Girls." In *Law, Society, and History: Themes in the Legal Sociology and Legal History of Lawrence M. Friedman,* Robert W. Gordon & Morton J. Horwitz, (eds.), 309–336. Cambridge, Cambridge University Press.

Ruttan, Rachel, Mary-Hunter McDonnell, & Loran Nordgren (2015) "Having 'Been There' Doesn't Mean I Care: When Prior Experience Reduces Compassion for Emotional Distress." *Journal of Personality and Social Psychology* 108 (4), 610–622.

Saer, D. J. (1923) "The Effect of Bilingualism on Intelligence." *British Journal of Psychology* 14 (1), 25–38.

Salimbene, Franklyn P. (1997) "Court Interpreters: Standards of Practice and Standards for Training." *Cornell Journal of Law and Public Policy* 6, 645–672.

Salomone, Rosemary C. (2010) *True American. Language, Identity, and the Education of Immigrant Children.* Cambridge, MA, Harvard University Press.

San Miguel, Guadalupe, Jr. (1987) *Let Them All Take Heed: Mexican Americans and the Campaign for Educational Equality in Texas, 1910–1981.* Austin, TX, University of Texas Press.

San Miguel, Guadalupe, Jr. (2004) *Contested Policy. The Rise and Fall of Federal Bilingual Education in the United States, 1960–2001.* Denton, TX, University of North Texas Press.

Sarason, Seymour B. & John Doris (1979) *Educational Handicap, Public Policy, and Social History: A Broadened Perspective on Mental Retardation.* New York, Free Press.

Scanlon, T. M. (2000) "The Diversity of Objections to Inequality." In *The Ideal of Equality,* Matthew Clayton and Andrew Williams (eds.), 41–59. Basingstoke, Macmillan.

Scaperlanda, Michael (2005) "Illusions of Liberty and Equality: An 'Alien's' View of Tiered Scrutiny, *ad hoc* Balancing, Governmental Power and Judicial Imperialism." *Catholic University Law Review* 55, 5–53.

Schlieben-Lange, Brigitte (1996) *Idéologie, révolution et uniformité de la langue.* Bruxelles, Éditions Mardaga.

Sealing, Keith (2001) "Peligro! Failure to Warn of a Product's Inherent Risk in Spanish Could Constitute a Product Defect." *Temple Political and Civil Rights Law Review* 11, 153–179.

Seller, Maxine S. (1979) *Ethnic Communities and Education in Buffalo, New York: Politics, Power and Group Identity 1833–1979.* Buffalo, State University of New York at Buffalo.

Selmi, Michael (2014) "The Evolution of Employment Discrimination Law: Changed Doctrine for Changed Social Conditions." *Wisconsin Law Review* 2014, 937–1000.

Sen, Amartya (1999) "Democracy as a Universal Value." *Journal of Democracy* 10 (3), 3–17.

Sen, Amartya (2009) *The Idea of Justice.* Cambridge, MA, The Belknap Press of Harvard University Press.

Sharif, Iman & Julia Tse (2010) "Accuracy of Computer-Generated Spanish-Language Medicine Labels." *Pediatrics* 125 (5), 960–965.

Sheridan, Clare (2003) "'Another White Race': Mexican Americans and the Paradox of Whiteness in Jury Selection." *Law and History Review* 21, 109–144.

Shockley, John S. (1974) *Chicano Revolt in a Texas Town.* Notre Dame, IN/London, University of Notre Dame Press.

Shradar, Victor L. (1974) "Ethnic Politics, Religion and the Public Schools of San Francisco, 1849–1933)." Unpublished PhD dissertation, Stanford University.

Siegel, Reva (2011) "From Colorblindness to Antibalkanization: An Emerging Ground of Decision in Racial Equality Cases." *Yale Law Journal* 120, 1278–1366.

Siegel, Reva (2013) "The Supreme Court 2012: Foreword." *Harvard Law Review* 127, 1–94.

Sivasubrahmaniam, Diane & Larry Heuer (2007) "Decision Makers and Decision Recipients: Understanding Disparities in the Meaning of Fairness." *Court Review* 44, 62–70.

Skogly, Sigrun (1992) "Article 2." In *The Universal Declaration of Human Rights: A Commentary*, Asbjørn Eide, Gudmundur Alfredsson, Göran Melander, Lars Adam Rehof, & Allan Rosas (eds.), 57–72. Oslo, Scandinavian University Press.

Smith, David Barton (2003) "Healthcare's Hidden Civil Rights Legacy." *Saint Louis University Law Journal* 48, 37–60.

Smith, Frank (1923) "Bilingualism and Mental Development." *British Journal of Psychology* 13 (3), 272–282.

Sommerfeld, Linda L. (1986) "An Historical Descriptive Study of the Circumstances That Led to the Elimination of German from the Cleveland Schools, 1860–1918." Unpublished PhD dissertation, Kent State University.

Spack, Ruth (2002) *America's Second Tongue. American Indian Education and the Ownership of English, 1860–1900*. Lincoln, NE/London, University of Nebraska Press.

Sperino, Sandra F. (2011) "Rethinking Discrimination Law." *Michigan Law Review* 110, 69–125.

Sracic, Paul A. (2006) *San Antonio v. Rodriguez and the Pursuit of Equal Education. The Debate over Discrimination and School Funding*. Lawrence, KS, University Press of Kansas.

State Justice Institute/National Center for State Courts (2013) *A National Call to Action: Access to Justice for Limited English Proficient Litigants: Creating Solutions to Language Barriers in State Courts*. Williamsburg, VA, National Center for State Courts.

Steele, Richard W. (1991) "'No Racials': Discrimination Against Ethnics in American Defense Industry, 1940–1942." *Labor History* 32 (1), 66–90.

Strauss, Marcy (2011) "Re-evaluating Suspect Classifications." *Seattle University Law Review* 35, 135–174.

Strong, Edward K., Jr. & Reginald Bell (1933) *Vocational Aptitudes of Second-Generation Japanese in the United States*. Stanford, CA, Stanford University Press.

Strum, Philippa (2010) *Mendez v. Westminster: School Desegregation and Mexican-American Rights*. Lawrence, KS, University Press of Kansas.

Sutherland, Brian J. (2009) "Patchwork of State and Federal Language Assistance for Minority Voters: A Proposal for Model State Legislation." *New York University Annual Survey of American Law* 65, 323–380.

Sweeney, Arthur (1922) "Mental Tests for Immigrants." *North American Review* 215 (798), 600–612.

Szasz, Margaret Connell (1999) *Education and the American Indian: The Road to Self-Determination since 1928*. 3rd Ed. Albuquerque, NM, University of New Mexico Press.

Taylor, Paul S. (1971[1934]) *An American Mexican Frontier: Nueces County, Texas*. Chapel Hill, NC, University of North Carolina Press.

Teitelbaum, Joel, Lara Cartwright-Smith, & Sara Rosenbaum (2012) "Translating Rights into Access: Language Access and the Affordable Care Act." *American Journal of Law & Medicine* 38, 348–373.

Thompson, Frank V. (1920) *Schooling of the Immigrant*. New York/London, Harper and Brothers.

Tokaji, Daniel P. (2014) "Responding to *Shelby County*: A Grand Election Bargain." *Harvard Law & Policy Review* 8, 71–108.

Toth, Carolyn (1990) *German-English Bilingual Schools in America: The Cincinnati Tradition in Historical Context*. New York, Peter Lang.

Treadwell, Harriette Taylor (1919) "Better Speech Week." *Primary Education* 27, 604.

Tucker, James T. (2009) *The Battle Over Bilingual Ballots: Language Minorities and Political Access Under the Voting Rights Act*. Farnham, Surrey, UK, Ashgate.

Tussman, Joseph & Jacobus tenBroek (1949) "Equal Protection of the Laws." *California Law Review* 37, 341–381.

Tyack, David B. (1974) *The One Best System. A History of American Urban Education*. Cambridge, MA, Harvard University Press.

Ulrich, Robert J. (1980) "The Bennett Law of 1889: Education and Politics in Wisconsin." Unpublished PhD dissertation, University of Wisconsin.

Umansky, Ilana & Sean Reardon (2014) "Reclassification Patterns Among Latino English Learner Students in Bilingual, Dual Immersion, and English Immersion Classrooms." *American Educational Research Journal* 51 (5), 879–912.

United States Commission on Civil Rights (1975) *A Better Chance to Learn: Bilingual Bicultural Education*. Washington, DC, United States Commission on Civil Rights.

Uriarte, Miren, Rosann Tung, Nicole Lavan, & Virginia Diez (2010) "Impact of Restrictive Language Policies on Engagement and Academic Achievement of English Learners in Boston Public Schools." In *Forbidden Language. English Learners and Restrictive Language Policies*, Patricia Gándara & Megan Hopkins (eds.), pp. 65–85, New York/London, Teachers College Press.

Valencia, Richard R. (2008) *Chicano Students and the Courts. The Mexican American Legal Struggle for Educational Equality*. New York/London, New York University Press.

Volokh, Eugene (2001) "Freedom of Speech, Cyberspace, and Harassment." *Stanford Technology Law Review* 2001, 3 an online journal article found at https://journals .law.stanford.edu/sites/default/files/stanford-technology-law-review-stlr/online/v olokh-freedom-of-speech.pdf.

Warhol, Larisa (2012) "Creating Official Language Policy from Local Practice: The Example of the Native American Languages Act 1990/1992." *Language Policy* 11, 235–252.

Welch, Susan (1990) "The Impact of At-Large Elections on the Representation of Blacks and Hispanics." *Journal of Politics* 52, 1050–1076.

Wentworth, Laura, Nathan Pellegrin, Karen Thompson, & Kenji Hakuta (2010) "Proposition 227 in California: A Long-Term Appraisal of Its Impact on English Learner Student Achievement." In *Forbidden Language. English Learners and Restrictive Language Policies*, Patricia Gándara & Megan Hopkins (eds.), 37–49, New York/London, Teachers College Press.

Wertheimer, John (2009) *Law and Society in the South: A History of North Carolina Court Cases*. Lexington, KY, University Press of Kentucky.

Whelan, Frederick G. (1981) "Language and Its Abuses in Hobbes' Political Philosophy." *American Political Science Review* 75 (1), 59–75.

Wiese, Ann-Marie & Eugene E. García (1998) "The Bilingual Education Act: Language Minority Students and Equal Educational Opportunity." *Bilingual Research Journal* 22, 1–18.

Wilson, Steven H. (2003) "Whiteness and Others: Mexican Americans and American Law. Brown Over 'Other White': Mexican American Legal Arguments and Litigation Strategy in School Desegregation Lawsuits." *Law and History Review* 21, 145–194.

Winstead, Teresa, Adrea Lawrence, Edward J. Brantmeier, & Christopher J. Frey (2008) "Language, Sovereignty, Cultural Contestation, and American Indian Schools: No Child Left Behind and a Navajo Test Case." *Journal of American Indian Education* 47 (1), 46–64.

Wollenberg, Charles (1978) *All Deliberate Speed. Segregation and Exclusion in California Schools, 1855–1975.* Berkeley, CA, University of California Press.

Wyman, Roger E. (1968) "Wisconsin Ethnic Groups and the Election of 1890." *The Wisconsin Magazine of History* 51 (4), 269–293.

Yoshino, Kenji (2011) "The New Equal Protection." *Harvard Law Review* 124, 747–803.

Zeydel, Edwin H. (1964) "The Teaching of German in the United States from Colonial Times to the Present." *The German Quarterly* 37, 315–392.

Zimmerman, Jonathan (2002) "Ethnics against Ethnicity: European Immigrants and Foreign Language Instruction, 1890–1940." *Journal of American History* 88 (4), 1383–1404.

Index of Court Cases

Decisions filed by the U.S. Supreme Court are referenced as "U.S."
Decisions filed by U.S. Circuit Courts of Appeal are referenced as "F.2d" or "F.3d"
Decisions filed by U.S. District Courts are referenced as "F.Supp."
Other courts are specified as needed.

218

Index of Names

General Index